"*A Course in Miracles*" Dimensions of Awakening

≈ • ≈

See the Face of Christ and Awaken

Donald James Giacobbe

Miracle Yoga Services

Published by Miracle Yoga Services
— miracleyoga@gmail.com —
Cottonwood, Arizona

Printed in the United States of America

BISAC Subject Codes and Headings:

OCC027510 Body, Mind, and Spirit: Spirituality—*A Course in Miracles*

OCC014000 Body, Mind & Spirit—New Thought

REL012120 Religion: Christian Life—Spiritual Growth

Library of Congress Control Number: 2018911580

Author: Giacobbe, Donald James

A Course in Miracles Dimensions of Awakening:
    See the Face of Christ and Awaken

ISBN 978-0-9843790-6-4

CONTENTS

~ o ~

About the Author
Preface 1
Introduction and Acknowledgments 3
Part I:—The Third Floor Elevators of Awakening 5
    What is your only Choice and Purpose? 7
    Who Awakens? 11
    What is Salvation? 17
    The Plan of the Atonement 19
    The Forgiveness Elevator 25
    The Meditation Elevator 29
    The Holy Relationship Elevator 33
    The Miracles Elevator 35
    The Holy Instant Elevator 39
    The Christ's Vision Elevator 45
    The Atonement Elevator 49

Part II:—The Second Floor Content and Form 55
    The Second Floor Real World of Love 57
    The Second Floor Circle of Atonement 59
    The Second Floor Face of Christ 61
    The Second Floor Light Dimension 65

Part III:—The First and Second Dimensions Work Together 75
    The Two Light Dimensions 77
    The Hybrid of the Finite and the Infinite 81
    The World is in Your Mind 83
    The Content and Meaning of Light 85
    The Holy Meeting Place 93
    The Spark and the Great Rays 97

Part IV:—The Facilitators of Awakening 105
    The Holy Spirit and Awakening 107
    Jesus and the Holy Relationship 115
    Jesus is the Atonement 117
    The Resurrection and Einstein 121
    Jesus, True Light, and Christ's Vision 123
    The Bridge and the Law of Love 131
    Healing Your Two Major Fears 137
    One Mind and One Will with Jesus 145
    Your Role of Being a Teacher 153
    Recognizing That Truth is True 159
    Happy Learning That Truth is True 169
    Light Dimensions Leading to Heaven 175

Part V:—The Physics of Light in Three Dimensions 185
    Final Thoughts 211

ABOUT THE AUTHOR

≈ ۰ ≈

Don Giacobbe was employed for sixteen years as a case manager serving developmentally disabled clients. The professional nature of his work limited his ability to express his spiritual motivations overtly, so out of necessity, he served as an "undercover agent" for God.

A more direct approach to spirituality was facilitated by living with Zen Buddhist seekers and then being part of a yoga community. Later he was the director of the Aquarian Age Yoga Center in Virginia Beach, VA. He served as an instructor of meditation and yoga, teaching college courses and appearing on television. He specialized in providing yoga teacher training certification courses and leading meditation workshops and retreats. Don has attempted in his teaching of meditation to strip away the rituals of Zen Buddhism and yoga practices and transpose only the bare essence into a Christian context. Techniques of meditation inspired by Eastern sources open the mind to the influence of the Holy Spirit and enhance the use of traditional Christian practices, such as the "Jesus Prayer" and Christian contemplation. These techniques can be found in Don's book *Christian Meditation Inspired by Yoga and "A Course in Miracles": Opening to Divine Love in Contemplation*.

Don's goal is to do God's Will, be receptive to the Holy Spirit, and find Christ within the temple of his own heart. He is not affiliated with any religious group. Formerly Don used the term "Christian yoga" to describe his path, which combines following Christ with yoga disciplines. In recent years he has adopted the term "Miracle Yoga" to describe his type of Christian yoga. This spiritual path is a combination of yoga and the philosophy of *A Course in Miracles* that encourages seeing with "forgiving eyes" and perceiving Christ in everyone. Don seeks to maintain a balance between opening to divine love inwardly and allowing love to be extended outwardly to others. Don recorded his life story in his autobiography, *Memory Walk in the Light*. You are welcome to contact Don at miracleyoga@gmail.com and read his teachings on the following websites:

www.miracleyoga.org
www.christianyoga.org
www.christianmeditation.org

PREFACE

~ o ~

If you have not already learned to listen very attentively to the Holy Spirit and persistently follow His guidance, the ego will present you with many roadblocks to learning *A Course in Miracles*.[1] "The ego's whole continuance depends on its belief you cannot learn this course."[2] If you have not already accepted the Holy Spirit as your Guide, the Course asks you to "Resign now as your own teacher."[3] Your resignation is needed so you can choose the Holy Spirit to be your new Teacher. Even with the Holy Spirit as your Guide, the Course turns your perception of the world upside down. Therefore, the Course can be disorienting and difficult to comprehend, and even harder to apply. The book you are reading now is just one way of overcoming the difficulty that studying the Course presents.

As you study the Course, the ego will ask you many questions designed to confuse you and remind you of your littleness, weakness, and limitations. "Remember that the Holy Spirit is the Answer, not the question. The ego always speaks first."[4] If you listen to the Holy Spirit, He will bring clarity and peace to your mind. "Hear, then, the one answer of the Holy Spirit to all the questions the ego raises: You are a child of God, a priceless part of His Kingdom, which He created as part of Him. Nothing else exists and only this is real."[5] Although you are the Son of God, you have forgotten your home in Heaven. "Yet the Holy Spirit remembers it for you, and He will guide you to your home because that is His mission."[6] Because you have fallen asleep in Heaven, you are now dreaming of an illusory world of separation.

> You have chosen a sleep in which you have had bad dreams, but the sleep is not real and God calls you to awake. There will be nothing left of your dream when you hear Him, because you will awaken. Your dreams contain many of the ego's symbols and they have confused you. Yet that was only because you were asleep and did not know. When you wake you will see the truth around you and in you, and you will no longer believe in dreams because they will have no reality for you. Yet the Kingdom and all that you have created there will have great reality for you, because they are beautiful and true.[7]

Your journey of awakening requires a transition from the earth to Heaven, from the concrete to the abstract, from illusion to truth, from time to timelessness, from separation to Oneness, and from the self to the Self. *"A Course in Miracles" Dimensions of Awakening* is about this transition from the illusory three-dimensional world of form to the formlessness of Heaven. The Course uses many different names to identify and emphasize the importance of a specific place of transition between the earth and Heaven. Some examples of these names are "the real world," "the happy dream," "the bridge," "the borderland," "the altar of God," "the holy meeting place," "the face of Christ," and "the vision of the Son of God."

The Course never employs the word "dimensions" to describe this journey of transition. Yet reason will tell you that the transition from form to formlessness must involve changes in dimensions. There are two dimensions of light that enable you to make the transition from the partial awareness of your three-dimensional perception to the total awareness of knowledge in Heaven. This book focuses on these two light dimensions that help you to awaken to the truth that "you *are* light."[8] When you see "the blazing light upon the altar to the Son of God,"[9] you will awaken to your light and remember your Father and your Self. "Who could behold the face of Christ and not recall His Father as He really is?"[10]

Your transition is from past nightmares to present happiness in this world and then to eternal happiness in Heaven. "Be not content with future happiness."[11] You are being called to awaken and so you are being called to happiness. "The Holy Spirit is the Call to awaken and be glad.... Our task is the joyous one of waking it [the world] to the Call for God."[12] Your purpose is to remove the illusory separation between your brother and you so you can both experience happiness not just in the future, but also *now*. "The Holy Spirit's purpose now is yours. Should not His happiness be yours as well?"[13]

The Course requires only that you have the "little willingness" to make the transition from an old way of thinking to a new perception of the world, others, and yourself. The Holy Spirit Himself will guide you: "He will direct your efforts, telling you exactly what to do, how to direct your mind, and when to come to Him in silence, asking for His sure direction and His certain Word."[14]

ACKNOWLEDGMENTS

≈ • ≈

In bringing this book to publication, I very much appreciate the encouragement and help of Jon Pratt, David Luma, Linda Garger, John Francis, Heather Clarke, Cynthia Fawcett, Sharon Watson, Tya Schrader, and Gordon and Deborah Poisson.

INTRODUCTION

~ o ~

God's Will, which is your true will, is for you to awaken. This book focuses on the process of awakening to reality and increasing your understanding, motivation, and participation in the role the Holy Spirit has assigned to you. Here is a very simple analogy that will be used in the first half of this book to discuss how the mind is unified to bring about awakening: Simply imagine that your mind is symbolized by a three-story hospital. The third floor represents intensive care. Your mind needs healing because you have amnesia, having forgotten who you are. Your mind is split between true and false perceptions, between loving and unloving perceptions. Your mind needs intensive care to be healed and returned to wholeness. This intensive care floor where healing is needed is your everyday three-dimensional world.

The first floor represents your discharge from the hospital when your amnesia has been healed. This first floor symbolizes Heaven, the place where your limited perception has been replaced by the total awareness of knowledge. This is where the full memory of God returns when you have awakened from your amnesia. The goal of awakening is to go from the third floor of intensive care to the first floor of your discharge. But you cannot go directly from the third floor to the first floor. The third floor of intensive care is the place of nightmares of death and unhappy dreams of never being cured of amnesia. The first floor stands for pure joy because it transcends all dreams, sickness, and death. You cannot go from the trauma of nightmares directly into the bliss of Heaven unless you first go to and then through the second floor.

What is the second floor of the hospital? It is the recovery room for amnesia patients, which the Course calls the "real world." After the intensive care of the third floor, you go to the second floor to help you recover your memory by releasing the false identities you have made up, but you have not yet remembered your true Identity. On the second floor, you replace your nightmares of the third floor with happy dreams that prepare you for eternal happiness. While you are on the second floor, your memory is partially recovered, and you rest as you prepare for being completely cured of your amnesia. "The real world holds a counterpart for each unhappy thought reflected in your world... The real world shows a world seen differently, through quiet eyes and with a mind at peace. Nothing but rest is there."[15] The Course describes the recovery room as "the world of happy dreams, from which awaking is so easy and so natural."[16] Your happy dreams in the real world prepare you to regain your complete memory of who you are when you are transported to the first floor. "You will first dream of peace, and then awaken to it. Your first exchange of what you made for what you want is the exchange of nightmares for the happy dreams of love."[17]

The second floor is the place of transition from the third floor to the first floor. But you must meet the condition of awakening on the first floor, symbolic of Heaven. This condition is reaching the second floor and leaving the third floor behind. Thus the focus of this book is on going from the third floor to the second floor. Why is there less focus on going from the second floor to the first floor? The answer is that once you fully accept the second floor and reject the third floor, God Himself will surely take the final step of transporting you to the first floor of total awakening. If you do your part of letting the Holy Spirit bring you to the second floor, God will do His part of bringing you Home. "For we wait in quiet expectation for our God and Father. He has promised He will take the final step Himself. And we are sure His promises are kept. We have come far along the road, and now we wait for Him."[18]

This book presents a new theory of dimensions related to the Course. Why learn about these dimensions? "What is it *for?*"[19] The answer is that your understanding of these dimensions can help you to prepare for your awakening in Heaven. In the amnesia analogy, the three floors of the hospital are related to the three dimensions in which you live. The third floor is *the third dimension*, which is your everyday world. The second floor is *the second dimension*, which is the "real world" or "happy dream." The first floor is *the first dimension*, which is reality or Heaven. The title "Dimensions of Awakening" refers to the first and second dimensions that have only light in contrast to the third dimension of darkness and light. The second half of this book explains how these light dimensions work together to prepare you to make the transition from the partial awareness of three-dimensional perception to the total awareness of the knowledge of Heaven in the first dimension. When you have made the necessary preparations for unifying your mind, your loving Father will gladly take the final step of giving you His Divine Embrace, restoring you to the awareness of eternal Oneness.

> Perfect [loving true] perception, then, has many elements in common with knowledge [in Heaven], making transfer to it possible. Yet the last step must be taken by God, because the last step in your redemption, which seems to be in the future, was accomplished by God in your creation.... Aspects of reality can still be seen, and they will replace aspects of unreality. Aspects of reality can be seen in everything and everywhere. Yet only God can gather them together, by crowning them as one with the final gift of eternity.[20]

PART I

~ • ~

THE THIRD FLOOR

ELEVATORS

OF AWAKENING

Part I of this book lays the foundation for sharing the new theory of dimensions in relation to the whole process of awakening. The focus will be on asking and answering the questions of who, what, when, where, why, and how in regard to salvation. For example, the first three sections address these questions: "What is your only choice and purpose?" "Who awakens?" and "What is salvation?" Then God's plan for salvation will be addressed because only His plan will bring about awakening. "Only God's plan for salvation will work."[21] By God's grace, you have help from the Holy Spirit Who will guide you.

But ask yourself if it is possible that God would have a plan for your salvation that does not work. Once you accept His plan as the one function that you would fulfill, there will be nothing else the Holy Spirit will not arrange for you without your effort. He will go before you making straight your path, and leaving in your way no stones to trip on, and no obstacles to bar your way. Nothing you need will be denied you. Not one seeming difficulty but will melt away before you reach it. You need take thought for nothing, careless of everything except the only purpose that you would fulfill. As that was given you, so will its fulfillment be.[22]

The remainder of Part I describes the seven instruments of the Holy Spirit, called "elevators" because they will be the tools given to you as a means of transporting you from the third floor, meaning from the familiar third dimension, to higher levels of awareness in the other two dimensions that will be introduced in Part II and Part III.

The seven instruments of the Holy Spirit, described in Part I, are the tools that He uses and asks the sleeping Son of God to use to awaken from his amnesia. In this process of awakening, the Holy Spirit has one function and you have another function related to His. The Holy Spirit's function is correction leading to healing. Your function is forgiveness leading to healing. Both the Holy Spirit and you have the single united purpose of wanting to heal your mind. But you must not attempt to assume the Holy Spirit's function of correction or you will be unable to perform your function of forgiveness. "Correction is not your function. It belongs to One [the Holy Spirit] Who knows of fairness, not of guilt. If you assume correction's role, you lose the function of forgiveness. No one can forgive until he learns correction is but to forgive, and never to accuse. Alone [without the Holy Spirit], you cannot see they are the same, and therefore is correction not of you."[23]

Correction and forgiveness are the same because both require the absence of judgment and result in healing. Because of the ego, you will mistakenly believe correction involves judging your brother and finding guilt in him, which will prevent you from performing your function of forgiveness. "*You* cannot correct yourself. Is it possible, then, for you to correct another? Yet you can see him truly, because it is possible for you to see yourself truly. It is not up to you to change your brother, but merely to accept him as he is."[24] You must allow the Holy Spirit to first perform his function of correction by removing judgment from your mind. After the Holy Spirit has performed his function of correction, only then are you capable of performing your function of forgiveness by perceiving your brother without judgment and without guilt.

Your function of forgiveness is just one of the seven tools of the Holy Spirit that are the focus of Part I. The others are Christ's vision, miracles, the holy relationship, the holy instant, and the Atonement. All these are learning aids that work together to lead you to awakening from your amnesia. As you read Part I, bear in mind that these tools of the Holy Spirit will only benefit you if you actively welcome His presence into your mind so you can apply these instruments to your daily life.

Part I:—The Third Floor Elevators of Awakening 5
    What is your only Choice and Purpose? 7
    Who Awakens? 11
    What is Salvation? 17
    The Plan of the Atonement 19
    The Forgiveness Elevator 25
    The Meditation Elevator 29
    The Holy Relationship Elevator 33
    The Miracles Elevator 35
    The Holy Instant Elevator 39
    The Christ's Vision Elevator 45
    The Atonement Elevator 49

WHAT IS YOUR ONLY
CHOICE AND PURPOSE?

≈ ∘ ≈

There is a "secret bargain made with the ego"[25] to forget your Father and accept "the great amnesia in which the memory of God seems quite forgotten."[26] But before focusing on healing your mind of forgetfulness, let's consider what you are remembering to replace the memory of God. At times, you may focus on the memory of past events in your life, but recalling any past event brings your awareness to the unfortunate and unpleasant "fearful instant" of the original separation when the illusion of time began. "And do you want that fearful instant kept, when Heaven seemed to disappear and God was feared and made a symbol of your hate?"[27] At least consciously, you do not want to be reliving that fearful instant of the separation, yet the Course says that every day you are reliving what it calls the "time of terror."

Notice that the word "terror" has the word "error" within it. Your first experience of terror was also your first experience of error. This "fearful instant" was the separation in which you lost the awareness of Heaven and became afraid of your Father. The "time of terror" was the beginning of time. Ironically, it was also the end of time because in the instant that the illusion of time was made as an error, it was immediately corrected and undone by the Holy Spirit Who was created by God in that same instant of the separation. With the undoing of that error, the past was gone. But you have kept the past alive in your mind by bringing the illusion of time into the present, appearing to contradict God's Will.

Perhaps you recall the movie titled "Groundhog Day" in which the main character keeps reliving the same day. You are doing something similar in that you are reliving the same instant of the separation. "Each day, and every minute in each day, and every instant that each minute holds, you but relive the single instant when the time of terror took the place of love."[28] This reliving of the instant of terror relates to your daily experience of the peace of deep sleep at night and seemingly waking up every morning to the discontent found in daily life in the physical world of separation. "And so you die each day to live again, until you cross the gap between the past and present, which is not a gap at all."[29] The alternation between times of separation also relates to each person's life span of living as a body, death of the body, and reincarnation. "Such is each life; a seeming interval from birth to death and on to life again, a repetition of an instant gone by long ago that cannot be relived."[30]

Time is merely like a videotape that you keep playing over and over again, each time pretending you have never seen this videotape before. "And all of time is but the mad belief that what is over is still here and now."[31] What kind of videotape is this that you are replaying? Because you are reliving "the single instant when the time of terror took the place of love," the tape you are replaying is a scary movie you watch to experience fear instead of love. You are familiar with PTSD, which is post-traumatic stress disorder. The ongoing distress caused by PTSD is the result of witnessing or participating in a life-threatening event, such as military combat, a sexual attack, a car accident, or a natural disaster. However, reliving "the time of terror," which was the separation, can also be called PTSD. In this case, the word "stress" can be replaced by the word "separation." Therefore, PTSD can stand for "post-traumatic *separation* disorder." An aspect of waking up from your self-induced amnesia is not just remembering God, but also forgetting your PTSD "time of terror." "Forget the time of terror that has been so long ago corrected and undone. Can sin withstand the Will of God?"[32]

Along with time, the illusions of fear, sin, and guilt entered your mind at the separation when you believed you had attacked reality and succeeded in overcoming God's Will. But what keeps you clinging to the past so that you relive the instant of terror when you first experienced fear, sin, and guilt? Whatever you do not forgive causes you to replace the present with the past. "The unforgiven is a voice that calls out from a past forevermore gone by. And everything that points to it as real is but a wish that what is gone could be made real again and seen as here and now, in place of what is *really* now and here."[33]

How do you free yourself from the illusion of time based on the belief that you have separated yourself from the eternal now of Heaven? You can practice forgiveness to let go of illusions of separation and accept the reality of the present. Since forgiveness releases illusions of fear, sin, and guilt, it enables you to let go of the illusion of the time when fear, sin, and guilt began. "Forgiveness is the great release from time."[34] Thus forgiveness allows you to release reliving the past that is gone as you accept the present. "It [forgiveness] is the key to learning that the past is over. Madness [of illusions] speaks no more."[35] You might think that your past experience is your teacher, but your past is what must be undone. Actually forgiveness is your teacher, freeing you from the past. Forgiveness teaches you to undo illusions you made in the past when influenced by the ego. "There *is* no other teacher and no other way [besides forgiveness]. For what has been undone no longer is."[36]

You are in Heaven now. Yet you imagine you are a body within the limitations of time and space. "And who can stand upon a distant shore [Heaven], and dream himself across an ocean [the illusory world], to a place and time that have long since gone by?"[37] When you imagine the past is in the present, you think that what is unreal has replaced reality. But you cannot go back to a past that is not there and is not anywhere. "Can it be up to you to see the past and put it in the present? You can *not* go back. And everything that points the way in the direction of the past but sets you on a mission whose accomplishment can only be unreal."[38] At the separation, you accepted the "mission impossible" of separating yourself from your oneness with your loving Father. You attempted to disown your inheritance as the holy Son of God.

But your Father knew that disowning your oneness with Him would make you unhappy, imagining you do not deserve love. In spite of your attempt to disown your divine inheritance, God's justice protected you. Unlike worldly justice in which someone must lose, God's justice ensures that you will always deserve and receive only love and blessings. If you had accomplished your mission impossible of separation, you would have been the loser. Thus you would have imposed the unfairness of worldly justice upon yourself. Since the fairness of God's justice always affirms you are worthy of love, you cannot change your true nature of love no matter how many dreams you fabricate, based on your belief that the past can replace the present and separate you from your home in Heaven. "Such is the justice your All-Loving Father has ensured must come to you. And from your own unfairness to yourself has He protected you. You cannot lose your way because there is no way but His, and nowhere can you go except to Him."[39]

Although God's justice and His Will have determined that you will awaken, He cannot violate your free will. Thus you must express your free will by your choice to awaken. But consider the nature of choice. In Heaven there is only the one joyful expression of always extending God's Love and Truth. After you have awakened in Heaven, you will never have any reason to decide against God's Will of Love and Truth. In God's Creation that is Heaven, there are no opposites, and there is nothing to choose between. "Creation knows no opposite."[40] Choice is only required when there are opposites so you must choose one or the other. "Choice is the obvious escape from what appears as opposites. Decision lets one of conflicting goals become the aim of effort and expenditure of time."[41] Since Heaven has no conflicting goals, choice itself is meaningless, and so there is no need to make any choice.

In your worldly experience of time and form, there are opposites and conflicting goals so the idea of choice is meaningful. You are constantly choosing between using your time and effort to awaken to reality and the opposite purpose of wasting your time by darkening your mind with illusions. "There are but two directions you can take, while time remains and choice is meaningful. For never will another road be made except the way to Heaven. You but choose whether to go toward Heaven, or away to nowhere. There is nothing else to choose."[42] You can only make the one choice to awaken since the option of never awakening is not God's Will or your true will. "You need to be reminded that you think a thousand choices are confronting you, when there is really only one to make. And even this but seems to be a choice."[43]

In the world, you need to make the one meaningful choice to awaken from your dreams of separation and accept you are in Heaven and have been in Heaven all along. Choosing against awakening seems to be a viable option, but it is meaningless to choose against the truth, which has no opposite. Once you choose to awaken to Truth in Heaven, you will realize "there is nothing else to choose." There's no other choice you could reasonably make because only the truth is meaningful. "And when that one [choice for the truth of Heaven] is made, you will perceive it was no choice at all. For truth is true, and nothing else is true. There is no opposite to choose instead. There is no contradiction to the truth."[44]

What if you insist on the choice of continuing to sleep instead of the choice to awaken? You will delay your only true choice, which is your inevitable choice to awaken. It is God's Will and your own true will for you to awaken after you make the only choice that God and you really want. The delay of time caused by choosing to continue sleeping is only a small obstacle to your awakening because it is meaningless. "Nothing is ever lost but time, which in the end is meaningless."[45]

Time is a meaningless illusion and only a small hindrance, yet you do believe time is real. The only power of time is to delay you, but there is no reason to allow yourself to be delayed, which only prolongs your self-imposed ways of limiting yourself. "Yet since you do believe in it [time], why should you waste it going nowhere, when it can be used to reach a goal as high as learning can achieve?"[46] Instead of allowing yourself to be delayed in time, you can choose to use time for the highest aim of learning, which is the purpose of awakening and helping others to awaken in Heaven. "Think not the way to Heaven's gate is difficult at all. Nothing you undertake with certain purpose and high resolve and happy confidence, holding your brother's hand and keeping step to Heaven's song, is difficult to do."[47] Heaven is perfectly peaceful. Even your firm dedication to the purpose of awakening brings peace to your mind. Since the choice to awaken is inevitable, you might as well make your only meaningful choice sooner rather than later. "Salvation cannot be withheld from you. It is your purpose. You cannot choose apart from this. You have no purpose apart from your brother, nor apart from the one [purpose] you asked the Holy Spirit to share with you."[48] Your purpose is to fully awaken to your true Self. "My Self is holy beyond all the thoughts of holiness of which I now conceive. Its shimmering and perfect purity is far more brilliant than is any light that I have ever looked upon. Its love is limitless, with an intensity that holds all things within it, in the calm of quiet certainty."[49]

WHO AWAKENS?

≈ ∘ ≈

Before discussing healing your amnesia and awakening any further, there is this question that arises: Who awakens? I lead a Course study group, and in one session I was explaining that we seem to make many decisions in daily life, but actually we are always deciding between only two choices: either the Holy Spirit or the ego. Then I said, "You are the decider!" One student, Xianti, looked perplexed, and asked, "But who is the decider?" I was startled by her question because I did not want to give her a superficial answer. Xianti is very smart, and she could easily see that the ego could not be the decider because you are choosing for or against identification with the ego. My answer to her was, "The sleeping Son of God is the decider." This answer satisfied her and the others in the study group, but it did not satisfy me. Yes, it was the correct answer, but my intuition told me I must ponder this further.

If I had said, "Christ is the decider because that is who you are," that answer would be incorrect. Christ is indeed who you are, but Christ in Heaven only uses knowledge and not perception. The decider is making choices using perception, so the decider cannot be the Christ. Thus the correct answer was that the decider is the sleeping Son of God. But that correct answer was not completely in alignment with the very precise thinking in the Course. The question arises then: Who is the sleeping Son of God? This question is similar to the question: "Who awakens?" These two questions must have the same answer. The answer cannot be Christ, Who is your Self, because Christ is already awake in Heaven and never sleeps. "Christ has never slept."[50]

I felt it was important to find one answer that satisfied me so I could bring clarity to others, and after much pondering, I did find that answer. Since finding that one answer, I have had many occasions to share the answer with others who needed this particular answer. The best example of someone who needed this specific answer was Judith, whom I met at a miracles conference. I cannot remember the exact words of our conversation, but the following is my best attempt to retain the basic content of our conversation:

Don: I have been wanting to talk with you because of something you said yesterday as you and I were walking along the corridor. You said, "I have always felt in my life as though I was looking for a missing piece of me." Then I saw you glance backward for emphasis, when you said, "It is as though that part of me is right behind me following me like a shadow." Do you remember saying that to me yesterday?

Judith: No, I don't remember saying those words, but that is how I do feel. I have been trying to figure out what that missing piece of me is for years. So what is that missing piece?

Don: Your missing piece is really about, "What is your true nature?" But let me share my similar question because the answer I found for me is the answer that will explain your missing piece. Before studying the Course, my background spiritually was in attempting to find a balance between the East and West. But I had a problem with the identity issue that I could not resolve. Western spirituality teaches the dualistic idea that I have an individual soul that is separate from God. I can be mystically united to God, but there will always be some separation from God. The most profound Eastern philosophies teach complete nondualism in which the individual dissolves completely into God like the raindrop dissolving into the divine ocean. Here was my problem: I liked the Western idea of having some individual identity, but I did not like the dualistic idea of being separate from God. On the other hand, I liked the Eastern idea of nondualism. I liked the idea that this world is an illusion of separation, and we have never actually been separated from God. Thus we are merely waking up to our pre-existing condition of always having been united to God. But I did not like the Eastern idea that complete waking up means I will lose all my individuality. I did not mind giving up my ego, yet I felt that when I finally wake up to God, I wanted there to be some individual identity. Does this problem make sense to you?

Judith: Yes, I've studied Eastern philosophy. You want to dissolve the raindrop into God, and you want there to still be some of you left.

Don: Yes, that's the problem of reconciling Western individuality with Eastern nondualism. Then *A Course in Miracles* came along and solved my problem. The Course says that I am part of the one Christ and I am the whole of the one Christ at the same time. This paradox is the genius of the Course. God took pity on us and gave us the answers in the Course that we could not figure out for ourselves. Without the Course, we could not have figured out that we are a part of Christ and the whole of Christ at the same time. In this world, a part of a watch cannot be the whole watch. But in Heaven the Course tells us that every part *is* the whole. The paradox can be explained by a variation of the idea of the raindrop dissolving into the divine ocean. Let's say that the raindrop is a unique red color, and when the red raindrop dissolves completely into the Ocean, it retains its unique redness as its "part-ness" even though it accepts its wholeness in the fullness of the divine ocean. Therefore, it retains its individuality and is not completely lost in the acceptance of its wholeness.

Judith, this paradox is at the heart of answering your question about the nature of the missing piece in your life, but first, let's talk about the cause and the result of the separation. Since you have been studying the Course, you know that some parts of the Sonship, including you and I, decided to ask God for "special favor."[51] This was a request that God the Father give more love to some parts of the Sonship than other parts. God had already given all of Himself, including all of His Love, equally to every part of the Sonship. To be the God of Love, your Father could not give more love to some parts of the Sonship than other parts. The small number of parts of the Sonship that were refused special love decided to get together and form what I call the "collusion illusion."

You and I are parts of the Sonship that caused the separation. To pull off the separation, we could not really separate from God, but we gave ourselves what amounts to an "amnesia pill." The Course calls this the "great amnesia."[52] We made up a false identity that we call the "ego," which is another name for the "amnesia pill," that enables us to forget our true nature and believe in the idea of separation. Our true identity is that we are each part of the one Christ and the whole of the one Christ. The separation was the rejection of our wholeness in Christ and an exaggeration of our "part-ness." Our true nature of wholeness in Christ never left Heaven when the separation happened. Let's go back to your feeling that you have been looking for a missing piece of yourself. Your ego-based individuality is an exaggeration of your true individuality as a part of the one Christ, but you have totally forgotten your wholeness in Christ. So you are part of the Christ in search of your wholeness. You said you were "looking for the missing piece of yourself," but you are really looking for your missing *wholeness*. You have not really lost your wholeness in Christ, but because of the ego, you have lost your *awareness* of your wholeness in Christ. Remembering your wholeness releases the ego and is your key to awakening in Heaven.

Judith: Yes, of course, my ego-based part-ness in this world must be an illusion because my true part-ness in Christ only has reality in the wholeness of Christ in Heaven.

Don: I can see the lights turn on in your mind so you do immediately get that you are a part of the Christ in search of your wholeness in Christ to complete yourself.

The answer I gave Judith that she is a part of the one Christ in search of her wholeness in Christ is the same answer to Xianti's question: "Who is the decider?" You are part of the Christ in search of your wholeness is also the answer to: "Who awakens?" It also answers these questions: "Who is studying the Course? Who is reading this book right now? And why?" Thus it is absolutely essential that you understand that you are a part of Christ in search of your wholeness in Christ.

The terms "Christ," the "Self," and the "Sonship" mean the same thing. They each describe the one Son of God in His Wholeness. Each term describes you as you truly are now and forever. Your Identity is in the Wholeness of the Father and the Son, since neither is separate nor complete without the other. If you were only this divine Wholeness, you would have no divine individuality, which is the complete "nondualism" of Eastern philosophy. The Course offers "qualified nondualism" that includes the nondualistic idea of completely merging with God, but the qualifying factor is that your individuality is not lost in this complete merging with God. Rather, in your union with God, your ego-based individuality is undone and replaced by your true individuality within God. However, your Father created you with a two-part nature of both your individuality and your wholeness as part of God Himself.

One part of your two-part nature is that you are one individual part of the one Christ. The other part of your two-part nature is you are the whole Christ. Your two-part nature seems to be a paradox when seen from the perspective of perception. The partial awareness of perception will logically tell you that you cannot be a unique part of the Christ and also be the whole Christ. But perception brings the partial awareness of separate parts that can combine to make wholeness in their combination. Yet the total awareness of knowledge in Heaven knows this: "Though every aspect [every part of the Sonship] is the whole, you cannot know this until you see that every aspect is the same, perceived in the same light and therefore one."[53] Knowledge in Heaven fully recognizes the wholeness in every part of the one Christ, but perception in this world sees every part as only a small part of a larger whole.

> The whole does define the part, but the part does not define the whole. Yet to know in part is to know entirely because of the fundamental difference between knowledge and perception. In perception the whole is built up of parts that can separate and reassemble in different constellations. But knowledge never changes, so its constellation is permanent. The idea of part-whole relationships has meaning only at the level of perception, where change is possible. Otherwise, there is no difference between the part and whole.[54]

Since the normal logic of perception cannot understand this paradox that the whole is in every part of the one Christ, how can you accept this belief? If you believe the true Author of the Course is the combination of Holy Spirit speaking through Jesus, then you must also believe that the knowledge of the Christ Mind is communicating to you some ideas that transcend your ability to understand them within the limits of perception.

What appears to be a paradox in perception of this world is a perfectly natural awareness in Heaven. Yet when you threw away knowledge in Heaven, you forgot your former natural way of knowing and accepted perception as an unnatural way of thinking.

> The very real difference between perception and knowledge becomes quite apparent if you consider this: There is nothing partial about knowledge. Every aspect is whole, and therefore no aspect is separate. You are an aspect of knowledge, being in the Mind of God, Who knows you. All knowledge must be yours, for in you is all knowledge.[55]

The partial awareness of perception itself is a barrier between God and His children because it blocks the total awareness of knowledge in Heaven. "When no perception stands between God and His creations, or between His children and their own, the knowledge of creation must continue forever."[56] False perceptions or "wrong-mindedness" bring you further away from awakening to knowledge. True perception or "right-mindedness" corrects "wrong-mindedness." Since the separation when you threw away knowledge, your whole mind has been split so it is filled with both true perceptions and false perceptions. The function of the Holy Spirit is to help you prepare to again accept knowledge by first filling your perceptual mind with only true perceptions. Within perception it is difficult to understand the paradox of being part of Christ and the whole of Christ. Yet the awareness of the part as the whole is perfectly natural in the knowledge of Heaven. However, in this world of illusions, perception has blocked your awareness of what is natural to you in your true nature.

> And when you are told what is natural, you cannot understand it. The recognition of the part as whole, and of the whole in every part is perfectly natural, for it is the way God thinks, and what is natural to Him is natural to you.[57]

You cannot rely on your perception alone to obtain the "recognition of the part as whole, and of the whole in every part." You will have to rely on faith in the Source of the Course to accept what seems unnatural to you. You will have to accept that your true Identity is limitless so it transcends your limited perception. You will have to rely on your faith to accept this: You are a part of the one Self and the whole of the one Self. You are part of the Sonship and the whole of the Sonship. You are part of the one Son of God and the whole of the one Son of God. You are part of the one Christ and the whole of the one Christ.

If you believe the previous quotations from the Course about the nature of the part and the whole, you may decide to believe the paradox that you are part of Christ and you are the whole of Christ. But that intellectual affirmation is not enough to experientially awaken you to your true nature. Since your brother is also part of Christ and the whole of Christ, he can be your savior and help you awaken.

> When you meet anyone, remember it is a holy encounter. As you see him you will see yourself. As you treat him you will treat yourself. As you think of him you will think of yourself. Never forget this, for in him you will find yourself or lose yourself. Whenever two Sons of God meet, they are given another chance at salvation. Do not leave anyone without giving salvation to him and receiving it yourself. For I [Jesus] am always there with you, in remembrance of *you*.[58]

What is it about your brother that enables him to be your savior and you to be his savior? Your brother is a part of Christ and you are a part of Christ. Therefore, if you can look past the form of your brother's body and past your judgments of him, you can see that you are both joined in Christ. You can recognize that you are both equal parts of one Christ and have a sense of true brotherhood and oneness with him. Now let's consider that your brother is *more* than a brother. *He is part of you and you are part of him.* "As part of you, he [your brother] is holy."[59]

Here is a form-related analogy to explain why your brother and you are part of each other. Imagine the whole Christ is the "body of Christ" and you are a part of this body and the whole body. You are a part of Christ because you are one "hand" of Christ. Your brother is also a part of Christ because he is one "foot" of Christ. Also, you are the whole body of Christ, so your brother as one foot of Christ is part of your wholeness in Christ. Likewise, your brother is the whole body of Christ, so you as one hand of Christ are part of your brother's wholeness in Christ.

Here's the message of this analogy: Of course, the whole Christ is not really a body, and you are not really a hand of Christ and your brother is not a foot of Christ. Nevertheless, if your true spiritual part-ness in Christ was missing, your brother could not be the whole Christ. Likewise, if your brother's unique part-ness in Christ were missing, you could not be the whole Christ. The conclusion is that for you to be the whole Christ, your brother must be part of your wholeness and you must be part of his wholeness. If you reject your brother who is part of Christ and part of you, you will be denying your shared Identity as the whole Christ. If you recognize your brother as part of you, you will recognize both your brother and yourself as a part of Christ and the whole Christ.

WHAT IS SALVATION?

~ o ~

"Never forget that the Sonship is your salvation, for the Sonship is your Self. As God's creation It is yours, and belonging to you It is His."[60] Your salvation is fully waking up to your true Identity in God, but the wholeness of your Identity always belongs to you. Your wholeness in Christ, in the Self, and in the Sonship doesn't need salvation since your wholeness has never fallen asleep. In Heaven there is no distinction between your part-ness and your wholeness because every part is the whole. But it is your part-ness that became distorted in your mind after the separation so you have forgotten about your wholeness. You have devoted only a small part of your mind to your part-ness and entirely excluded your awareness of your wholeness in Heaven. The small part of your whole mind is dominated by the ego and needs salvation produced by undoing the ego. The ego doesn't recognize your wholeness in Christ and has replaced your part-ness in Christ with "apart-ness" from God and from your brothers. The small part of your whole mind devoted to disordered thinking needs to accept your true nature and let go of your false identity based on the ego's belief in separation. "Your Self does not need salvation, but your mind needs to learn what salvation is."[61]

God has given you Himself and His Glory as your inheritance, but you have to heal your mind to accept His gift of your true Identity and accept the gift of His Glory. "You are not saved *from* anything, but you are saved *for* glory. Glory is your inheritance, given you by your Creator that you might extend it."[62] Salvation is simply the acceptance of your true nature—acceptance of who you already are and must be forever. Your true nature is love just as your Father is Love. If you do not express love, you cannot accept salvation because you cannot accept your true nature. "Yet if you hate part of your Self [your brother] all your understanding is lost, because you are looking on what God created as yourself without love. And since what He created is part of Him, you are denying Him His place in His Own altar."[63]

Your true nature is peace because you are just like your Father in His Peace. If you are not at peace, you cannot accept salvation because you cannot accept your true nature. "Your peace lies in its limitlessness. Limit the peace you share, and your Self must be unknown to you. Every altar to God [your brother] is part of you, because the light He created is one with Him."[64] Your peace must extend to every brother who is a part of wholeness in the Sonship, or you will reject salvation by darkening your mind. "Would you cut off a brother from the light that is yours? You would not do so if you realized that you can darken only your own mind. As you bring him [your brother] back [to Heaven], so will you return. That is the law of God, for the protection of the Wholeness of His Son."[65]

The ego uses denial and projection to convince you that others have done to you what you have really done to yourself. This misperception of the ego must be overcome to accept your true nature. Full acceptance of your true nature will result in awakening to salvation because the ego is undone in the presence of the light and love that you are. *"Only you can deprive yourself of anything.* Do not oppose this realization, for it is truly the beginning of the dawn of light."[66] This acceptance of your full responsibility for inviting all your experiences is very important. "This is a crucial step in the reawakening. The beginning phases of this reversal are often quite painful, for as blame is withdrawn from without, there is a strong tendency to harbor it within. It is difficult at first to realize that this is exactly the same thing, for there is no distinction between within and without."[67]

When you learn to let go of blaming others, you could make the mistake of blaming yourself. Accepting responsibility for your mistakes does not mean shifting blame from others to yourself. It means undoing the whole idea that blame, including self-imposed guilt, has any value or reality. "If your brothers are part of you and you blame them for your deprivation, you are blaming yourself. And you cannot blame yourself without blaming them. That is why blame must be undone, not seen elsewhere."[68] If you blame yourself, you cannot accept salvation since your self-condemnation prevents you from accepting your true nature of love. "Lay it [blame] to yourself and you cannot know yourself, for only the ego blames at all. Self-blame is therefore ego identification, and as much an ego defense as blaming others. *You cannot enter God's Presence if you attack His Son."*[69]

Salvation requires the appreciation and acceptance of your brother and yourself. The kind of self-acceptance that you need can be called "Self-acceptance." True Self-acceptance is accepting your true nature in which you see yourself or, more correctly, see your Self in the face of Christ. "God knows His Son as wholly blameless as Himself, and He is approached through the appreciation of His Son. Christ waits for your acceptance of Him as yourself, and of His Wholeness as yours." To accept yourself is to accept your innocence and the innocence of all your brothers in Christ who are part of you. "There is no condemnation in the Son, for there is no condemnation in the Father. Sharing the perfect Love of the Father the Son must share what belongs to Him, for otherwise he will not know the Father or the Son."[70]

THE PLAN OF
THE ATONEMENT

~ o ~

The Introduction to this book describes the analogy of a three-story hospital that represents healing your mind of its amnesia. The focus is on awakening to your true nature by bringing your awareness from the third floor of intensive care to the second floor of the recovery room and then God will take the final step of transporting you to the first floor that is the final cure of your amnesia as you wake up in Heaven. Although God Himself takes the final step of your awakening, He has a plan that He set in motion when He created the Holy Spirit. His plan is the Atonement designed to heal you of your amnesia. "Healing and Atonement are not related; they are identical."[71]

Following God's plan of Atonement heals your amnesia by returning your mind to the total awareness of knowledge in Heaven. You have amnesia because you now have only the partial awareness of perception that limits your ability to accept your true nature as part of Christ and the whole of Christ. Your perception on the third floor requires intensive care because your mind is split between false and true perceptions. There are seven elevators on the third floor that help carry out the plan of salvation by healing your split mind. These elevators are forgiveness, Christ's vision, the holy relationship, the holy instant, miracles, meditation, and the Atonement itself. These are the seven tools of the Holy Spirit that elevate your consciousness and bring your awareness from the third floor of intensive care to the second floor of the recovery room.

On the third floor, you have perception that fluctuates between loving and unloving thoughts. But using the seven tools of the Holy Spirit brings your awareness to the second-floor recovery room where your mind has "perfect perception" or "total perception" of only loving thoughts and no unloving thoughts. Total perception is also called "redeemed perception," because the mind is completely filled with only loving perceptions. Therefore, your split mind is healed and saved from the illusion of separation and from the mistaken belief in guilt. "Redeemed perception is easily translated into knowledge, for only perception is capable of error and perception has never been."[72]

What does it mean that "perception has never been"? Perception has never been because it is an illusion, and all illusions have never existed because anything outside of reality has never happened in the Mind of God. Perception is an illusion because it is an awareness mechanism based on separation. You are the perceiver, and what you perceive is separate from you. You have never been separate from reality in spite of your perceptual illusions of separation. Yet if your mind has only true perceptions of loving thoughts, your loving mind will prepare you for God taking the final step of transporting your awareness to the first floor for your full recovery from amnesia. God Himself restores your total awareness of knowledge in Heaven. Following God's plan of Atonement makes the transfer of perception to knowledge possible. Perception is fully corrected by God's Love. "Perception is not knowledge, but it can be transferred to knowledge, or cross over into it. It might even be more helpful here to use the literal meaning of transferred or 'carried over,' since the last step is taken by God."[73] Perceptual love becomes so much like the love in the knowledge of Heaven that the transfer from the lesser love of perception can be made to the greater love of knowledge.

> For the Holy Spirit will lead everyone home to his Father, where Christ waits as his Self. Every child of God is one in Christ, for his being is in Christ as Christ's is in God. Christ's Love for you is His Love for His Father, which He knows because He knows His Father's Love for Him. When the Holy Spirit has at last led you to Christ at the altar to His Father, perception fuses into knowledge because perception has become so holy that its transfer to holiness is merely its natural extension. Love transfers to love without any interference, for the two are one.[74]

Love is attracted to love. That is its power. God is Love. And "you are love. Love is your power, which the ego must deny. It must also deny everything this power gives you *because* it gives you everything." [75] The attraction of love to love can't be resisted. Although the ego denies love, love will enable you to deny the ego. The attraction of love in you to the Love in God will bring back the memory of your Father. "What God did not give you has no power over you, and the attraction of love for love remains irresistible. For it is the function of love to unite all things unto itself, and to hold all things together by extending its wholeness."[76]

There are two aspects of the Atonement. One aspect is the Atonement progressing within time on the third floor of intensive care using the seven tools of the Holy Spirit to heal your brother's mind and your own mind. This first aspect of the Atonement is the elevator that helps you navigate through the world of time and space by expressing love. You must accept the Atonement for yourself. Then you become a healer of others and your own mind is also healed. On the third floor of intensive care, you repeatedly accept the Atonement and grow toward the day when you will finally accept the *whole* Atonement. The second aspect of the Atonement focuses on this final acceptance of the whole Atonement that happens on the second-floor recovery room. The purpose of the final acceptance of the whole Atonement is to enable you to permanently overcome the illusions of time and space and accept reality as God created it. "The Atonement was built into the space-time belief to set a limit on the need for the belief itself, and ultimately to make learning complete. The Atonement is the final lesson."[77]

The first aspect of the Atonement is within time and corrects and heals your mind. The second aspect of the Atonement prepares your mind for God's final step in which you ultimately transcend time and space as perception itself is translated into the knowledge of Heaven. This second aspect of the Atonement is at the end of time. "But the Atonement as a completed plan has a unique relationship to time. Until the Atonement is complete, its various phases will proceed in time, but the whole Atonement stands at time's end. At that point the bridge of return has been built."[78] The second aspect of the Atonement as a whole is the fulfillment of God's plan to prepare your mind for His final step. The Atonement heals your mind of all false and unloving perceptions and thus "the bridge of return has been built."[79] Then the ultimate blessing of God completely heals the mind, allowing loving perception to be elevated to the total awareness of the knowledge of Heaven.

The Course describes the Atonement in this way, "Perfect love is the Atonement."[80] Accepting the Atonement naturally means the choice to accept perfect love into the mind. During your life, you can practice accepting perfect love into your mind as you utilized the seven tools of the Holy Spirit: forgiveness, meditation, the holy relationship, miracles, the holy instant, Christ's vision, and the Atonement itself. Accepting the Atonement allows you to perform miracles. "*The sole responsibility of the miracle worker is to accept the Atonement for himself.* This means you recognize that mind is the only creative level, and that its errors are healed by the Atonement. Once you accept this, your mind can only heal."[81] Miracles are expressions of love. By performing miracles, you prepare your mind for the final acceptance of the whole Atonement at the end of time. "The Atonement is but the way back to what was never lost. Your Father could not cease to love His Son."[82]

The Atonement is God's blessing. "You have a part to play in the Atonement, but the plan of the Atonement is beyond you."[83] The plan of Atonement is "beyond you" because it is not *your* plan. It is God's gift to you. "The plan is not yours because of your limited ideas about what you are. This sense of limitation is where all errors arise. The way to undo them, therefore, is not *of* you but *for* you."[84] God's gift of the Atonement enables you to share love and to fully awaken to your true guiltlessness, untouched by illusory errors. "Atonement is for all, because it is the way to undo the belief that anything is for you alone."[85]

The Atonement teaches you how to share. "The Atonement is a lesson in sharing, which is given you because *you have forgotten how to do it*. The Holy Spirit merely reminds you of the natural use of your abilities. By reinterpreting the ability to attack into the ability to share, He translates what you have made into what God created."[86] To accept the Atonement means accepting perfect love, which enables you to forgive your brother and forgive yourself. Every act of forgiveness contributes to the overall plan of the Atonement that will bring salvation to all the sleeping Sons of God.

Practicing forgiveness as your function in God's plan of Atonement will relieve you of your false belief in guilt. "You will feel guilty till you learn this [function of forgiveness]. For in the end, whatever form it takes, your guilt arises from your failure to fulfill your function [of creating in Heaven] in God's Mind with all of yours [your mind]. Can you escape this guilt by failing to fulfill your function [of forgiveness] here?"[87] When you fulfill your function of forgiveness in God's plan of Atonement, you remove the barriers you made to your awareness of God and His knowledge. "You need not understand creation to do what must be done [forgiveness] before that knowledge would be meaningful to you. God breaks no barriers [that you made]; neither did He make them."[88] God does not remove the barriers that you have made to the awareness of Him because He would never violate your free will by forcing you to release your self-imposed illusions. Yet by fulfilling your function of forgiveness in the Atonement, you can undo the illusory barriers that you have made. "When you release them [your illusory barriers] they are gone. God will not fail, nor ever has in anything. Decide that God is right and you are wrong about yourself."[89]

God is the First Cause. His Son, who you are, is His Effect. God created you as part of Himself. Therefore, you are like Him in every way except you cannot be the First Cause. Thus you have His eternal holiness. "He created you out of Himself, but still within Him. He knows what you are. Remember that there is no second to Him. There cannot, therefore, be anyone without His Holiness, nor anyone unworthy of His perfect Love."[90] Your function is to receive and express the perfect love of the Atonement. "Fail not in your function of loving in a loveless place made out of darkness and deceit, for thus are darkness and deceit undone. Fail not yourself, but instead offer [love] to God and you His blameless Son."[91] Fulfilling your function of expressing love and affirming guiltlessness is the gift of gratitude you give to God. He will reward your gratitude by restoring your full awareness of your true nature in Him. "For this small gift of appreciation for His Love, God will Himself exchange your gift for His."[92]

Your awakening is achieved by fulfilling your function of accepting and then expressing the perfect love of the Atonement. But you cannot fulfill your function of expressing love unless you make all your choices with the guidance of the Holy Spirit deciding for you. "Before you make any decisions for yourself, remember that you have decided against your function in Heaven, and then consider carefully whether you want to make decisions here."[93] Part of your function is to decide that you do not know your best interests. "Your function here is only to decide against deciding what you want, in recognition that you do not know. How, then, can you decide what you should do?"[94]

Only the Holy Spirit knows how to truly manifest your function, so He must be allowed to decide for God for you. "Leave all decisions to the One [the Holy Spirit] Who speaks for God, and for your function as He knows it."[95] The Holy Spirit teaches you to replace your belief in guilt with His teaching of your true guiltlessness. "So will He teach you to remove the awful burden you have laid upon yourself by loving not the Son of God, and trying to teach him guilt instead of love."[96] You will be able to fulfill your function of giving up your mistaken belief that guilt is real. "Give up this frantic and insane attempt that cheats you of the joy of living with your God and Father, and of waking gladly to His Love and Holiness that join together as the truth in you, making you one with Him."[97]

If you think for yourself alone, you will think destructively. If you think with God, you will find peace of mind that is already within you but unrecognized. "When you have learned how to decide with God, all decisions become as easy and as right as breathing. There is no effort, and you will be led as gently as if you were being carried down a quiet path in summer. Only your own volition seems to make deciding hard."[98] The Holy Spirit can be trusted to do His part of guiding you. "The Holy Spirit will not delay in answering your every question what to do. He knows."[99] The Holy Spirit will guide you and will help you accomplish your function because with your permission, He will function through you to accomplish God's Will of expressing His Love. "And He will tell you, and then do it for you. You who are tired will find this is more restful than sleep. For you can bring your guilt into sleeping, but not into this."[100]

Because perception is only partial awareness, you cannot possibly fully comprehend God and His Love. "You cannot understand how much your Father loves you, for there is no parallel in your experience of the world to help you understand it. There is nothing on earth with which it can compare, and nothing you have ever felt apart from Him resembles it ever so faintly."[101] Because your awareness is limited, you cannot give in this world as completely as you will be able to give of yourself when you awaken in Heaven. "You cannot even give a blessing in perfect gentleness. Would you know of One Who gives forever, and Who knows of nothing except giving?"[102] When you wake up in Heaven, you will fully realize how truly blessed you have always been. "The children of Heaven live in the light of the blessing of their Father, because they know that they are sinless."[103]

Your function in the Atonement is to awaken your awareness of your brother's guiltlessness and your own guiltlessness. "The Atonement was established as the means of restoring guiltlessness to minds that have denied it, and thus denied Heaven to themselves."[104] The belief in guilt blocks your awareness of your true nature. "Atonement teaches you the true condition of the Son of God."[105] That condition is guiltlessness. The Atonement doesn't tell you your true nature but does remove the blocks to the light, love, and truth that you are as the holy Son of God. The Atonement "does not teach you what you are, or what your Father is. The Holy Spirit, Who remembers this for you, merely teaches you how to remove the blocks that stand between you and what you know."[106] What you have made with illusions will block your awareness of reality, so you must let go of the illusions you have made. The Holy Spirit's "memory [of what you are and what God is] is yours. If you remember what you have made, you are remembering nothing. Remembrance of reality is in Him, and therefore in you."[107]

There is no compromise between guilt and guiltlessness because only one is true. Those who identify with guilt cannot communicate with those who identify with guiltlessness. "The guiltless and the guilty are totally incapable of understanding one another. Each perceives the other as like himself, making both unable to communicate, because each sees the other unlike the way he sees himself."[108] The Holy Spirit is God's Communication Link with you. "God can communicate only to the Holy Spirit in your mind, because only He shares the knowledge of what you are with God. And only the Holy Spirit can answer God for you, for only He knows what God is."[109] Thoughts that are not in accord with God and the Holy Spirit can seem very real to you because you made them. But all the thoughts you made by yourself, such as the thought of guilt, do not exist except in your imagination. "Everything else [what you made without God and without the Holy Spirit] that you have placed within your mind cannot exist, for what is not in communication with the Mind of God has never been. Communication with God is life. Nothing without it is at all."[110] The next section will describe forgiveness as the recognition of guiltlessness.

THE FORGIVENESS ELEVATOR

~ o ~

Using the analogy in the Introduction of the three-story hospital where your amnesia is healed, there are seven "elevators" on the third floor of intensive care that will bring you to the second-floor recovery room. This section emphasizes the "forgiveness elevator." Forgiveness is the primary means advocated in the Course for healing your amnesia. "That forgiveness is healing needs to be understood..."[111]

The main idea of the previous section titled "Who Awakens?" is that you are the part of the one Christ in search of your wholeness in Christ. But how can you apply the awareness of your part-ness and wholeness in Christ to your learning of the Course? This book is designed to help you affirm your part-ness and wholeness in Christ as you learn about how to awaken. Among the previous quotations about the part and the whole, this is the one that is most helpful: "The recognition of the part as whole, and of the whole in every part is perfectly natural, for it is the way God thinks, and what is natural to Him is natural to you."[112]

According to this quotation, it is natural for you to recognize "the part as whole, and of the whole in every part." You are the learner of this Course, and you have already learned that you are the decider who must in all situations choose between the Holy Spirit and the ego. When you decide for the ego, it will teach you to identify with your "apart-ness" because the ego itself is the idea of separation. When you decide for the Holy Spirit, He will remind you to identify with your true part-ness in Christ and your wholeness in the Christ. Also, deciding for the Holy Spirit means allowing Him to make all other decisions to help you awaken.

Let's apply this understanding to the forgiveness elevator. Forgiveness is your primary means of bringing your awareness from the third floor to the second floor because it discriminates in favor of acknowledging your part-ness and wholeness in Christ and it discriminates against your apart-ness. "Forgiveness is the healing of the perception of separation."[113] Therefore, forgiveness restores your awareness of your part-ness and wholeness in Christ and heals your perception of apart-ness. Because forgiveness affirms the part-ness and wholeness of your brother and overcomes your apparent apart-ness from your brother, you join with him and recognize your equality in the Sonship.

> Forgiveness recognizes what you thought your brother did to you has not occurred. It does not pardon sins and make them real. It sees there was no sin. And in that view are all your sins forgiven. What is sin, except a false idea about God's Son? Forgiveness merely sees its falsity, and therefore lets it go.[114]

The sleeping Son of God can make mistakes but can't sin and can't be guilty since he deserves only love. Forgiveness recognizes that your brother deserves only love and is never guilty just as you deserve only love and are never guilty. Forgiveness recognizes that your brother has not harmed you. Also, forgiveness recognizes that your brother is part of the one Christ and the whole of the one Christ just as you are. Thus forgiveness recognizes who your brother really is and who you are.

Let's draw a contrast between *false forgiveness* and *true forgiveness.* False forgiveness claims to forgive a person while still seeing him as a guilty sinner. True forgiveness in the Course is the practice of forgiving by recognizing that guilt and sin are unreal and that everyone deserves love. True forgiveness, which is based on right-mindedness, involves both *"overlooking and looking."* The "overlooking" part of forgiveness looks past what is forgiven, perceiving that it is entirely an illusion that never happened in reality. Thus "overlooking" consists of looking beyond error from the beginning, and therefore keeps it unreal for you. Overlooking requires only that you recognize immediately that all fearful appearances of sin and guilt are illusory. Such illusions are unreal and untrue because they contradict the truth that every Son of God is just as holy now as when God created him in the eternal present moment.

> Forgiveness through the Holy Spirit lies simply in looking beyond error from the beginning, and thus keeping it unreal for you. Do not let any belief in its realness enter your mind, or you will also believe that you must undo what you have made in order to be forgiven. What has no effect does not exist, and to the Holy Spirit the effects of error are nonexistent. By steadily and consistently cancelling out all its effects, everywhere and in all respects, He teaches that the ego does not exist and proves it.[115]

The "looking" part of forgiveness sees only the divine holiness and true reality of the one who is forgiven, realizing he is always worthy of only love. Since he deserves love, you join with him. Forgiveness removes the illusory gap between you and your brother and proves to yourself that the ego, the whole idea of separation, is an illusion. The looking part of forgiveness looks for what is real because your brother's true nature and your true nature is reality. The overlooking part of forgiveness overlooks what is unreal because it has never been and will never be your brother's true nature or your true nature as God created you. Forgiveness as discrimination between the real and the unreal is the central message of the Course, described in the Introduction:

Nothing real can be threatened.
Nothing unreal exists.[116]

The question that most students of the Course ask is this: How do I manifest forgiveness in a practical way? The answer is the two-part process of "looking and overlooking," which is the practical aspect of forgiveness that I call *"focused forgiveness."* It is a form of meditation applied outwardly toward others in which you focus on looking for the divine in your brother and overlooking everything else. Forgiveness therefore looks for your brother's reality and overlooks his unreality. Thus it affirms your own reality and overlooks your own unreality. With forgiveness you look for and see your brother as a part of Christ and also see his wholeness in Christ. You do that by seeing everything divine in your brother. You see light, love, truth, and everything eternal in him. In order to succeed in seeing the divine in your brother, you must overlook everything that is not divine. You overlook his body, his judgments of himself, your judgments of him, anything temporary, and anything that would distract you from seeing the divine in him.

If you were practicing an inner form of meditation with your eyes closed, you wouldn't expect to be able to focus your mind continuously. Your mind would wander because of distracting stray thoughts. But without blaming yourself, you would gently return your mind to your focus for inner meditation. Exactly the same thing happens in your outer meditation of focused forgiveness. Although you are focusing on the divine in your brother and overlooking everything not divine, your mind will wander to stray thoughts and judgments will float into your mind. But then you can return to focusing only on the divine.

Here is an analogy of how to deal with stray thoughts: Imagine you are sitting on the bank of a river and see garbage floating by. You must not look upstream to see where the garbage is coming from and must not look downstream to see where the garbage is going. Allow your vision to look straight ahead, so you will still see the garbage. The garbage represents your stray thoughts of judgment that will float through your mind. This analogy shows you how to limit the distracting effect of stray thoughts. When your mind temporarily wanders away from perceiving the divine in your brother, you gently refocus your mind on seeing the divine and overlooking everything else.

You cannot overlook your brother's errors if you think they are real and if you think he is guilty. But you can easily overlook his errors if you immediately recognize they are unreal. However, if you examine your brother's errors by paying attention to them, you will be following the ego's advice on forgiveness.

> The ego, too, has a plan of forgiveness because you are asking for one, though not of the right teacher... The ego's plan is to have you see error clearly first, and then overlook it. Yet how can you overlook what you have made real? By seeing it clearly, you have made it real and *cannot* overlook it.[117]

The ego's plan of forgiveness is to clearly examine errors in detail and then overlook them, which makes errors seem real so they cannot be overlooked. The Holy Spirit's plan of forgiveness is to overlook errors immediately in order to keep them unreal for you. Instead of looking at errors, even just to examine them, the Holy Spirit wants you to look at your brother's reality in Christ because doing so reminds you of your own reality in Christ. Because your Identity in Christ is shared, your perception of your brother will be your perception of yourself. If you identify with your brother's errors and not his reality, you will identify with your own errors and not with your reality. True forgiveness always recognizes the difference between your reality and the unreality of errors. Thus you forgive *what never happened to you* because the error that is forgiven is not real and so does not exist. However, if you think the error is real, you will imagine that you have to do something more to correct it than simply handing it over to the Holy Spirit and accepting the Atonement, which corrects all errors and their effects.

It is easy to forgive when you realize that you always forgive your brother for what he never did to you. True forgiveness sees that there is nothing to forgive, so it is correct to say that God did not forgive you because He knows there was nothing to forgive. "God does not forgive because He has never condemned."[118] Christ in you also knows there is nothing to forgive, and He would gladly share His awareness of your sinlessness, bringing peace to your mind if you identify with Him.

> Where could your peace arise *but* from forgiveness? The Christ in you looks only on the truth, and sees no condemnation that could need forgiveness. He is at peace *because* He sees no sin. Identify with Him, and what has He that you have not? He is your eyes, your ears, your hands, your feet. How gentle are the sights He sees, the sounds He hears.[119]

THE MEDITATON
ELEVATOR

≈ ● ≈

The next elevator bringing you from the third floor to the second floor is the "meditation elevator." The previous section describes focused forgiveness as meditation applied outwardly toward others. Forgiveness and meditation have a reciprocal relationship. Since forgiveness is meditation applied outwardly, the inverse is equally true: *Meditation is forgiveness applied inwardly toward yourself.* When you forgive your brother by letting go of your grievances, you are helping your brother to heal his mind and simultaneously helping to heal your own mind. Your forgiveness of others is really a means of forgiving yourself. Yet this process of forgiving yourself can also be done directly by the inner practices of meditation. After all, when you go within, you are letting go of distracting thoughts and judgments. You are attempting to go past these distractions, which are inner grievances that you are holding against yourself. These grievances hide your true nature. Just as you can see the divine in your brother by letting go of grievances, you can apply forgiveness toward yourself by looking past your inner grievances to find the divine within.

Forgiveness is your means of transferring your awareness from the third floor to the second floor because it discriminates in favor of your part-ness and wholeness in Christ and discriminates against your apart-ness. But does meditation perform this same function? At first glance it may seem that meditation is a solitary activity and therefore it appears to be unlike forgiveness because it emphasizes your apart-ness from your brother. But does meditation really separate you from your brother and is it really a solitary activity?

No path to God can be complete if it is a solitary path that excludes your brothers. Meditation is not the solitary practice that it appears to be, and the goal of meditation is not an individual goal. The following quotation from *Absence From Felicity* was part of the early dictation received by Helen. In this quotation, Jesus commented to Bill regarding his daily practice of traditional meditation in which he emptied his mind of all thoughts to become inwardly silent:

> Your [Bill's] giant step forward was to *insist* on a collaborative venture. This does not go against the true spirit of meditation at all. It is inherent *in* it. Meditation is a collaborative venture with God. It *cannot* be undertaken successfully by those who disengage themselves from the Sonship....[120]

Some early parts of the dictation, in which Helen and Bill were addressed directly by Jesus, were altered so that the Course as a whole would be addressed to all seekers. The above quotation made its way into the Course in an altered manner in which the first usage of the word "meditation" was omitted altogether and the second reference to the word "meditation" was changed to the word "salvation," stated as follows:

> Salvation is a collaborative venture. It cannot be undertaken successfully by those who disengage themselves from the Sonship....[121]

The original words of Jesus gave a new definition of the "true spirit of meditation" as inherently a joining with God and the Sonship. The idea that true meditation "cannot be undertaken successfully by those who disengage themselves from the Sonship" was dictated by Jesus as a correction of the idea of isolation that is inherent in the old concept of meditation. If the original version of the new definition of the "true spirit of meditation" had been included in the Course, it may have prevented some misinterpretations of the value of meditation. Including the new definition from Jesus would have alerted Course students to the fact that meditation is helpful as a means of joining with others, as long as it is practiced without reinforcing the belief in sin and separation.

The original meaning of the quotation in which Jesus addressed Bill indicated that meditation is a good practice if its purpose is properly understood as a means of joining with God *and* with all your brothers. The combination of meditation with relationships is not an alteration of meditation but rather its true purpose. Meditating with a sense of being isolated from the rest of the Sonship defeats its purpose and will not succeed. If you separate yourself from the Sonship, you will separate yourself from God. If you draw closer to the Sonship, you will draw closer to God. In the same way that forgiveness discriminates in favor of your part-ness and wholeness in Christ and against your apart-ness, meditation, if properly understood, performs this same function.

When the Course refers to setting aside periods for daily "quiet time," it is referring to what is generally called "meditation." All meditation methods involve ignoring distracting thoughts that come from the ego and simultaneously focusing on a sacred goal. Thus meditation brings detachment from the ego and attraction to the divine. In the Manual for Teachers, the Course recommends a daily quiet time for both the morning and evening. This quiet time is described as being very similar to, but less structured than, the practices learned in your Workbook lessons, such as the focusing methods of meditation.

> ... as soon as possible after waking take your quiet time, continuing a minute or two after you begin to find it difficult....
>
> The same procedures should be followed at night. Perhaps your quiet time should be fairly early in the evening, if it is not feasible for you to take it just before going to sleep. It is not wise to lie down for it. It is better to sit up, in whatever position you prefer. Having gone through the workbook, you must have come to some conclusions in this respect.[122]

Meditation is important in your spiritual growth, yet it plays only a secondary role in the Course. Ingrained ego flaws need to be addressed at the form level in which they operate. The difficult work of spiritual growth is done at the level of perception, where the ego dwells. For this reason, the teachings of the Course are mainly concerned with changing your perceptions and only secondarily on affirming one perception or one set of perceptions, as often occurs in meditation. The goal of the Course is to change your entire thought system in order to grow toward unifying your mind with all loving and true perceptions. The primary means of facilitating this gradual transformation and unification of the mind is forgiveness, rather than meditation. Nevertheless, meditation can be a powerful elevator of your awareness. Helen's Song of Prayer speaks of the term "true prayer" but is actually talking about meditation. Prayer is normally considered as to be asking God for something. But true prayer is meditation because it merely consists of opening your heart and mind, while accepting the light, love, and truth you already are as the Son of God. "Through prayer [meditation] love is received, and through miracles love is expressed."[123]

No one specific meditation method is recommended for the daily quiet times. It is obvious that the Workbook lessons offer a variety of methods that lead in the direction of experiencing the divine presence. The Course seems to be saying that any technique will be sufficient. The method most often advocated in the Course is repeating an idea in your mind, and then letting go of that thought in order to experience the divine presence without words. If the mind becomes distracted, then you return to the central thought for the day. When the mind is no longer distracted, you return to experiencing the divine presence in wordless contemplation.

The type of meditation that is *not* recommended in the Course is any method that reinforces a sense of sinfulness as an attempt to reach

God while simultaneously feeling you are unworthy of Him. You do not need to do anything to make yourself worthy of God since He has already created you holy. This is explained in the Text in the section titled "I Need Do Nothing."

> It is extremely difficult to reach Atonement [God's Plan for your Salvation] by fighting against sin. Enormous effort is expended in the attempt to make holy what is hated and despised. Nor is a lifetime of contemplation and long periods of meditation aimed at detachment from the body necessary. All such attempts will ultimately succeed because of their purpose. Yet the means are tedious and very time consuming, for all of them look to the future for release from a state of present unworthiness and inadequacy.[124]

The Course statement "I need do nothing" does not mean you do not have to do any meditation as part of your mind training. It merely means that you do not have to do anything to make yourself worthy of God. In addition, it is clear from the context of this section that the Course is offering an alternative to the tediousness and ineffectiveness of methods that remind you of sinfulness that has no basis in reality.

> To do nothing is to rest, and make a place within you where the activity of the body ceases to demand attention. Into this place the Holy Spirit comes, and there abides. He will remain when you forget, and the body's activities return to occupy your conscious mind.
>   Yet there will always be this place of rest to which you can return. And you will be more aware of this quiet center of the storm than all its raging activity. This quiet center, in which you do nothing, will remain with you, giving you rest in the midst of every busy doing on which you are sent. For from this center will you be directed how to use the body sinlessly. It is this center, from which the body is absent, that will keep it so in your awareness of it.[125]

Meditation is a way of doing nothing in regard to worldly mental and physical activity. Since most doing involves the body, when you do nothing with the body, you can find the place of rest within your mind where the Holy Spirit abides. To do nothing means finding the "quiet center, in which you do nothing." This quiet center of rest can be found now instead of using tedious methods that involve years of seeking future release from present unworthiness. In fact, this quiet center can and must be found in the holy instant that is in the real world.

THE HOLY
RELATIONSHIP
ELEVATOR

≈ ○ ≈

The "holy relationship elevator" strongly emphasizes that you can't transfer your awareness from the third floor to the second floor all by yourself. "The Kingdom cannot be found alone, and you who are the Kingdom cannot find yourself alone."[126] You need the help of your brother because, if you exclude him, you would be excluding the fact that your brother and you are both equal parts of the one Christ and are joined in the wholeness of Christ that is his true nature and your true nature.

> The Holy Spirit teaches you that if you look only at yourself you cannot find yourself, because that is not what you are. Whenever you are with a brother, you are learning what you are because you are teaching what you are. Give him his place in the Kingdom and you will have yours.[127]

Certainly you can experience some divine aspects by looking within, but you cannot entirely awaken to your true nature by looking within yourself *alone*. You can find your place in God's Kingdom only by acknowledging and appreciating your brother's place with you in the Sonship. You can never actually be alone because your true nature is in the Father, the Son, and the Holy Spirit. As you perceive your brother, you will perceive yourself. In your partner you will see your part-ness and wholeness in Christ and you will remember your own part-ness and wholeness in Christ.

> You can encounter only part of yourself because you are part of God, Who is everything. His power and glory are everywhere, and you cannot be excluded from them. The ego teaches that your strength is in you alone. The Holy Spirit teaches that all strength is in God and *therefore* in you.[128]

In the holy relationship, two people join for a common purpose. Also, they must have common interests in the pursuit of that common purpose so they have the same motivation for pursuing that purpose. If both partners have the same unselfish interests, they will be united in a holy relationship. Holy relationship partners join for what they can gain together rather than for what they can gain separately with separate motivations. When the partners join in a holy relationship, the Holy Spirit enters the relationship. Although they may initially have only a mundane common purpose, the Holy Spirit will help them accept His higher purpose of perceiving holiness in each other instead of their mundane purpose. By joining in the purpose of holiness, they overcome the ego's purpose of guilt and limit their identification with the ego itself.

> Those who have joined their brothers have detached themselves from their belief that their identity lies in the ego. A holy relationship is one in which you join with what is part of you in truth.[129]

Unlike the holy relationship, the special relationship acts like an exclusive club of two in which each partner feels he is trading his lack of specialness for the greater specialness taken from his partner. This forms an ivory tower mentality of separation. The two partners in their specialness are pitted against the world of less special people so differences are highlighted.

In contrast to the special relationship, the holy relationship fosters a deep sense of equality between each partner and, just as importantly, equality with everyone else. "Here [in the holy relationship] is belief in differences undone. Here is the faith in differences shifted to sameness."[130] This sense of sameness and equality with your brother means you can see how everything you learn about relating to your partner also applies to how you need to relate to everyone else. You will learn from your holy relationship to place your faith in the truth and in the holiness you see in every brother in every situation.

In the holy relationship, you forgive each other, and you become saviors for each other. Then you generalize your learning to realize that everyone to whom you extend forgiveness becomes your savior and you become his savior. Instead of the exclusiveness of the special relationship, the holy relationship "must extend, as you extended when you and he [your partner] joined."[131] The holy relationship is a means of extending holiness to other relationships. "The extension of the Holy Spirit's purpose [of holiness] from your relationship to others, to bring them gently in, is the way in which He will bring means and goal in line."[132] Your holy relationship is not only the means of your salvation; it is the means through which salvation comes to many others through the Holy Spirit.

THE MIRACLES ELEVATOR

~ ⚬ ~

The "miracles elevator" affirms that your brother is part of Christ and the whole of Christ, and so it proves to you that you are part of Christ and the whole of Christ since you and your brother are one. "Wholeness is the perceptual content of miracles."[133] Miracles are expressions of love that remind you of your wholeness with your brother in the Sonship.

Miracles occur naturally as expressions of love. The real miracle is the love that inspires them. In this sense everything that comes from love is a miracle.[134]

Perhaps you have been told that *miracles are changes in perception.* Since you know cows produce milk, would you conclude that cows *are* milk? The *result* of miracles is that they produce changes in perception. However, miracles themselves are not changes in perception. Similarly, although miracles produce healing, miracles themselves are not healing, but they are the expressions of love that bring healing.

The miracle is the means, the Atonement is the principle, and healing is the result. To speak of "a miracle of healing" is to combine two orders of reality inappropriately. Healing is not a miracle. The Atonement, or the final miracle, is a remedy and any type of healing is a result.[135]

The result of a miracle is old perceptions of fear are replaced by new perceptions of love and forgiveness. "Miracles are examples of right thinking, aligning your perceptions with truth as God created it. A miracle is a correction introduced into false thinking by me. It acts as a catalyst, breaking up erroneous perception and reorganizing it properly. This places you under the Atonement principle, where perception is healed."[136]

Miracles are an exchange of light and love going to the receiver of the miracle and returning equally to the giver of the miracle. This loving mutual exchange is a miracle, which brings healing to both the mind of the giver and receiver of forgiveness. "Miracles are a kind of exchange. Like all expressions of love, which are always miraculous in the true sense, the exchange reverses the physical laws. They bring more love both to the giver *and* the receiver."[137]

The awareness of oneness in Heaven is a direct experience. In the world of form, miracles are indirect experiences of Heaven that can lead to awakening to the direct experience of Heaven in which knowledge of God is restored. Miracles express love and so express sharing since love is sharing. The sharing of loving perceptions in this world leads to the direct sharing of love that happens in the knowledge of Heaven.

> In Heaven reality is shared and not reflected. By sharing its reflection here, its truth becomes the only perception the Son of God accepts. And thus, remembrance of his Father dawns on him, and he can no longer be satisfied with anything but his own reality.[138]

You seem to live in a world where it appears that everything is limited. "You on earth have no conception of limitlessness, for the world you seem to live in is a world of limits."[139] In this world of limitations and differences, it seems that all activities must have a range of difficulty. But there is one activity that has no limits and no range of difficulty.

> In this world, it is not true that anything without order of difficulty can occur. The miracle, therefore, has a unique function, and is motivated by a unique Teacher Who brings the laws of another world to this one. The miracle is the one thing you can do that transcends order, being based not on differences but on equality.[140]

Miracles are reflections of Heaven that introduce heavenly laws into this world. There is no competition in Heaven, and there everything is unlimited. Thus miracles bring into this world both equality and limitlessness. "Miracles are not in competition, and the number of them that you can do is limitless. They can be simultaneous and legion. This is not difficult to understand, once you conceive of them as possible at all."[141] All miracles are equal in difficulty.

> There is no order of difficulty in miracles because all of God's Sons are of equal value, and their equality is their oneness. The whole power of God is in every part of Him, and nothing contradictory to His Will is either great or small. What does not exist has no size and no measure. To God all things are possible. And to Christ it is given to be like the Father.[142]

No miracle is harder or easier than any other miracle, but this is hard to understand in a world of differences. "What is more difficult to grasp is the lack of order of difficulty that stamps the miracle as something that must come from elsewhere, not from here. From the world's viewpoint, this is impossible."[143] All miracles are equal in difficulty because God's unlimited power is behind every miracle. Also, miracles manifest the equality of all parts of the one Christ and restore the oneness that God's sleeping Sons had forgotten in dreams of separation.

The miracle demonstrates the truth of the Holy Spirit's judgment that your brothers can only express love or a call for love. "The miracle is the recognition that this is true."[144] The miracle expresses both love and a call for love. The miracle worker expresses love by responding to his brother with a miracle, recognizing he is calling for love. If you are a miracle worker, you must accept the perfect love of the Atonement as your sole responsibility. When you accept the Atonement for yourself, your mind is joined with your brother's mind so your love is shared with him. Thus God's perfect Love is expressed through you to your brother. This sharing of love helps you remember God.

Since you asked for God's Love by accepting the Atonement, you can recognize that your brother is asking for love that he has refused to give to himself. Yet your brother has the option of opening directly to God's Love by accepting the Atonement. When your brother and you have accepted God's Love and the Atonement, you can quite naturally share love with each other. "Where there is love, your brother must give it to you because of what it is."[145] If your brother does not accept God's Love directly and does not accept the Atonement, he will call for love from you since you have accepted God's Love and the Atonement. In the miracle, you give your brother the love he is asking for. "But where there is a call for love, you must give it because of what you are."[146] During a miracle when your brother receives love from God indirectly through you, he sends love back to you out of gratitude. This sharing helps your brother to remember God, just as the miracle helps you to remember God, since God is remembered through sharing love.

Miracles are interpersonal so you cannot perform a miracle alone. "You have done miracles, but it is quite apparent that you have not done them alone."[147] Since miracles express love, they always involve joining. "You have succeeded [in performing miracles] whenever you have reached another mind and joined with it."[148] When you join with one brother in a miracle, you begin to open your mind to the whole Sonship and you connect with your brother's and your own unique part-ness in Christ. You begin to recognize your brother's and your own true nature of being the Christ, the one Self you share. "When two minds join as one and share one idea equally, the first link in the awareness of the Sonship as One has been made."[149]

Just as a long-term holy relationship is a relationship in which two people join in a common purpose, a miracle is a very temporary holy relationship in which both participants join in the common purpose of sharing the one idea of exchanging light and love. By sharing one idea, one person's part in Christ and another person's part in Christ are joined. Since each part of Christ is also the whole Christ, joining two parts of Christ reminds both participants that they are joined in the wholeness of the Self. Joining with your brother's mind is facilitated by the Holy Spirit. "When you have made this joining as the Holy Spirit bids you, and have offered it to Him to use as He sees fit, His natural perception of your gift enables Him to understand it, and you to use His understanding on your behalf."[150]

In Heaven you share love fully with every part of the Sonship. In this world you share love in miracles that confirm your shared Identity. "Earlier I [Jesus] said this course will teach you how to remember what you are, restoring your Identity to you. We have already learned that this Identity is shared. The miracle becomes the means of sharing It."[151] Your Identity is your shared love nature as the Christ. In the miracle, you see your brother's Identity and accept your own shared Identity with him. "By supplying your Identity wherever It is not recognized, you will recognize It."[152] Recognizing your shared Identity means you are remembering God because your Identity is part of Him.

This is the miracle of creation; *that it is one forever.* Every miracle you offer to the Son of God is but the true perception of one aspect of the whole [Sonship]. Though every aspect *is* the whole, you cannot know this until you *see* that every aspect is the same, perceived in the same light and therefore one.[153]

You are an aspect of the whole and you are the whole, just as your brother is an equal aspect of the whole and he is the whole. God blesses you for every miracle you perform since you have recognized His Son Whom He loves. "And God Himself, Who wills to be with His Son forever, will bless each recognition of His Son with all the Love He holds for him."[154] God gives all of His power to every miracle so there is no miracle that is more or less difficult than any other miracle. "Nor will the power of all His Love be absent from any miracle you offer to His Son. How, then, can there be any order of difficulty among them?"[155] Miracles remind you of your equality and oneness with your brothers. Just as there is only one reality, there is only one great miracle. You are God's one and only miracle!

They [miracles] are all the same; all beautiful and equal in their holiness. And He will offer them unto His Father as they were offered unto Him. There is one miracle, as there is one reality. And every miracle you do contains them all, as every aspect of reality you see blends quietly into the one reality of God. The only miracle that ever was is God's most holy Son, created in the one reality that is his Father.[156]

THE HOLY INSTANT
ELEVATOR

≈ • ≈

The "holy instant elevator" takes only one instant to bring you from the third floor to the second floor, but it is only a temporary move until you allow it to be permanent. The holy instant is always there awaiting your acceptance of it. The holy instant reminds you that you are part of Christ and the whole of Christ by connecting you with the entire Sonship and your Father. The holy instant is a time of perfect communication, of giving and receiving in which God and the whole Sonship participate. Thus your mind is open to receive the divine truth that reflects Heaven. "Yet in the holy instant you unite directly with God, and all your brothers join in Christ. Those who are joined in Christ are in no way separate. For Christ is the Self the Sonship shares, as God shares His Self with Christ."[157]

The holy instant is a time of joining in which normal habits of thinking and feeling are set aside. The past and future are gone in the holy instant, and you are transported to the eternal present moment of *now* in eternity. The holy instant overcomes the ego because: "'Now' has no meaning to the ego. The present merely reminds it of past hurts, and it reacts to the present as if it *were* the past."[158] When you are releasing the past and future in the holy instant, you are releasing the ego. The holy instant is your window to Heaven. Though it only lasts for an instant of time, it leads toward experiencing the eternal now. But you may ask: *What is so significant about experiencing "now"?* This question implies that you already experience now all the time so there is nothing unusual about the present moment. You may believe that you currently understand what the word "now" means and that every day you experience now all the time. Yet your belief is based on your past learning. The Course repeatedly asks you to release your past learning because if you think you already understand, you have removed your motivation for learning. The Course offers you a definition of now by explaining the nature of the holy instant, but the understanding of now that the Course provides is very different from the false perceptions that the ego offers. Perhaps your past learning has taught you about the commonly accepted idea of "being here now" or in other words "being fully present" with another person. This typically means bringing the full awareness of your heart and mind in the present moment to each individual you encounter. Being fully present is wonderful and very beneficial, but is this really a direct experience of now? If you perceive yourself as a body being fully present with another person who is a body, you cannot experience now with him.

Consider what science tells you about experiencing now. When you are outside and look at the sun, are you seeing the sun now? No, you are not. The sun is 93 million miles away from earth. Sunlight travels at a rate of 186,282 miles per second. At that rate, it takes 8.3 minutes for sunlight to reach the earth. If the sun suddenly became totally black, you would not see the blackness when it happens. You could only see it 8.3 minutes after it happens. Thus you are never seeing the sun now since you are seeing the sun 8.3 minutes ago. You are seeing the past. How does this long-distance time delay apply to looking at closer objects? Most television shows are prerecorded, but even live television shows have some small amount of delay before you see them because it takes a short time for electrical impulses to travel to your television. It is easy for you to understand the 8.3 minute delay in looking at the sun and the shorter delay of looking at a live television show. But if you look at a person in front of you, are you seeing that person now or is there a time delay? Your past learning will typically tell you that you are seeing him now, but actually you are not seeing that person now. It takes a tiny amount of time for light to travel from that person to your eyes. Then it takes more time for your brain to register the image of the person. Next, it takes another small amount of time for your brain to process the meaning of what you see. Finally, it takes time to provide a response to the visual information. Thus you are always seeing the past since everything you see is delayed. This delay is always happening because of the apparatus of the body being separate from what it sees and because of the time it takes for electrical impulses to travel within your body to receive, interpret, and respond to information.

Why is it important to understand that this time delay is always happening within the world of form? If there were no time delay, your ego would not be able to maintain the illusion of time itself. "Time is a trick, a sleight of hand, a vast illusion in which figures come and go as if by magic."[159] The holy instant is your means of removing the time delay and overcoming the illusion of time itself. The holy instant is needed because your ego-based body awareness deceives you into believing you are experiencing the present, when in fact you are experiencing only the past. You think you are seeing the present because the delay is so small, but the fact is that you are always seeing only the past and not now. Your spirit lives now, but your physical body is not equipped to prevent the experience of delay that separates you from being aware of now. You live in the present as if it were the past because everything is delayed in your brain. This delay is the nature of this world that modern science calls "space-time" because space and time depend upon each other. For centuries, time was believed to be a never-changing constant.

But then Einstein gave science the theory of relativity that showed that time varies depending on space and speed factors. In fact, time will almost stop altogether for a man in a rocketship traveling close to the speed of light. Because time and space are both illusions, they will both end in your final experience of the holy instant when you accept the timelessness and formlessness of Heaven.

But even before you have your final holy instant of release that will bring ultimate salvation, you may have some direct experiences of the holy instant in which you are freed from the illusory past and future and receive a glimpse of the reality of the eternal now. The holy instant releases you from fear and opens you to love. "Do not be concerned with time, and fear not the instant of holiness that will remove all fear. For the instant of peace is eternal *because* it is without fear."[160] The holy instant releases weakness in your brother and you. Because you are joined with your brothers in reality, the release of your ego-based thinking in the holy instant is a release you share with your brothers. Thus your release of limitations in the holy instant offers your brothers freedom from their limitations. "You who have spent days, hours and even years in chaining your brothers to your ego in an attempt to support it and uphold its weakness, do not perceive the Source of strength. In this holy instant, you will unchain all your brothers, and refuse to support either their weakness or your own."[161]

In order to accept the holy instant, you must let go of the littleness of the ego so you can accept your magnitude in God. "You can claim the holy instant any time and anywhere you want it. In your practice, try to give over every plan you have accepted for finding magnitude in littleness. *It is not there.*"[162] There is a simple reason why you find it difficult to accept the holy instant. "You could live forever in the holy instant, beginning now and reaching to eternity, but for a very simple reason. Do not obscure the simplicity of this reason, for if you do, it will be only because you prefer not to recognize it and not to let it go. The simple reason, simply stated, is this: The holy instant is a time in which you receive and give perfect communication."[163]

Why is the receiving and giving of perfect communication of the holy instant the reason why you cannot immediately "live forever in the holy instant, beginning now and reaching to eternity"? The reason why you are not now consciously living within the holy instant and staying there forever is the fact you currently do *not want* to receive and give perfect communication. Instead, you currently *do want* to keep your ego-based commitment to having a private mind. Your private mind limits sharing so you cannot give and receive perfect communication. "The body is the symbol of the ego, as the ego is the symbol of the separation. And both are nothing more than attempts to limit communication, and thereby to make it impossible. For communication must be unlimited in order to have meaning, and deprived of meaning, it will not satisfy you completely."[164] Your real relationships are with God, the Holy Spirit, and the Sonship. The holy instant offers you real relationships. "Yet it [perfect unlimited communication in the holy instant] remains the only means by which you can establish real relationships, which have no limits, having been established by God."[165]

The meaning of love is found in inclusiveness and wholeness. The meaning of love is lost in any expression of exclusiveness, specialness, or separation. You cannot understand love if you limit it since love is not limited. God has defined love as unconditional sharing of oneness in reality. If you love conditionally or selectively, you cannot understand love's meaning. "You cannot love parts of reality [some of your brothers and not others] and understand what love means. If you would love unlike to God, Who knows no special love, how can you understand it?"[166] The meaning of love is distorted by judgments that focus on the past and fail to recognize now. The holy instant removes judgments because it removes the past that is the basis for judgment. Therefore, the holy instant eliminates distortions of love that rely on the past and reveals the true meaning of love. "The holy instant is the Holy Spirit's most useful learning device for teaching you love's meaning. For its purpose is to suspend judgment entirely. Judgment always rests on the past, for past experience is the basis on which you judge."[167]

The experience of the holy instant is the Holy Spirit's most valuable teaching device. The holy instant is such a valuable tool for learning because it teaches you that perfect love is within you and brings the recognition of God as the Source of love. God holds all of the Sonship within His Mind and by connecting with His Mind, you hold all of the Sonship within your mind just as God does. In that divine connection, there is no loss but only the gaining of love in which you experience your wholeness. "In the holy instant you recognize the idea of love in you, and unite this idea with the Mind that thought it, and could not relinquish it. By holding it within itself, there *is* no loss. The holy instant thus becomes a lesson in how to hold all of your brothers in your mind, experiencing not loss but completion."[168] By accepting your wholeness in the Sonship, you naturally want to give love to the whole Sonship because the whole Sonship gives love to you. "From this [recognition of your completeness in the Sonship] it follows you can only give. And this *is* love, for this alone is natural under the laws of God."[169]

You are a Thought of love within the Mind of God. His Love in you is unlimited. In the holy instant, you will experience the freedom of being unlimited and freedom from the limitations of time and space imposed by the ego and identification with the body. "In that [holy] instant he is as free as God would have him be. For the instant he refuses to be bound, he is not bound."[170]

Everyone has experienced what he would call a sense of being transported beyond himself. This feeling of liberation far exceeds the dream of freedom sometimes hoped for in special relationships. It is a sense of actual escape from limitations. If you will consider what this "transportation" really entails, you will realize that it is a sudden unawareness of the body, and a joining of yourself and something else in which your mind enlarges to encompass it. It becomes part of you, as you unite with it. And both become whole, as neither is perceived as separate.[171]

The feeling of going beyond the body happens to everyone. You experience a decrease or a complete absence of body awareness. You also experience being united with something or someone beyond the limitations of your small self. You let go of the illusion of separation and directly experience that love is union. In this state that is a holy instant, you have let go of fear and you have accepted that your true identity is love.

What really happens is that you have given up the illusion of a limited awareness, and lost your fear of union. The love that instantly replaces it extends to what has freed you, and unites with it. And while this lasts you are not uncertain of your Identity, and would not limit It. You have escaped from fear to peace, asking no questions of reality, but merely accepting it. You have accepted this instead of the body, and have let yourself be one with something beyond it, simply by not letting your mind be limited by it.[172]

In your experience of love as union, you can unite with anything and transcend the ordinarily accepted "laws" of time and space that govern the body and limit you. This transportation is just an increase in your awareness of your true Self. Also, this transportation is a clear example of the holy instant in which there is a release from time and space, an experience of joy and peace, a release of body awareness, and a reassessment of your true identity.

There is no violence at all in this escape. The body is not attacked, but simply properly perceived. It does not limit you, merely because you would not have it so. You are not really "lifted out" of it; it cannot contain you. You go where you would be, gaining, not losing, a sense of Self. In these instants of re-lease from physical restrictions, you experience much of what happens in the holy instant; the lifting of the barriers of time and space, the sudden experience of peace and joy, and, above all, the lack of awareness of the body, and of the questioning whether or not all this is possible.[173]

When you experience a holy instant, you will imagine everything has changed because you have released the past and future and released judgment. Certainly your ego awareness has changed, but nothing about reality has changed. Time is an illusion of change, and reality is changeless. The holy instant is a hybrid of time and timelessness. It is the smallest unit of time in the real world, yet it leads to timelessness in Heaven. Similarly, the holy instant is also a hybrid of change and changelessness. It is the smallest unit of change, and so it serves as a transition to the changelessness of reality. The holy instant, suddenly reveals what has always been. "In the holy instant nothing happens that has not always been. Only the veil that has been drawn across reality is lifted. Nothing has changed."[174] If you experience the holy instant of receiving and giving of perfect communication, you will understand love without fear. But without experiencing the holy instant, you will fail to believe in love without fear. "Yet the awareness of changelessness comes swiftly as the veil of time is pushed aside. No one who has not yet experienced the lifting of the veil, and felt himself drawn irresistibly into the light behind it, can have faith in love without fear."[175]

Although you cannot believe in love without fear unless you have the experience of the holy instant, there is no reason why you will be denied this experience. The Holy Spirit will give you the experience of the holy instant if you welcome His gift. "Yet the Holy Spirit gives you this faith [in love without fear], because He offered it to me [Jesus] and I accepted it. Fear not the holy instant will be denied you, for I denied it not. And through me the Holy Spirit gives it unto you, as you will give it."[176] To open your mind to receiving the gift of the holy instant from the Holy Spirit, you must recognize your need for this experience of love. "Let no need you perceive obscure your need of this [the holy instant]."[177]

Miracles of love are waiting for you to express them by inviting the holy instant. "The holy instant is the miracle's abiding place."[178] Where is the holy instant? It is not in Heaven, but it is a reflection of Heaven. "The holy instant is a miniature of Heaven, sent you *from* Heaven."[179] The holy instant is in time, yet it reflects eternity. "The holy instant is a miniature of eternity. It is a picture of timelessness, set in a frame of time."[180] The holy instant is in the real world of only loving thoughts and peace without fear. This lack of fear invites the love that brings healing. "Do not be concerned with time, and fear not the instant of holiness that will remove all fear. For the instant of peace is eternal *because* it is without fear."[181] You might imagine you must do the job of releasing all fear from your mind before you invite the holy instant, but that is not true. "Never approach the holy instant after you have tried to remove all fear and hatred from your mind. That is *its* function."[182] At any time, you can enter the real world for a holy instant, bringing peace, love, and healing to your mind with the Holy Spirit's help.

THE CHRIST'S VISION ELEVATOR

≈ ◦ ≈

The "Christ's vision elevator" allows you to perceive beyond the third floor intensive care. It requires a loving state of mind that sees holiness in everyone. Christ's vision is also called "vision," "real vision," "spiritual vision," "true vision," "perfect vision," "forgiving vision," "the savior's vision," "His vision," and "the Holy Spirit's vision." All these terms refer to the same ability of being able to see the divine presence and meaning of holiness. This divine perceiving reflects the meaning of the presence of God and His Love, which is everywhere. This ability is made possible through welcoming the Holy Spirit and light into the mind and is sometimes called seeing with the "eyes of Christ," the "eyes of love," or the "eyes of forgiveness."

> You have but two emotions, and one [fear] you made and one [love] was given you. Each is a way of seeing, and different worlds arise from their different sights. See through the vision that is given you, for through Christ's vision He beholds Himself. And seeing what He is, He knows His Father. Beyond your darkest dreams He sees God's guiltless Son within you, shining in perfect radiance that is undimmed by your dreams. And this *you* will see as you look with Him, for His vision is His gift of love to you, given Him of the Father for you.[183]

Christ's vision is an extension of love that replaces the ego's projection of guilt. Christ's vision enables you to see light and love in others and in the world. This is not seeing with your physical eyes, but rather perceiving the inner mental content of holiness in others. Perceiving holiness, light, and love outwardly helps you to recognize this same holiness, light, and love must be in your own mind. In this process of perceiving holiness, light, and love outwardly and inwardly, you are joining with what you see, instead of producing the sense of separation that is the result of projecting guilt. This vision of holiness, light, and love is a gift of divine grace from the Holy Spirit and from Christ, requiring only your willingness to receive it.

Christ's eyes are open, and He will look upon whatever you see with love if you accept His vision as yours. The Holy Spirit keeps the vision of Christ for every Son of God who sleeps. In His sight the Son of God is perfect, and He longs to share His vision with you.... Through Him your Father calls His Son to remember.[184]

Christ's vision is the gift from the Holy Spirit that allows you to perceive holiness in everyone and in everything. Thus Christ's vision lets you perceive your brother's part-ness and wholeness in Christ and reminds you of your own part-ness and wholeness in Christ. "Christ's vision is the holy ground in which the lilies of forgiveness set their roots."[185] Therefore, Christ's vision is the power that enables you to practice forgiveness. Christ's vision lets you overlook illusions of guilt and instead perceive the holiness in your brother revealing that he is worthy of your forgiveness. Christ's vision that perceives the reflections of the divine presence in everyone is the power behind the application of the other elevators that require the perception of holiness.

Christ's vision is the miracle in which all miracles are born. It is their source, remaining with each miracle you give, and yet remaining yours. It is the bond by which the giver and receiver are united in extension here on earth, as they are one in Heaven. Christ beholds no sin in anyone. And in His sight the sinless are as one. Their holiness was given by His Father and Himself.[186]

Using Christ's vision, you switch from the ego's vision to the Holy Spirit's vision. This change in vision manifests the looking aspect of forgiveness, which enables you to look for holiness in your brother instead of grievances. Using the Holy Spirit's gift of vision results in joining with your brother. This joining is a miracle resulting in healing in which there is an exchange of light and love. You become a savior for your brother and your brother becomes your savior as you see holiness rather than guilt in each other. Guided by the Holy Spirit, you can learn to forgive by this new kind of looking that looks for the divine presence in the world and in all reflections of reality.

This do the body's eyes behold in one whom Heaven cherishes, the angels love and God created perfect. This is his reality. And in Christ's vision is his loveliness reflected in a form so holy and so beautiful that you could scarce refrain from kneeling at his feet. Yet you will take his hand instead, for you are like him in the sight that sees him thus.[187]

If you use Christ's vision, you can look past the body and can literally see the radiant light hidden by the physical form. "Its [refers to aspects of God, including you] radiance shines through each body that it [Christ's vision] looks upon, and brushes all its [the body's] darkness into light merely by looking past it [the body] *to the light*."[188] But can you really see light if you look past the physical body? The Course teaches that your perception depends upon your purpose. Your purpose is closely related to your desire for what you want and your choice of expressing your will. "And always is it [perception] faithful to your purpose, from which it never separates, nor gives the slightest witness unto anything the purpose in your mind upholdeth not."[189] Your purpose is the end result you want to achieve. Perception is a means of achieving your purpose because it provides only the witnesses that would support the end result you have previously decided you want.

In relation to Christ's vision, your perception means it depends upon what you *want* to see. Since perception is the means you use to obtain the end result that you want, you cannot see light by looking past the body unless you make it your purpose to see that light. The second thing to keep in mind is that there are two kinds of light. There is physical light that can be seen with the physical eyes. Yet physical three-dimensional light is not the kind of light that can be seen by "looking past it [the body] to the light." The other kind of light is not a physical three-dimensional light, and this kind of light *can* be seen, if you really desire to see it and make that part of your purpose of perceiving holiness.

Those who do not believe they can see this light or do not want to see this light will interpret many Course references to light as figurative rather than literal. But those who want to see this light will be able to do so as an experience. Those who have already had the experience of seeing this light will confirm that the Course references to seeing light can be interpreted literally in most cases. For instance, based on the personal experience of others and my own personal experience, it is correct to maintain a literal interpretation of the following quotation regarding seeing light by using Christ's vision to look past the body:

> Christ's vision has one law. It does not look upon a body, and mistake it for the Son whom God created. It beholds a light beyond the body; an idea beyond what can be touched, a purity undimmed by errors, pitiful mistakes, and fearful thoughts of guilt from dreams of sin. It sees no separation. And it looks on everyone, on every circumstance, all happenings and all events, without the slightest fading of the light it sees. This can be taught; and must be taught by all who would achieve it.[190]

Notice that the previous quotation speaks of beholding both a "light" and an "idea" when it says that Christ's vision "beholds a light beyond the body; an idea beyond what can be touched..." This means that when you are seeing this light, you are simultaneously perceiving an idea of holiness. I believe it is possible to see holiness in another person without seeing this light. But I do not believe it is possible to see this light without also perceiving the idea of holiness that comes inherently with perceiving the light. Light and the idea of holiness go hand in hand because "light *is* understanding."[191] Since this light is actually understanding, it must bring the understanding of your holiness when you see it instead of seeing the body and instead of perceiving only physical three-dimensional light.

The final line in the previous quotation is a reminder to teach by example what you want to learn: "This [Christ's vision of light] can be taught; and must be taught by all who would achieve it." In the study groups that I have led, there is a portion of the time devoted to reading the Course and gaining and sharing intellectual insights. But while one person at a time shares his or her insights, everyone else in the group is asked to focus on using Christ's vision to overlook the body and look for the divine presence in each person who is speaking. This entire study group functions as a temporary holy relationship in which everyone is joined with the common interest and common purpose of seeing the divine in each participant. Through joining in this common purpose and common practice, we are both teaching each other and learning from each other how to perceive with the *eyes of Christ*.

After learning how to practice Christ's vision with a small number of people, you can generalize your practice to seeing the divine presence in everyone. Christ's vision allows you to lift the veil that is the fear of God and fear of your brother and enables you to see the face of Christ in your brother as a reflection of your own Christ Identity. "The veil [of the fear of God and fear of your brother] is lifted through its [Christ's vision's] gentleness, and nothing hides the face of Christ from its beholders. You and your brother stand before Him now, to let Him draw aside the veil that seems to keep you separate and apart."[192] When you leave the body awareness of this world behind at the time called "death," it is actually your best opportunity for awakening because you will no longer be distracted by attention given to the body. I believe you will have the opportunity to perceive the face of Christ at the deepest level of the real world, which will overcome your fear of God and will return the memory of your loving Father. "*The face of Christ* has to be seen before the memory of God can return."[193] The face of Christ is a vision of light expanding infinitely, and Christ's vision is preparing you to see this vision that will awaken you to your true nature with God in Heaven.

THE ATONEMENT
ELEVATOR

≈ ◦ ≈

My previous book *"A Course in Miracles" Seven Keys to Heaven* discussed the seven elevators as the seven tools of the Holy Spirit. First, the tools were described as seven distinctly different tools, but then the book clarified that the seven tools are totally interrelated. Also, the seven tools use only one process that provides a unified approach to awakening. This is the process of forgiveness that I call "looking and overlooking." Each tool emphasizes a similar but slightly different aspect of overlooking what is unreal and looking for what is real.

THE FORGIVENESS ELEVATOR —
    Overlooking all your projections of guilt
    Looking for the divine holiness in others

THE MEDITATION ELEVATOR —
    Overlooking multiple mental distractions and inner grievances
    Looking for one sacred thought and then for the Divine Presence

THE HOLY RELATIONSHIP ELEVATOR—
    Overlooking differences and separateness from others
    Looking for union with others in the common purpose of holiness

THE MIRACLES ELEVATOR —
    Overlooking false perceptions of grievances
    Looking for miracles as equal exchanges of light and love

THE HOLY INSTANT ELEVATOR—
    Overlooking time to release focusing on the past and future
    Looking for the timelessness of now and connection with the Sonship

THE CHRIST'S VISION ELEVATOR—
    Overlooking the body and your own judgments of your brother
    Looking for light, Christ, and the Holy Spirit's judgment of holiness

THE ATONEMENT ELEVATOR—
    Overlooking sickness and errors
    Looking for healing and correction that eventually lead to awakening

The central message of the Course is the practice of forgiveness that I call "looking and overlooking." You can see in the list of elevators that the looking and overlooking of forgiveness permeates each tool of the Holy Spirit. In order to build upon the information in my previous book, this book elaborates on the dual role of being the "Atonement elevator" within time and also being the whole Atonement that stands at the end of time as the final miracle.

Since perception emphasizes differences, you may not realize that the seven elevators of the Holy Spirit are really only one elevator that is seen from different perspectives. The one all-inclusive elevator could be called the "forgiveness elevator," but here will instead be described as the "Atonement elevator." The reason is that the power of looking and overlooking actually comes from the Atonement. The other elevators express that power. But what actually is the looking and overlooking power of the Atonement that activates all six of the seemingly different elevators? That power is actually the Mind of the Holy Spirit.

> God honored even the miscreations of His children because they had made them. But He also blessed His children with a way of thinking that could raise their perceptions so high they could reach almost back to Him. The Holy Spirit is the Mind of the Atonement. He represents a state of mind close enough to One-mindedness that transfer to it is at last possible. The Holy Spirit, the shared Inspiration of all the Sonship, induces a kind of perception in which many elements are like those in the Kingdom of Heaven itself.[194]

Because the "Holy Spirit is the Mind of the Atonement," His Mind provides the power behind all healing. The practice of looking and overlooking that occurs in forgiveness, meditation, holy relationships, miracles, the holy instant, and Christ's vision would be ineffective and without purpose if not supported by the Mind of the Holy Spirit providing the transforming power of the Atonement. The one process of looking and overlooking relies on discrimination between truth and illusions that your mind is not capable of without the power of the Mind of the Holy Spirit because judgment is His function, not yours.

> If you already understood the difference between truth and illusion, the Atonement would have no meaning. The holy instant, the holy relationship, the Holy Spirit's teaching, and all the means by which salvation is accomplished, would have no purpose. For they are all but aspects of the plan [of Atonement] to change your dreams of fear to happy dreams, from which you waken easily to knowledge.[195]

You cannot awaken yourself because your judgment is so poor, but you can rely on the discrimination and power of the Holy Spirit to act through you to bring healing to your brother and to you. By avoiding the temptation to believe that you can correct yourself, you can accept God's gift of the Atonement to bring correction and healing. "Peace abides in every mind that quietly accepts the plan God set for its Atonement, relinquishing its own."[196] You will not come up with your own plan of salvation if you realize you cannot make that decision for yourself or by yourself. "You know not of salvation, for you do not understand it. Make no decisions about what it is or where it lies, but ask the Holy Spirit everything, and leave all decisions to His gentle counsel."[197]

Your salvation is facilitated by accepting the Holy Spirit's guidance. "The One Who knows the plan of God that God would have you follow can teach you what it is. Only His wisdom is capable of guiding you to follow it."[198] If you make decisions alone, you will subconsciously define salvation as *saving the ego* from its undoing. Therefore, you will subconsciously and sometimes consciously want to *save the ego* from anything that threatens it. After all, the ego "judges only in terms of threat or non-threat to itself."[199] Light, love, and truth are perceived as threats by the ego. If you are identified with the ego, salvation would be perceived as being *saved from* light, love, and truth. By accepting decisions made for you by the Holy Spirit, you will be accepting that salvation consists of freedom from guilt and welcoming light, love, and truth. "Every decision you undertake alone but signifies that you would define what salvation *is*, and what you would be saved *from*. The Holy Spirit knows that all salvation is escape from guilt. You have no other 'enemy,' and against this strange distortion of the purity of the Son of God the Holy Spirit is your only Friend."[200]

The Atonement elevator that encompasses all the other elevators and supplies the power of healing is the Mind of the Holy Spirit active on the third floor of intensive care. Accepting the Atonement can be most easily understood as your decision to accept perfect love into your mind. "Perfect love is the Atonement."[201] Since the Holy Spirit is the Mind of the Atonement, accepting the Atonement means accepting the Mind of the Holy Spirit. The Holy Spirit has been placed in your mind by God Himself at the instant of the separation. Thus accepting the Atonement means accepting the *awareness* of the Holy Spirit that has been blocked by the ego. When you accept the awareness of the Holy Spirit, you are accepting your part-ness and wholeness in Christ since the Holy Spirit always sees you are in your true Identity.

The acceptance of the Atonement provides the power of healing to the six other elevators of awakening. The power of the Atonement recognizes and affirms your divine nature and releases guilt, fear, and every other illusion. Looking and overlooking is a practice you must learn to do, but actually the Holy Spirit in the Atonement accomplishes the function of looking only for the divine and overlooking all that is not divine. You can think of the Atonement elevator as the "electricity" that empowers the other elevators to function as healing agents. Supplying healing power to the forgiveness elevator, the Atonement connects your brother and you. "Forgiveness is the healing of the perception of separation."[202] The Atonement enables you to see that your brother has no guilt and there is nothing to forgive. You see your brother's part-ness and wholeness in Christ and connect with your own part-ness and wholeness in Christ.

Similarly, when you use the meditation elevator, your acceptance of the Atonement enables you to manifest the true spirit of meditation that connects you with all of your brothers in the Sonship by affirming your equality with them. As you see guiltlessness in the Sonship, you recognize your own guiltlessness. Therefore, you forgive yourself for all your former illusions of guilt that you had mistakenly harbored in your mind and projected upon your brothers in the past.

When you accept the Atonement as the Mind of the Holy Spirit in your experience of the holy relationship elevator, you also connect at the divine level with your holy relationship partner. When you joined, the Holy Spirit entered your relationship, establishing His purpose of seeing holiness in each other. Thus you remind each other of your part-ness and wholeness in Christ through your joint awareness of the Mind of the Holy Spirit in each other. You become healing saviors for each other. It only takes one partner to faithfully accept the Atonement and the other partner's mind is healed because your minds are joined in spirit.

In order to perform miracles, the miracle worker must accept the awareness of the Mind of the Holy Spirit in the Atonement. When the miracle worker accepts the Atonement, the Mind of the Holy Spirit provides the healing power of the miracle elevator to both the giver and the receiver of the miracle. The Mind of the Holy Spirit is why giving and receiving happen simultaneously and why both receive an increase in love and light without any loss of love or light. Without the power of the Mind of the Holy Spirit in the Atonement, there would be no exchange of love and light that is the miracle itself and no result of a shift in perception bringing healing. "The miracle is an expression of an inner awareness of Christ and the acceptance of His Atonement."[203]

Accepting the Atonement only occurs within the holy instant elevator because the Mind of the Holy Spirit only functions now. The power of the Atonement allows you to let go of the past and of all guilt as well as the future with all of its fear of punishment. Through the power of the Mind of the Holy Spirit, the holy instant elevator temporarily releases you for an instant from all the third-floor limitations of the three-dimensional world of space and time. In the holy instant, you temporarily reestablish perfect communication with God and with the entire Sonship, therefore you recognize your part-ness and wholeness in Christ.

The power of the Christ's vision elevator also comes from the Mind of the Holy Spirit acting through the Atonement supplying divine light and love. You cannot see the divine holiness, truth, love, and guiltlessness in your brother with the physical eyes of your body. You require a blessing from the Mind of the Holy Spirit imparted by accepting the Atonement to enable you to perceive the part-ness and wholeness of Christ in your brother. "The wish to see calls down the grace of God upon your eyes, and brings the gift of light that makes sight possible."[204]

The basic idea in all these examples is that the Atonement as the Mind of the Holy Spirit manifests as the power of healing. Thus God's grace comes to you through the Mind of the Holy Spirit as the activating agent of God's plan of the Atonement. "The purpose of the Atonement is to restore everything to you; or rather, to restore it to your awareness."[205]

> The Holy Spirit uses time, but does not believe in it. Coming from God He uses everything for good, but He does not believe in what is not true. Since the Holy Spirit is in your mind, your mind can also believe only what is true. The Holy Spirit can speak only for this, because He speaks for God. He tells you to return your whole mind to God, because it has never left Him. If it has never left Him, you need only perceive it as it is to be returned. The full awareness of the Atonement, then, is the recognition that *the separation never occurred.* The ego cannot prevail against this because it is an explicit statement that the ego never occurred.[206]

Because the Holy Spirit is the Mind of the Atonement, when you accept the Atonement or accept perfect love that is the Atonement, you are accepting the awareness of the Holy Spirit already in your mind. Certainly the Holy Spirit wants to share His Mind with you, but He also wants you to share your true nature with all parts of the Sonship. That is why the Atonement is an experience of sharing.

> The Atonement must be understood as a pure act of sharing. That is what I meant when I said it is possible even in this world to listen to one Voice. If you are part of God and the Sonship is One, you cannot be limited to the self the ego sees.
> Every loving thought held in any part of the Sonship belongs to every part. It is shared *because* it is loving. Sharing is God's way of creating, and also yours.[207]

What does it mean that the Atonement as the Mind of the Holy Spirit functions as "a pure act of sharing"? The reason why the Atonement is the one elevator on the third floor that encompasses the other elevators is that the Holy Spirit uses forgiveness, meditation, the holy relationship, miracles, the holy instant, and Christ's vision as His means of sharing His Mind and helping you share your mind with the whole Sonship. The Holy Spirit knows you only as the guiltless Son of God, and He guides you to practice forgiveness to affirm the innocence of the whole Sonship. Your forgiveness removes judgment that blocks the awareness of love within and reestablishes the thought of love in your mind.

The previous quotation states: "Every loving thought held in any part of the Sonship belongs to every part. It is shared *because* it is loving." The Holy Spirit encourages you to receive perfect love into your mind in meditation, and this thought of love is shared with the whole Sonship. The Holy Spirit inspires you to join in holy relationships so you can have the common purpose of seeing holiness in each other. That perception of holiness is a thought of love shared with the whole Sonship. The Holy Spirit encourages you to perform miracles that are expressions of love that go to the entire Sonship. The Holy Spirit facilitates your experience of the holy instant in which you accept the eternal now and let go of the past and future. In the holy instant, you reestablish perfect loving communication with God and with the whole Sonship.

Finally, the Holy Spirit is the power behind your practice of Christ's vision that enables you to perceive the divine light and love in your brother. Your perception of love in Christ's vision is shared with the entire Sonship. At first, the Atonement elevator, like all the other elevators contained within it, goes only temporarily to the second floor. To bring your full awareness to the second floor where your mind can become filled with only love, you must generalize your learning by accepting the Atonement as your only function that you apply to everyone and every situation. "The offer of Atonement is universal. It is equally applicable to all individuals in all circumstances."[208]

In addition to the Atonement elevator on the third floor of intensive care, the other aspect of the Atonement is active on the second floor of your recovery and facilitates the final miracle of your awakening. This other aspect of the Atonement is at the end of time awaiting the completion of your awakening. This aspect of the Atonement as the Mind of the Holy Spirit will be elaborated upon later in this book.

> The Holy Spirit has no need of time when it has served His purpose. Now He waits but that one instant more for God to take His final step, and time has disappeared, taking perception with it as it goes, and leaving but the truth to be itself. That instant is our goal, for it contains the memory of God. And as we look upon a world forgiven, it is He Who calls to us and comes to take us home, reminding us of our Identity which our forgiveness has restored to us.[209]

PART II

~ ○ ~

THE SECOND FLOOR
CONTENT AND FORM

Part II of this book describes some commonly used terms in the Course, such as "the real world," "the circle of Atonement," "the face of Christ," and "vision of the Son of God." Because perception sees everything in separation, these terms are presented in the Course as different ideas. Part II alerts you to the understanding that these are different terms that express the same content and the same form. The content that these have in common is that they are all the same reflection of Heaven with the same meaning of light, love, and true perception, without any darkness, fear, or false perceptions.

> For true perception is a remedy with many names. Forgiveness, salvation, Atonement, true perception, all are one. They are the one beginning, with the end to lead to oneness far beyond themselves. True perception is the means by which the world is saved from sin, for sin does not exist. And it is this that true perception sees.[210]

In addition to having the common content of light, love and truth, these terms described in Part II also have a common form. Surprisingly, they have the common form of what is called here the "second floor." When you apply the seven instruments of the Holy Spirit, your learning brings your awareness to this "second floor," as the transition bridge between the three-dimensional world and Heaven. The last section in Part II is titled, "The Second Floor Light Dimension," and this section introduces the first explanation of why this second floor is actually the second dimension. It also explains why the first floor is actually the first dimension, which is Heaven. When you awaken from your dreams of separation, you will realize that you never really left your Father's Home and your Home in the first dimension.

You are at home in God, dreaming of exile but perfectly capable of awakening to reality. Is it your decision to do so? You recognize from your own experience that what you see in dreams you think is real while you are asleep. Yet the instant you waken you realize that everything that seemed to happen in the dream did not happen at all. You do not think this strange, even though all the laws of what you awaken to were violated while you slept. Is it not possible that you merely shifted from one dream to another, without really waking?[211]

At first, the most significant block to awakening is the false belief that you are already awake because such a belief robs you of your motivation for waking. After you recognize that you have amnesia and need to wake up from your dreaming state of mind, you are still every day tempted to believe that the three-dimensional world is real and not just an illusion you have manufactured. Every time you brush your teeth, take a shower, eat a meal, or sit on a toilet, you are tempted once again to believe you are a body.

The Course gives you many reminders to resist this temptation to believe that three-dimensional awareness is real. For emphasis, the Course reminds you 46 times: "I am not a body." Also, 46 times it reminds you: "I am free," meaning free of body awareness and limitations. But if you are not a body and are free, what are you free to be? You are free to be "as God created you," repeated 24 times in the Course. God created you as spirit without form in Heaven where you are now, while dreaming of being a body.

In spite of these many Course reminders, your attachment to body awareness may be so great that you are afraid of the formlessness of your true nature because you perceive formlessness to be death rather than eternal life. Therefore, it is difficult to make the leap in consciousness from a dream state of all form to the awareness of complete formlessness in the reality of Heaven. This leap would be impossible if it were not for the Holy Spirit and the second dimension that stands between the third dimension and the first dimension. In the second dimension, you learn to let go of your attachment to three-dimensional body awareness and prepare for accepting your true Self in the formlessness of Heaven that is the first dimension. Part II begins to explain how the second dimension functions as a transition place, symbolized by the second floor of the three-story hospital where you recover from your amnesia.

Part II:—The Second Floor Content and Form 55
    The Second Floor Real World of Love 57
    The Second Floor Circle of Atonement 59
    The Second Floor Face of Christ 61
    The Second Floor Light Dimension 65

THE SECOND FLOOR
REAL WORLD OF LOVE

≈ ● ≈

The second-floor recovery room of the three-story hospital is where the third-floor elevators have brought you. Here you have been lifted out of the three-dimensional world where perceptions fluctuate between loving and unloving thoughts, between false and true thoughts. The third floor has seven elevators that were described separately. But then it was explained that the seven elevators are really just one Atonement elevator including all the other elevators. Similarly, the second-floor recovery area will be described as separate rooms with different names, but bear in mind that the second floor is actually just one place of transition to the first floor of awakening. Although this second floor has many names in the Course, the most frequently used name is the "real world."

The real world is the second floor of only loving thoughts and none of the unloving thoughts of the third floor. Here you dwell in perfect perception in which the perceptual mind is unified by thoughts of love. Love itself leads you to the real world. "Love leads so gladly!"[212] Christ also leads you to the real world because that is God's Will and your true will. Why do Christ and God's Will lead you to the real world? The role of the real world in your spiritual growth is to be the bridge that transports you from your world of denial to your home in Heaven. "As you follow Him [Christ], you will rejoice that you have found His company, and learned of Him the joyful journey home."[213] Christ leads you from within because you in your true nature are the Christ. "You wait but for yourself."[214] But you must release the world of denial that makes you unhappy. "To give this sad world over and exchange your errors for the peace of God is but *your* will. And Christ will always offer you the Will of God, in recognition that you share it with Him."[215]

Your world has denied the peace of God, so giving up this unhappy world means the acceptance of God's peace and safety from suffering. "It is God's Will that nothing touch His Son except Himself, and nothing else comes nigh unto him. He is as safe from pain as God Himself, Who watches over him in everything. The world about him shines with love because God placed him in Himself where pain is not, and love surrounds him without end or flaw."[216] God has given you His eternal peace, and you still have it. "Disturbance of his peace can never be.

In perfect sanity he looks on love, for it is all about him and within him."[217] You will deny the world you made if you experience God's loving embrace. "He must deny the world of pain the instant he perceives the arms of love around him. And from this point of safety he looks quietly about him and recognizes that the world is one with him."[218]

You cannot understand God's peace if you disturb your mind with events from the past. But if you focus on the present, you can understand the peace of God. "The peace of God passeth your understanding only in the past. Yet here it *is*, and you can understand it *now*."[219] The peace of God comes from awakening to God's love for you and your love for God. The role of the real world is to lead you to remember God's Love for you and your love for God. "God loves His Son forever, and His Son returns his Father's Love forever. The real world is the way that leads you to remembrance of the one thing that is wholly true and wholly yours."[220] You have mistakenly invested in temporary distractions from God's Love. "For all else you have lent yourself in time, and it will fade." But God's Love awaits your recognition. "But this one thing [God's Love] is always yours, being the gift of God unto His Son. Your one reality was given you, and by it God created you as one with Him."[221]

How does the real world help you to let go of illusions and lead you to fully awakening in the reality of God's Love in Heaven? "Perceiving only the real world will lead you to the real Heaven, because it will make you capable of understanding it."[222] The real world is called the "happy dream" of light and love because is it is a place of both happiness and illusion. Everything outside of Heaven is an illusion so even the real world is an illusion. Most illusions block the awareness of reality, but the real world is an illusion that leads to reality. "You will first dream of peace, and then awaken to it. Your first exchange of what you made for what you want is the exchange of nightmares for the happy dreams of love."[223] The real world is the home of the holy instant and miracles.

The real world is a world of true perceptions, yet it leads beyond the partial awareness of perception to the total awareness of knowledge. The Holy Spirit offers you the gift of the real world of only true perceptions as a correction for your false perceptions. In your happy dreams of the real world "lie your true perceptions, for the Holy Spirit corrects the world of dreams, where all perception is. Knowledge needs no correction. Yet the dreams of love lead unto knowledge."[224] Although the real world is an illusion consisting of only loving and true perceptions, it is a reflection of Heaven and so serves as your doorway to divine love and knowledge. In your happy dreams of love "you see nothing fearful, and because of this they are the welcome that you offer knowledge. Love waits on welcome, not on time, and the real world is but your welcome of what always was. Therefore the call of joy is in it, and your glad response is your awakening to what you have not lost."[225]

THE SECOND FLOOR
CIRCLE OF ATONEMENT

~ • ~

The second floor is a place of love, but also a place of holiness called the "circle of Atonement." There is no guilt in the circle of Atonement, but it is not the Atonement itself. This circle is an image expressing the unity of those who have accepted the Atonement for themselves and become miracle workers and teachers of guiltlessness. All who have learned the lesson of guiltlessness will accept that they are safely within the circle of Atonement. They become convinced of their own holiness by inviting all their brothers to accept their place within this circle. "The circle of Atonement has no end. And you will find ever-increasing confidence in your safe inclusion in the circle with everyone you bring within its safety and its perfect peace."[226] Peace is found inside the circle of Atonement because guiltlessness invites the acceptance of your true nature. Peace is the proof of a mind no longer in pain caused by the mistaken belief in guilt. "Peace, then, be unto everyone who becomes a teacher of peace. For peace is the acknowledgment of perfect purity, from which no one is excluded."[227]

Ironically, everyone is already within the circle of Atonement that excludes no one since all are as pure as God Himself. Those who have not yet learned the lesson of guiltlessness will mistakenly believe they are outside the circle of Atonement. Only those who accept their own guiltlessness and the guiltlessness of everyone will perceive themselves to be within the circle of holiness and peace. "Within its holy circle is everyone whom God created as His Son. Joy is its unifying attribute, with no one left outside to suffer guilt alone."[228] Before you accept your guiltlessness you may feel you have been excluded from the circle without realizing that you had decided to exclude yourself by refusing to acknowledge your holiness. After you accept your guiltlessness, you will realize that you have always been in the circle because you are God's holy Son. Through the guidance of the Holy Spirit, God will help all seekers to eventually recognize they are within the circle of Atonement. Those who have accepted guiltlessness will be inspired by the Holy Spirit to welcome everyone to accept his rightful place within the circle. "The power of God draws everyone to its safe embrace of love and union. Stand quietly within this circle, and attract all tortured minds to join with you in the safety of its peace and holiness."[229]

The Holy Spirit is constantly aware of you as the Son of God who is as guiltless as God Himself. "The Holy Spirit sees only guiltlessness, and in His gentleness He would release from fear and re-establish the reign of love."[230] Love is the true power that is restored with the acceptance of the guiltlessness of the Atonement. "The power of love is in His [the Holy Spirit's] gentleness, which is of God and therefore cannot crucify nor suffer crucifixion."[231]

You made the body as a place of guilt and hiding from God, yet the body can become a temple of worship. "The temple you restore becomes your altar, for it was rebuilt through you."[232] You worship God with the temple of your body by giving love to your brothers. As you give love to your brothers and to God, you receive love in return and awaken your recognition that your true nature is love. God created you with love and as love. You restore the awareness of God and His Love by accepting the Atonement and your guiltlessness. "And everything you give to God is yours. Thus He creates, and thus must you restore."[233]

With your beliefs, you decide whether to place your brother within the circle of Atonement where he is redeemed or place him outside the circle of Atonement where he is condemned. "Each one you see you place within the holy circle of Atonement or leave outside, judging him fit for crucifixion or for redemption."[234] Seeing your brother outside the circle of Atonement tells you that you must be outside with him. By seeing your brother inside the circle of Atonement, you take your rightful place inside the circle with him. "If you bring him into the circle of purity, you will rest there with him. If you leave him without, you join him there."[235] Judgment can be used negatively to affirm guilt or used positively with the guidance of the Holy Spirit to affirm guiltlessness. Before you decide how to perceive your brother, it is wise to allow your mind to rest in the silence and peace of God so you will hear the Holy Spirit and judge correctly. "Judge not except in quietness which is not of you."[236]

You have been blessed by God with His Love, so you are called to bless your brothers. "Refuse to accept anyone as without the blessing of Atonement, and bring him into it by blessing him. Holiness must be shared, for therein lies everything that makes it holy."[237] The Atonement is a plan of holiness because it is a plan of sharing guiltlessness. "Come gladly to the holy circle, and look out in peace on all who think they are outside."[238] Your brother outside is in pain and seeks the peace that you have within the circle of Atonement. You can only keep your peace of mind by sharing it for what you give away you keep in your own mind. "Cast no one out, for here is what he seeks along with you. Come, let us join him in the holy place of peace which is for all of us, united as one within the Cause of peace."[239] God is the only Cause so He is the Cause of peace. By realizing you are within the circle of Atonement, you open your mind to His peace and to the awareness of God Himself.

THE SECOND FLOOR
FACE OF CHRIST

≈ ○ ≈

In addition to the circle of Atonement being an image on the second floor, there is another image on the second floor. The real world is the content of love on the second floor of the recovery of your mind, but the Course clearly states that the real world can be seen. The content of the real world of only loving thoughts is the only reality of the world.

Every loving thought that the Son of God ever had is eternal. The loving thoughts his mind perceives in this world are the world's only reality. They are still perceptions, because he still believes that he is separate. Yet they are eternal because they are loving. And being loving they are like the Father, and therefore cannot die. The real world can actually be perceived. All that is necessary is a willingness to perceive nothing else. For if you perceive both good and evil, you are accepting both the false and the true and making no distinction between them.[240]

Since the real world is a world having only the content of loving thoughts, how can it be seen? Can thoughts be seen? A reading by Edgar Cayce, the sleeping prophet, stated: "Thoughts are things and take form."[241] Certainly things can be seen. "There *are* no idle thoughts. All thinking produces form at some level."[242] Therefore, thoughts are things that can be seen because the content of thoughts cannot be seen, but the form of thoughts can be seen. Since the content of all thoughts produces form, the real world containing only loving thoughts must produce a form that is the image of the real world that can be seen. This image of the real world is called "the face of Christ." If you saw a picture of Christ, seeing that image would call to mind the thought of Christ. Similarly, Christ's vision enables you to see the image of the face of Christ, and it reminds you of the content of the real world. But in addition, it reminds you of Christ. Of course, Christ Himself is in Heaven and is not this image, but the face of Christ is such a perfect reflection of Heaven that it calls to mind Christ. Because you are part of the Christ and you are the whole Christ, seeing the face of Christ reminds you of your own true nature as the Son of God. Since it reminds you of your Sonship, it enables you to remember your Father.

When brothers join in purpose in the world of fear, they stand already at the edge of the real world. Perhaps they still look back, and think they see an idol that they want. Yet has their path been surely set away from idols toward reality. For when they joined their hands it was Christ's hand they took, and they will look on Him Whose hand they hold. The face of Christ is looked upon before the Father is remembered. For He must be unremembered till His Son has reached beyond forgiveness to the Love of God. Yet is the Love of Christ accepted first. And then will come the knowledge They are One.[243]

Just as the physical sun always shines brightly while clouds obscure its bright rays of light, the face of Christ shines its light brightly while being clouded over by illusions of fear. The entire purpose of the Course is to remove all the illusions covering the face of Christ through the application of forgiveness. When all the clouds of illusion are removed, forgiveness has done its job of revealing the face of Christ:

No clouds remain to hide the face of Christ. Now is the goal achieved. Forgiveness is the final goal of the curriculum. It paves the way for what goes far beyond all learning. The curriculum makes no effort to exceed its legitimate goal. Forgiveness is its single aim, at which all learning ultimately converges. It is indeed enough.[244]

Since the face of Christ is only an image reflecting Heaven, it is an illusion and not reality. But it is the final illusion you will ever see because it is such a pure reflection of Heaven that seeing it brings back the memory of God. What is the effect of remembering God? All false perception is replaced by true perception, and then perception itself is replaced by knowledge as God Himself takes the final step of bringing about your awakening. This transformation happens because you have seen the face of Christ that is "the great symbol of forgiveness" and the "symbol of the real world."

The face of Christ has to be seen before the memory of God can return. The reason is obvious. Seeing the face of Christ involves perception. No one can look on knowledge. But the face of Christ is the great symbol of forgiveness. It is salvation. It is the symbol of the real world. Whoever looks on this no longer sees the world. He is as near to Heaven as is possible outside the gate. Yet from this gate it is no more than just a step inside. It is the final step. And this we leave to God.[245]

The face of Christ is more than an ordinary vision because it is the final vision of perception that ends perception and makes the transfer to knowledge possible. The following analogy is described in my book *"A Course in Miracles" Seven Keys to Heaven.* I am reprinting this analogy below because the book you are reading now will elaborate upon this analogy and add new information not shared previously.

Here is an analogy to describe what this profound vision [of the face of Christ] does: Imagine you are looking at a supernatural mirror. As you look at this mirror, you see yourself reflected there. Then you notice "little edges of light around"[246] the image of your body. You step closer to the mirror to get a better look, and as you do, you see your whole body shining in light. You step even closer, and the light gets even brighter. The whole mirror fills with light, and the image of your body fades and becomes transparent in your sight. Then your mind merges with the mirror, and your body drops out of your awareness. Now you are in the mirror, and you are merging with the light, not observing the light from a distance. In fact, you feel at home in this light. You have left the three-dimensional world of bodies and entered a two-dimensional world of light. You are one with the light. Then one more strange thing happens: Without your body awareness, you feel you are actually *becoming* the light. Your center is a point of light, and your "arms" are rays of light extending outward infinitely. Finally, the two-dimensional world fades away, and then you are transported to a one-dimensional world, which is a "dimensionless dimension" that is everywhere all at once. Here you are a being of eternal light in union with all the other beings of light. Here "you *are* light."[247] Here "you *are* love,"[248] forever one with the Source of Light. You realize you have been here all along and have never left this state of mind, except in your former illusions of separation. Perhaps this analogy of being transported from the three-dimensional world to the two-dimensional world and finally to the one-dimensional world is close to what will really happen when you wake up in the Light of Heaven. Notice the parallels between this analogy and the following quotation:

> We share one life because we have one Source, a Source from which perfection comes to us, remaining always in the holy minds which He created perfect. As we were, so are we now and will forever be. A sleeping mind must waken, as it sees its own perfection mirroring the Lord of life so perfectly it fades into what is reflected there. And now it is no more a mere reflection. It becomes the thing reflected, and the light which makes reflection possible. No vision now is needed. For the wakened mind is one that knows its Source, its Self, its Holiness.[249]

The previous quotation indicates that your sleeping mind will see a vision of divine perfection, which is a reflection of your own perfection. Then your sleeping mind must awaken as it fades into its reflection and becomes more than a mere reflection. "It becomes the thing reflected, and the light which makes reflection possible."[250] Your sleeping mind becomes the light. You leave behind your last vision of light and become the awakened mind that knows your Source in God. This reflection of light that awakens your sleeping mind must be the face of Christ that has to be seen in order to bring back the memory of God.

This quotation referring to a reflection of light is very similar to the previously described mirror analogy. The face of Christ is like this two-dimensional mirror in the analogy that serves as a transition place between the three-dimensional world of form and the one-dimensional world, which is really the *One-dimensional* world of Heaven. Although the image of a mirror is used as an analogy, this mirror of light is a close representation of the face of Christ

The reprinted section above from *"A Course in Miracles" Seven Keys to Heaven* describes an analogy of what it is like to have the final vision of the face of Christ. One of the ideas I will expand upon next is that seeing the face of Christ is the seeing of a blazing light that awakens the memory of God. Seeing this blazing light brings your awareness from the second floor to the first floor of awakening. Notice the reference to blazing light and the face of Christ in the following quotation:

> God has come to claim His Own. Forgiveness is complete.
> And now God's *knowledge*, changeless, certain, pure and wholly understandable, enters its kingdom. Gone is perception false and true alike. Gone is forgiveness, for its task is done. And gone are bodies in the blazing light upon the altar to the Son of God. God knows it is His Own, as it is his. And here They join, for here the face of Christ has shone away time's final instant, and now is the last perception of the world without a purpose and without a cause. For where God's memory has come at last there is no journey, no belief in sin, no walls, no bodies, and the grim appeal of guilt and death is there snuffed out forever.
> O my brothers, if you only knew the peace that will envelop you and hold you safe and pure and lovely in the Mind of God, you could but rush to meet Him where His altar is. Hallowed your Name and His, for they are joined here in this holy place. Here He leans down to lift you up to Him, out of illusions into holiness; out of the world and to eternity; out of all fear and given back to love.[251]

THE SECOND FLOOR
LIGHT DIMENSION

~ • ~

This book was inspired by a conversation I had with my friend Jon Pratt as he was giving me a ride back to Arizona after we attended a Miracle Conference held in Las Vegas, Nevada. I do not recall the exact wording of my conversation with Jon, but below I will convey the basic content of our sharing. Between some lines of the dialogue of our conversation below, I have inserted quotations from the Course that expand upon the ideas we were discussing. Jon and I had already had a lively sharing of many Course teachings, but then I said:

Don: I would like to share something with you that I have known for many years, but I have only shared it with one person who was not a committed Course student. You understand the Course so I am looking forward to your feedback after I share this. To set this up, I have to go back to before the separation. I am sure you remember that some parts of the one Christ asked for "special favor." God couldn't give more love to some parts of the Sonship so He refused the request. Those Sons of God responded by having the radical thought of separation or actually the thought of making the illusion of separation.

Jon: Sure, I remember the quote that said that one mistake was so incredible that "a world of total unreality *had* to emerge."

> You may be surprised to hear how very different is reality from what you see. You do not realize the magnitude of that one error. It was so vast and so completely incredible that from it a world of total unreality *had* to emerge. What else could come of it? Its fragmented aspects are fearful enough, as you begin to look at them. But nothing you have seen begins to show you the enormity of the original error, which seemed to cast you out of Heaven, to shatter knowledge into meaningless bits of disunited perceptions, and to force you to make further substitutions.[252]

Don: The Course says the sleeping parts of the Son of God had the opportunity to awaken immediately after their mistake, but their first experience of fear and guilt prevented them from waking up.

Jon: "The Son of God remembered not to laugh."

> Into eternity, where all is one, there crept a tiny, mad idea, at which the Son of God remembered not to laugh. In his forgetting did the thought become a serious idea, and possible of both accomplishment and real effects. Together, we can laugh them both away, and understand that time cannot intrude upon eternity. It is a joke to think that time can come to circumvent eternity, which *means* there is no time.[253]

Don: Yes, they forgot to laugh. I have asked myself: *What happened in relation to the world as an effect of the instant of the separation?* We know that the misguided parts of the Sonship never left Heaven. Instead, they produced the illusion of the separation. The instant of the separation is what scientists call the "Big Bang." Scientists have traced time itself all the way back to the Big Bang and have proven that there is no time before that event. That's a scientific confirmation that the Big Bang was the effect of the separation producing the illusion of the world and at the same time manufactured the illusion of time.

Jon: Just recently I was reading about the Big Bang and learned that back then time was actually much slower than it is now.

Don: That's interesting. I didn't know that, but it makes sense. One of Einstein's thought experiments was the idea of a man in a rocketship traveling close to the speed of light. According to Einstein's theory of relativity, as the rocketship gets closer to the speed of light, two things would occur: Time would become slower for the man in the rocketship. For example, one minute of time might be equal to a year of time back on earth. The other thing that would happen is the rocketship would become shorter and shorter while simultaneously it would get wider. This shortening of length in the direction the rocketship is traveling is called the "Lorentz contraction." Although the laws of physics say the rocketship could never reach the speed of light, what would happen if the rocketship could reach the speed of light? Time that had been getting very slow would become one holy instant. The rocketship's length would be reduced to nothing, and its mass would be converted into the energy of light. But the rocketship's width and height would expand toward infinity but would not be infinite. The rocketship would become a finite two-dimensional circle expanding toward infinity.

Jon: OK, but what does that have to do with the Big Bang?

Don: Let's hypothetically consider the idea that the sleeping Sons of God created the illusion of the three-dimensional world by, in a sense, reversing Einstein's thought experiment, but without the rocketship. We know that Heaven is infinite, timeless, and dimensionless in reality. Since Heaven is infinite, then the finite can only be made by a contraction of the infinite so it becomes less than infinite. For example, the Son of God could have made what I call the "collusion illusion" of separation by somehow making an infinite circle and collapsing the circle inward upon itself so the circle became only a single dot. This contracting circle is a reversal of Einstein's rocketship becoming an expanding circle. Thus the collapsing of the circle by the sleeping Son of God would make an illusion of a finite world and would initiate the illusion of time. The collapsing of the circle would condense the infinite energy of Heaven into a dot. This totally energized dot would initiate the Big Bang.

Jon: So you are saying the collapsed dot with the condensed energy of Heaven would explode into the Big Bang?

Don: Not exactly. According to my study of the Big Bang, scientists now agree that the Big Bang was not actually an explosion, the way we think of a dynamite explosion. Rather, the current theory is that the Big Bang was really like an inflation or expansion without an explosion. You can think of it as the tiniest of balloons that is then blown up and keeps expanding. For many years scientists thought that the expansion of the universe would slow down so much that gravity would eventually cause the universe to collapse into itself. In recent years scientists discovered that the expansion of the universe is surprisingly accelerating. Anyway, my example of the collapsing circle is just a theory. Actually I don't really care exactly how the sleeping Son of God made this three-dimensional illusion. But I am very much interested in how God responded to the making of this illusion by His sleeping Son.

Jon: Of course, you mean God's response of creating the Holy Spirit as His Answer to the separation.

Don: Yes, that's right. But I have put a lot of thought and prayer into understanding what that means. Now we have arrived at what I really want to share with you. Recently you and I had a conversation in which you referred to the Holy Spirit as the "simultaneous Corrector" because He corrects all our errors. But in that sentence, the Holy Spirit is called the "Maker of the world" with a capital "M." In the Course we know that creating is done in Heaven, but the word "make" has to do with making illusions. So my question to you is: *What did the Holy Spirit make?*

> There is another Maker [the Holy Spirit] of the world, the simultaneous Corrector of the mad belief that anything could be established and maintained without some link that kept it still within the laws of God; not as the law itself upholds the universe as God created it, but in some form adapted to the need the Son of God believes he has. Corrected error is the error's end. And thus has God protected still His Son, even in error.
>
> There is another purpose in the world that error made, because it has another Maker Who can reconcile its goal with His Creator's purpose. In His perception of the world, nothing is seen but justifies forgiveness and the sight of perfect sinlessness. Nothing arises but is met with instant and complete forgiveness.[254]

Jon: That's easy. The Holy Spirit made the real world. The real world is an illusion because it is not the same as the reality of Heaven, but is a perfect reflection of Heaven so it enables us to awaken to Heaven.

Don: That's true. But there is more to it than that. I have a theory I want to share with you. The instant when the Big Bang occurred, God created the Holy Spirit as you said as His Answer to the separation. And you said, "The Holy Spirit made the real world." However, here is the question I have pondered: *What actually is the real world?* We know the real world is a world of only loving thoughts and no unloving thoughts. Of course, our three-dimensional world has both loving and unloving thoughts, and our three-dimensional world has some beautiful forms and some forms of death. But what is the *form* of the real world?

Jon: Isn't the real world formless?

Don: Only Heaven is formless. Everything outside Heaven has a form, even though that form is always an illusion.

Jon: How can you be sure that everything outside of Heaven has a form?

Don: The Course says, "All thinking produces form at some level."[255]

Jon: So you are saying that the loving thoughts of the real world must have a form.

Don: Yes, also the real world can be seen. The content of loving thoughts cannot be seen. Since only forms can be seen, the real world must have a form that can be seen.

Jon: So what is the form of the real world?

Don: The Course describes the real world as a "world of light" and a "circle of brightness." That is your answer to the real world's form.

Jon: What are you saying exactly?

Don: I am saying that the Holy Spirit, as the Maker of the real world, made it as a circle of light. More than that I am saying that the Holy Spirit made the real world as the entire second dimension!

Jon: Do you mean the second dimension is like a pie plate that intersects the three-dimensional world?

Don: No. There is a tendency to think of the second dimension with what I call "three-dimensional thinking." That is why scientists can never understand what the second dimension really is. They think that the second dimension must have only length and width and so be smaller than the third dimension that has length, width, and depth. Also, they think that the first dimension is an infinitely small dot so it must be the smallest dimension of all. But they are mistaken. It is OK to think of the first dimension as an infinitely small dot, but where is that dot? That dot is everywhere but not limited to any one place in particular. The first dimension has no length, no width, and no depth. Therefore, the first dimension must be a dimensionless dimension. It has no size. Because it has no size, it must be infinite and everywhere. The first dimension is

Heaven. Heaven is infinite and everywhere, and so it must be larger than and encompass our three-dimensional world that has limited forms. Does it make sense that the first dimension of Heaven encompasses our illusory world of form and time?

Jon: But that does not explain why the second dimension is not a flat plane intersecting the three-dimensional world.

Don: It is hard to accept the concept that the second dimension is larger than the third dimension, but maybe that idea will become clearer as we share more about what the second dimension is. As you know, the Course uses different terms to describe the same thing.

Jon: Sure, like, "Forgiveness, salvation, Atonement, true perception, all are one."

> Knowledge is not the remedy for false perception since, being another level, they can never meet. The one correction possible for false perception must be *true perception*. It will not endure. But for the time it lasts it comes to heal. For true perception is a remedy with many names. Forgiveness, salvation, Atonement, true perception, all are one. They are the one beginning, with the end to lead to oneness far beyond themselves. True perception is the means by which the world is saved from sin, for sin does not exist. And it is this that true perception sees.[256]

Don: That's the perfect quote to illustrate the idea of many names for one thing. "Forgiveness, salvation, Atonement, true perception,"—those ideas seem to be different, but they have an underlying sameness. As you know the Course never talks directly about the second dimension, but the Course does have many names for it. The real world is the most frequently used name in the Course for the second dimension. Some other names are the "bridge" and the "borderland." The idea of the bridge is that it is a transition point from one side of the bridge to the other side of the bridge. The idea of the borderland is that it is on the border between two places and it is also a transition from one place to the other. Obviously this concept of the bridge or borderland world as a transition is directly related to the second dimension. If you realize that the first dimension is Heaven, then it is perfectly logical that in order to go from the third dimension to the first dimension, you must travel through the second dimension that is your transition place.

Jon: You're saying that the second dimension is a transition from the third dimension to the first dimension of Heaven, just as the real world is the bridge to Heaven. I understand how the loving thoughts of the real world are the transition between the loving and unloving thoughts of the three-dimensional world and God's perfect Love in Heaven. But how does the second dimension facilitate this transition from the lesser love of the real world to the greater perfect love of Heaven?

Don: Loving thoughts are the content of the real world. The loving thoughts of the real world cannot be seen, but there is another term describing the image of the second dimension. That term is the "face of Christ." This image of the second dimension is produced by the thought of love, and it can be seen. In fact, it *must* be seen in order to wake you up, because seeing this image awakens its underlying content in your mind like nothing else can. "*The face of Christ* has to be seen before the memory of God can return."[257] This image is a "blazing light" because every spiritual tradition describes this light that brings enlightenment. The Course says that the blazing light and the face of Christ are directly related and both are related to the memory of God returning.

> For this dark veil, which seems to make the face of Christ Himself like to a leper's, and the bright Rays of His Father's Love that light His face with glory appear as streams of blood, fades in the blazing light beyond it when the fear of death is gone.[258]

Jon: Does the Course make a link between the blazing light and the second dimension?

Don: The Course doesn't directly talk about the second dimension, but I believe it is implied. In addition to the real world and the face of Christ, another term is associated with the second dimension. It's the most undervalued term in the Course. What I am talking about is the "vision of the Son of God."[259] As the term implies, the vision of the Son of God must be the vision of Christ. Thus it must be the image of and face of Christ. The vision of the Son of God describes a vision of seeing an arc of golden light. As you approach this vision, the arc becomes larger and becomes a circle of light. This circle of light is expanding infinitely. As you look at it, the edges of the circle fade away and all you see is this expanding light that is all-encompassing.

Jon: Did this description of the vision of the Son of God inspire your idea that the Course is talking about the second dimension when it describes the real world as a transition to Heaven or was there something else?

Don: The importance of the second dimension as a dimension of light was an outgrowth of my personal experience. The vision of the Son of God was convincing, but it only confirmed something I had figured out earlier. The initial idea came from my personal experience of seeing light. I had a profound experience of light when I was twenty-four years old even before the Course was written in 1976. I have written about that experience, but I don't like talking about it. But there have been other experiences of light related to the second dimension that I don't mind sharing. I'm sure you remember that Workbook Lesson 15 talks about seeing "edges of light" around familiar objects.

You will begin to understand it when you have seen little edges of light around the same familiar objects which you see now. That is the beginning of real vision. You can be certain that real vision will come quickly when this has occurred.

As we go along, you may have many "light episodes." They may take many different forms, some of them quite unexpected. Do not be afraid of them. They are signs that you are opening your eyes at last. They will not persist, because they merely symbolize true perception, and they are not related to knowledge. These exercises will not reveal knowledge to you. But they will prepare the way to it. [260]

Jon: I am very familiar with Workbook Lesson 15.

Don: When I first formulated the idea of the second dimension, I was seeing light externally all the time in people and objects. I would have to still my body and then focus my mind on seeing light visually. But I found out that this would only work if I engaged my heart so I was extending love to a person or an object. I could have a loving state of mind and sometimes not see light externally. But I could not see light externally unless I had a loving state of mind. So I felt this external vision was a by-product of having a loving state of mind. First I would see edges of light around people and objects. Then, with more practice of focusing on the love in my heart and on seeing light, I could see people and objects filled with light. Next, I could look in any direction and see my whole panorama of vision filled with light. Everything would flatten out into a two-dimensional picture of shimmering light. Some objects were brighter than others, but everything in this flat panel of vision was shimmering with light. When I saw a flat image of light everywhere I looked, I realized that there must be a second dimension of light. I know it is hard to believe how the second dimension encompasses the third dimension, but they say "seeing is believing." I was seeing a flat vision of shimmering light everywhere, so I concluded the second dimension must be everywhere and must be transposed upon the three-dimensional world of forms. Since that experience occurred whenever I focused on it, I became convinced of the second dimension. Also, the description of the vision of the Son of God as a circle of light supported the idea of the second dimension. Does all this sound strange to you?

Jon: To most people it would be strange, but one time I had a similar experience, so what you are saying makes sense to me. [Then Jon told me about his own experience of seeing a two-dimensional world. And he also told me about an experience he had in relation to Jesus. When I attempted to write down what he told me, I realized I could not remember the details as well as he had told them to me. Consequently, I asked him to write about both experiences so I could use his written description for this book. Here is his written version of his experience of Jesus and of seeing a two-dimensional world:]

The instant I picked up ACIM at the age of forty I was intensely grateful for what seemed like validation to what I'd experienced and felt as a teenager and had looked for since. I was living in semi-remote Alaska so I had few distractions that kept me from reading and studying enthusiastically. There was some contact with other Course students via the internet even though it was in the dial-up days. It was always with a sense of excitement to hear the sound of the static-filled modem connecting to talk.religion.course-miracles.[261]

It was probably about a year and a half or two years into my intense immersion in the Course that I got frustrated that I wasn't able to talk directly with anyone about immediate questions or ideas since I was in semi-remote Alaska. This frustration grew strong. Late one evening, I was sitting in my recliner, and the winter moon was shining through the window. Though late, the light reflecting off the snow provided a winter landscape view of beauty. As I gazed out the window, I asked Jesus to share the view and to answer my questions and to sit on the couch next to the recliner and discuss what you've provided to Helen.

I felt frustration arise because this easy solution seemed impossible. The frustration turned to tears and even anger and my inner conversation went something like this: "The Course makes you, Jesus, sound close and infinitely willing to help but you can't or won't just sit on the couch and have a conversation with me. There is no one else here in the house to blow your cover. Just show up and do it. You claim you are real and didn't die and that you are so close to us that we cannot fail. If so, then why not show the hell up and help out." I was crying, angry, and frustrated.

And then a voice that was even more clear than an audible voice gently interrupted my hissy fit and said, "The next time a brother is sitting on the couch and you are talking with him, that is exactly what is happening." Oh my, the answer was so clear and pure, I immediately burst out laughing! I put my hands together and genuflected as I laughed and thanked my Brother for living in me.

It was four or five months after this experience, during the summer, that my wife and I decided to do the lessons again together. We had lurched our way through the Workbook somewhat before, but it felt our progress was haphazard at best. Though it was in June, we decided to start immediately with Lesson 1. We settled on the same furniture mentioned above, I was in the recliner and she was on the couch. We got settled in and I slowly read: "Nothing I see in this room [on this street, from this window, in this place] means anything."

I paused and then inexplicably the appearance of form paused it seemed. Perception itself changed as though from three-dimensional to two-dimensional. All that I saw was on the flimsiest of material barely existent to my eyesight. It was like a projection rather than material. I sat frozen for a time—I'm not sure how long—just moving my eyes, trying to grasp form without depth. An unknown amount of time went by and I rolled my eyes sideways to see what my wife was doing and if she thought I'd lost it. She was looking at me out of the corner of her eyes, too. Finally, I cleared my throat and mumbled something like, "Well, that was interesting."

I turned to face her and then asked her if she'd just had an unusual response to hearing that first line of Lesson 1. She said while shaking her head that she literally experienced nothing that she was seeing meaning anything and went on to describe almost identically the same experience I had. She said what she was seeing was like a painting on the thinnest of opaque material and it had no depth. I laughed and told her that was exactly what I experienced. We talked about it but never got beyond the experience just illustrating the unreality of perception. One other funny little footnote was that right after that experience, our desire or motivation to do the Lessons again evaporated. We laughed about it and decided all the lessons collapsed somehow into that glimpse into the dimensionless.

[After Jon shared his experiences of Jesus and the second dimension, he drove the car to a gas station to fill the tank. I got out to go to the bathroom. When I returned to the car, Jon was reading the Course, and I asked him what section he was reading.]

Jon: I am reading the first section of Chapter 21 that describes "the vision of the Son of God."

Don: Terrific! Read it aloud from "Beyond the body..."

Jon: "Beyond the body, beyond the sun and stars, past everything you see and yet somehow familiar, is an arc of golden light that stretches as you look into a great and shining circle. And all the circle fills with light before your eyes. The edges of the circle disappear, and what is in it is no longer contained at all."[262] So that's the second dimension you are talking about.

Don: Yes, and the next part says how it is everywhere and there is nowhere that it is not.

Jon: "The light expands and covers everything, extending to infinity forever shining and with no break or limit anywhere. Within it everything is joined in perfect continuity. Nor is it possible to imagine that anything could be outside, for there is nowhere that this light is not."[263]

Don: So it must encompass the entire third dimension.

Jon: "This is the vision of the Son of God, whom you know well. Here is the sight of him who knows his Father. Here is the memory of what you are; a part of this, with all of it within, and joined to all as surely as all is joined in you."[264]

Don: Wait a minute. Read that last line again.

Jon: "Here is the memory of what you are; a part of this, with all of it within, and joined to all as surely as all is joined in you."

Don: What a powerful line! First, it says, "Here is the memory of what you are." The memory of what you are is the same idea as the memory of God returning. The vision of the Son of God must be the same as the vision of the face of Christ because they both bring back the memory of God and the memory of our true nature.

Jon: The next quote says, "...a part of this, with all of it within..." This refers to the idea that each of us is a part of the one Christ as the Son of God and that all of the Christ is within each part.

Don: And then it ends by saying "...and joined to all as surely as all is joined in you..." to complete the idea that each of us is joined in the Sonship and every part of the whole Sonship is joined with every other part of the Whole Christ. What a power packed sentence!

Jon: This section is called "The Forgotten Song," and here is the part that refers to the song we have forgotten: "Accept the vision that can show you this, and not the body. You know the ancient song, and know it well. Nothing will ever be as dear to you as is this ancient hymn of love the Son of God sings to his Father still."[265]

Don: Talking about remembering an "ancient song" in praise of God is a poetic way of saying that when we see the vision of the Son of God, we will awaken the memory who we are as the Christ.

Jon: Here is what the last paragraph says about awakening that memory of yourself and of God: "And they will look upon the vision of the Son of God, remembering who he is they sing of. What is a miracle but this remembering? And who is there in whom this memory lies not?"[266] It's saying we all have this memory within us waiting for us to bring it back to our conscious awareness so we can wake up.

Don: The important thing for me is that this memory is not just an intellectual idea that needs to be restored. It is really about having a direct experience of the blazing light triggered by this vision.

Jon: The last two lines confirm the awakening to light and how this awakening of light is a shared experience in which we help everyone wake up. Here's the lines: "The light in one awakens it in all. And when you see it in your brother, you *are* remembering for everyone."[267]

Don: I can see you are excited about this idea of seeing the circle of blazing light in the second dimension and waking up.

Jon: Yes, I am. I have to ponder this more and see how it evolves in my mind.

PART III

~ • ~

THE FIRST AND
SECOND DIMENSIONS
WORK TOGETHER

Part III elaborates on the ideas related to the second dimension and the first dimension that were part of my conversation with Jon in the last section of Part II. The three-dimensional world consists of unhappy dreams of separate bodies, darkness, and death. The first dimension is Heaven, consisting of perfect oneness, light, love, and eternal life. In the third dimension, there are illusory forms that appear very real to you. You are identified with your body as a form among many other separate forms. These illusory forms offer the benefit of familiarity but also come with the baggage of fear. In the one-dimensional world of Heaven, there are no bodies and no other forms because there is only reality.

Almost everyone claims to want to go to Heaven, but no one wants to go to Heaven *right now*. No one wants to give up the familiarity of form because that means the death of the body in exchange for the uncertain promise of happiness to be found in unknown formlessness. The second dimension is between the two extremes of three-dimensional form and one-dimensional formlessness. The second dimension offers a middle ground where the transition from form to formlessness and from the fear of death to the joy of endless love can be made gracefully.

The gap between the everyday world and Heaven is so great that you cannot jump directly from the unhappiness of the three-dimensional world to the perfect happiness of Heaven. Some seekers mistakenly believe that they can make the leap directly from the fearful illusions of this world to Heaven where there is only love without any illusions. Yet it is foolhardy to believe you can go immediately from all fear to all love. First, you must release worldly dreams of fear before you can hear the Holy Spirit's Voice for God that calls you to awaken. Your fearful dream in which your brother is your enemy must be replaced with a "gentler dream" in which your brother is your friend.

Nothing more fearful than an idle dream has terrified God's Son, and made him think that he has lost his innocence, denied his Father, and made war upon himself. So fearful is the dream, so seeming real, he could not waken to reality without the sweat of terror and a scream of mortal fear, unless a gentler dream preceded his awaking and allowed his calmer mind to welcome, not to fear, the Voice [the Holy Spirit] that called with love to waken him. A gentler dream, in which his suffering was healed, and where his brother was his friend. God willed he waken gently and with joy, and gave him means to waken without fear.[268]

After you make the transition from fearful dreams to gentler dreams, you are ready to release all dreaming and accept the realty of Heaven. The second dimension, which the Course calls the "real world," is the place where you prepare yourself for the happiness of Heaven by having happy dreams. The second dimension is an illusion and not reality, but it is such a perfect and happy reflection of Heaven that the transfer from the real world to Heaven becomes possible. Another name for the two-dimensional real world is "the altar of God."

At the altar of God, the holy perception of God's Son becomes so enlightened that light streams into it, and the spirit of God's Son shines in the Mind of the Father and becomes one with it. Very gently does God shine upon Himself, loving the extension of Himself that is His Son. The world has no purpose as it blends into the purpose of God. For the real world has slipped quietly into Heaven, where everything eternal in it has always been. There the Redeemer and the redeemed join in perfect love of God and of each other. Heaven is your home, and being in God it must also be in you.[269]

The second dimension and first dimension are both light dimensions that lead from the perception of light to the ultimate reality of the Light of Heaven. Part III focuses on how these two dimensions work together to bring about your awakening.

Part III:—The First and Second Dimensions Work Together 75
    The Two Light Dimensions 77
    The Hybrid of the Finite and the Infinite 81
    The World is in Your Mind 83
    The Content and Meaning of Light 85
    The Holy Meeting Place 93
    The Spark and the Great Rays 97

THE TWO
LIGHT DIMENSIONS

≈ ○ ≈

Let's review the analogy of the three-story hospital. In this analogy, the third floor is the three-dimensional world where the Atonement elevator and the other six elevators are used by the Holy Spirit to bring your awareness to the second floor of recovery. The second floor can more specifically be called the second dimension of blazing light that goes by various names, such as *the real world, the face of Christ, and the vision of the Son of God.* The first floor of awakening can now be identified as the first dimension that is the dimensionless dimension of Heaven. The Course itself never talks directly about these three dimensions, so I am introducing an idea of dimensions that is my own interpretation, which you can choose to accept if you find it is helpful for you. Here at the beginning of Part III, I am introducing the idea that the first and second dimensions work together instead of functioning as separate dimensions.

The second dimension is the real world that serves as a transition place from the three-dimensional world to the one-dimensional world of Heaven. To bring about your awakening, I believe you must have the experience in the second dimension of seeing a circle of blazing light expanding infinitely. This experience is both the vision of the Son of God and the vision of the face of Christ that must be seen in order for you to remember your Father and your own place in the Sonship. The idea of a second dimension awakening is a new interpretation of the Course, but the idea of a transcendental circle of light is not unique. In Tantric Yoga, students are taught meditation in which they focus on an indivisible point of light called the "bindu" symbolized by a dot in the center of a circular mandala. The deepest level of this practice results in perceiving the bindu in the center suddenly expand into an infinitely expanding circle of light. Seeing this circle of light triggers the most profound transcendental awakening of the true Self. This is the same experience as seeing the expanding circle of light in the vision of the Son of God, which is the same as the vision of the face of Christ.

> And although yoga as "practice" requires concentration, the focusing inward of consciousness on the indivisible point of light (*bindu*), which is the Self, once the yogi realizes the Lord in the Self, the light radiates outward in a continuous expansion of consciousness which fills the universe, as Shiva himself.[270]

The *mandala's* form also suggests a "march toward the center," a rite of initiation in which the adept progressively penetrates into various levels until he or she reaches the inner sanctum of the *bindu*, the indivisible point which no longer has any meaning except on the level of yogic consciousness, where it paradoxically becomes an infinitely expanding circumference.[271]

In Tantric Yoga, the bindu is an individual point of light that has no length, width, or depth. It represents the dimensionless first dimension that is Heaven. The meditator meditates on this bindu that is seen within the circle of the mandala. It is not just a dot, but a *dimensionless* dot within a circle. The relationship between the dot and the circle is very important because the dot itself does not bring about awakening. Rather, the circle of light expanding infinitely with the dot at its center is what actually triggers the experience. The light is expanding from the dot outward to form the circle, so the dot and circle are interrelated.

This interrelationship between the dot and circle that is necessary for awakening in Tantric Yoga is also absolutely necessary for the awakening that occurs by seeing the blazing light of the face of Christ. In my former conversation with Jon, I described the second dimension as a separate dimension between the third dimension of this world and the first dimension of Heaven. Indeed, the second dimension is the "bridge" between these two dimensions, but I felt there was something not quite right about the description I conveyed to Jon.

When Jon returned to his home in Alaska, he sent me an email saying this: "I love trying to picture the 2nd dimension! I've thought lots about your dimensional descriptions and have enjoyed imagining (quite unsuccessfully) a 2D representation related to our 3D world." I felt Jon was still having trouble picturing why the second dimension was not a flat surface intersecting the three dimensions of this world. I was certain that the second dimension of blazing light is actually everywhere in the third dimension and encompasses it. Yes, I could see flat visions of light everywhere, and Jon himself had his own personal vision of a flat second dimension image of shimmering light just as I did. However, seeing flat images of light does not fully explain why the second dimension is everywhere in the third dimension. I felt I needed to have a better understanding myself so I could then explain how the second dimension overlapped the third dimension.

After pondering how I could explain why the second dimension was everywhere, I realized I had been using three-dimensional thinking to understand the second dimension. Three-dimensional thinking always defines everything by differences. By this limited thinking, the first, second, and third dimensions are all distinctly separate dimensions. After asking for guidance about this, I realized if the second dimension disappeared, the first dimension would still exist because the first dimension is the reality of Heaven. However, the second dimension is totally dependent upon the first dimension. Both the first dimension and second dimension are light dimensions. When God created the Holy Spirit at the instant of separation, the first dimension projected a circle of blazing light expanding infinitely. Thus the Holy Spirit became the Maker of the real world, the face of Christ, and the vision of the Son of God. In my first book, *An Overview of "A Course in Miracles,"* I wrote:

> Just what does the Holy Spirit have to do with form? The knowing part of the Holy Spirit resides in the formlessness of the Christ Mind. Where does the perceiving part of the Holy Spirit reside? According to the Course, the Holy Spirit, as the Voice for God, has "taken form. This form is not His reality...."[272] The Holy Spirit has taken the form of the blazing light. Although all form must be illusory, this one illusory form that the Holy Spirit has taken leads beyond all illusions to reality.

Although this overview book is an introduction to the Course, I included some mystical aspects such as the Holy Spirit taking the form of blazing light. Now I will expand upon that idea by stating that the Holy Spirit Himself has taken the form of the second dimension. The blazing light in the second dimension is the Holy Spirit's light. Thus the Holy Spirit Himself has the form that the Course calls the face of Christ and the vision of the Son of God that returns your memory of God.

> The Holy Spirit is described as the remaining Communication Link between God and His separated Sons. In order to fulfill this special function the Holy Spirit has assumed a dual function. He knows because He is part of God; He perceives because He was sent to save humanity. He is the great correction principle; the bringer of true perception, the inherent power of the vision of Christ. He is the light in which the forgiven world is perceived; in which the face of Christ alone is seen. He never forgets the Creator or His creation. He never forgets the Son of God. He never forgets you. And He brings the Love of your Father to you in an eternal shining that will never be obliterated because God has put it there.[273]

Although the second dimension of blazing light is the Holy Spirit's form, He is not limited by the second dimension because He is not limited to only true perception. He also includes the first dimension because He has knowledge as well as perception. The Holy Spirit, then, is the combination of the second dimension and the first dimension. However, only the second dimension is the form of the Holy Spirit, because the first dimension has no form. Therefore, the first dimension is the content of the Holy Spirit, and this content is reflected in the Holy Spirit's form and the true perception of the second dimension.

The second dimension is not a separate dimension because it has been projected from the first dimension. The Holy Spirit as the second dimension of true perception and as the first dimension of knowledge always functions in Oneness. Thus perfect perception and knowledge are never separated from each other in His Mind. The Holy Spirit always enables the transfer of perfect true perception into the One-mindedness of knowledge. The two light dimensions, which consist of the second dimension and first dimension combined, must function together since they represent the two joined aspects of the Mind of the Holy Spirit— true perception and the One-mindedness of knowledge.

A movie projector projects an image of light onto a flat screen to show a movie, so the movie on the flat screen does not exist without receiving its image of light from the one point of light coming from the projector. Similarly, the circular expanding light of the second dimension does not exist without receiving its image from its source coming from a single indivisible point of light originating in the first dimension, which is reality itself. Thus the reflection of expanding light seen in the face of Christ does not exist without reality and God's Presence of Light from which it is reflected. It is the second dimension's dependence on the first dimension that allows the Holy Spirit to bring salvation.

Salvation is nothing more than "right-mindedness," which is not the One-mindedness of the Holy Spirit, but which must be achieved before One-mindedness is restored.[274]

He [the Holy Spirit] represents a state of mind close enough to One-mindedness that transfer to it is at last possible. Perception is not knowledge, but it can be transferred to knowledge, or cross over into it.[275]

Now let's go back to my hope of finding a better way to understand and to explain how the second dimension encompasses the world of three-dimensional forms. One new answer I came up with is that it is really the combination of the second dimension and the first dimension that encompasses the entire third dimension. It is obvious that the first dimension alone symbolized by a dot is a dimensionless dimension, so this indivisible dot of light must be everywhere in the third dimension. Because the dot symbolizes the reality of Heaven, it transcends and encompasses all of the three-dimensional illusion of this world. Since the dot is everywhere in the third dimension, the dot's projection of the second dimension, as a reflection of Heaven, must also be everywhere in the third dimension. This is why anyone who can see light visually can perceive the flat images of light anywhere in the third dimension.

THE HYBRID OF THE FINITE AND INFINITE

~ • ~

Now let's elaborate on why an apparently flat second dimension can encompass the third dimension: Obviously the third dimension is entirely finite, since it has a limited length, width, and depth (up-down, left-right, and forward-backward). Every object within the third dimension is finite and has three limited measurements. Since the start of time at the Big Bang 13.8 billion years ago, the physical universe has been expanding and accelerating as it expands *toward* infinity. However, scientists cannot determine if the physical universe is infinite. The word "infinity" implies a state of being without limit so no number indicating size can be assigned to describe what is infinite. In my opinion, there is no such thing as an infinite physical universe because by the definition of infinity that would mean the universe has infinite size, which is no size limitation at all. Only the first dimension is infinite and therefore without size limitation of any kind. In fact, the third dimension is defined by its complete deviation from infinity in three directions.

Between the infinite first dimension and the finite third dimension, there is what I call the "second dimension." The title "The Hybrid of the Finite and Infinite" describes the second dimension's unique nature. If you make the mistake of using a three-dimensional perspective, you will describe the second dimension as having only length and width, but that is not the definition being used in this book. The word "hybrid" is used to emphasize that the second dimension has qualities of the finite third dimension and the infinite first dimension. Obviously the second dimension has limited length and limited width characteristic of the third dimension, without this world's limited third measurement.

What is less obvious is that the second dimension does have a third measurement that is *infinite*. The second dimension is defined by its deviation from infinity in two directions, but not in its third direction. The infinite third direction of the second dimension connects it with the first dimension. This enables the second dimension to work together with the first dimension. A circle with a dot in the center symbolizes the second dimension. The circle represents its two-dimensional nature. The dot in the center represents the infinite nature of its third measurement that links the second dimension to the first dimension. This dot allows the second dimension to encompass the third dimension. This infinite dot is really dimensionless, and it makes the leap from the second dimension to the first dimension possible, making salvation possible.

As a hybrid of the finite and infinite, the second dimension is also the home of the holy instant that is a hybrid of time and timelessness. In the second dimension's finite length and width, illusory time is reduced to one holy instant used to release the past and future. In the infinite depth of the second dimension, "the holy instant reaches to eternity."[276]

The goal of every spiritual seeker is to make the transition from the illusory three-dimensional world of form to the formless one-dimensional world of Heaven. But going directly from the nightmares of the third dimension to the bliss of the first dimension is not possible because the contrast between these two worlds is so great. The second dimension serves as a place of transition between these two worlds. Because the second dimension is a hybrid of these two worlds, it enables you to shift your awareness in a gentle way from the finite to the infinite.

The Course never uses the term "second dimension," but the term "real world" is used to indirectly refer to the second dimension. The real world as the second dimension is like the world of three-dimensional forms because it has loving and true perceptions, but it is unlike the physical world because it has no unloving and no false perceptions. The second dimension is like Heaven since it has one infinite direction, and its loving and true perceptions are reflections of God's perfect Love and Truth. The second dimension is called the "real world," not because it is real, but because it is a reflection of the reality of Heaven. If you identify with the ego and the body, you will believe the three-dimensional world is reality itself. Experiencing the real world will help you change your perspective on the nature of reality.

The Course terms "borderland," "bridge," and "the transition" are used to describe the function of the real world. "The bridge [real world] itself is nothing more than a transition in the perspective of reality."[277] Because the real world is the second dimension, it is not a place in the three-dimensional sense of the word "place." Rather, it is a transition place of thought. "There is a borderland [real world] of thought that stands between this world and Heaven. It is not a place, and when you reach it is apart from time."[278]

The real world offers different levels of awareness. The lowest level of the real world is the connecting link between the third dimension and the second dimension. The real world is also called the "meeting place" where you bring together your conflicting thoughts. Thus you learn to keep your loving and true perceptions and learn to release your unloving and false perceptions. "Here is the meeting place where thoughts are brought together; where conflicting values meet and all illusions are laid down beside the truth, where they are judged to be untrue."[279] The highest level of awareness in the real world is at the connecting link between the second dimension and the first dimension. This link is the face of Christ that must be seen to remember God and awaken.

THE WORLD IS
IN YOUR MIND

~ o ~

In addition to the explanation provided in the previous section, there is another answer to why the second dimension, combined with the first dimension, encompasses the three-dimensional world. Because you are identified with your body and your ego that perceives an outer world, you perceive the third dimension as a world of forms outside of yourself. *But actually the three-dimensional world is within your mind.* When your brother identifies with the ego, he will misperceive the world. "He always perceives this world as outside himself, for this is crucial to his adjustment. He does not realize that he makes this world, for there is no world outside of him."[280] The sleeping Son of God has a split mind because it has opposing thoughts within it. Just as the three-dimensional world is actually in your mind, the real world is also in your mind as the second dimension projected from the first dimension.

> If only the loving thoughts of God's Son are the world's reality, the real world [as the second dimension of blazing light coming from the first dimension] must be in his mind. His insane thoughts, too, must be in his mind, but an internal conflict of this magnitude he cannot tolerate. A split mind is endangered, and the recognition that it encompasses completely opposed thoughts within itself is intolerable.[281]

The ego-based mind contains loving and true perceptions that are in conflict with unloving and false perceptions. This condition of internal mental conflict is painful and intolerable. Consequently, you deny that there is a conflict in the mind by projecting the conflict so it is perceived as being outside the mind. "Therefore the mind projects the split, not the reality. Everything you perceive as the outside world is merely your attempt to maintain your ego identification, for everyone believes that identification is salvation."[282]

The conflict in your mind forces you to choose between the Holy Spirit and the ego. Choosing the Holy Spirit means perceiving the real world of loving thoughts in the second dimension projected from the first dimension. Choosing the ego means perceiving the three-dimensional world of both loving and unloving thoughts that is projected outwardly so you do not see the conflict within your mind. The Course encourages you to learn to recognize only the real world of loving thoughts within your mind and release all unloving thoughts in your mind by realizing that they are unreal and do not exist without your belief in them.

"God does love the real world, and those who perceive its reality cannot see the world of death. For death is not of the real world, in which everything reflects the eternal."[283] The real world of only loving thoughts is God's gift to you. "God gave you the real world in exchange for the one you made out of your split mind, and which is the symbol of death."[284] Since your world is an illusion of separation from God, it is a disordered dream. This outer world is not really outside because it is in your mind. "Yet this world is only in the mind of its maker, along with his real salvation. Do not believe it is outside of yourself, for only by recognizing where it is will you gain control over it. For you do have control over your mind, since the mind is the mechanism of decision."[285] By recognizing the world is within your mind, you can decide to withdraw your belief in the reality of this illusory world.

Since both the real world of the second dimension projected from the first dimension and the illusory world of the third dimension are both in your mind, how can you answer the question of which dimension is larger? I don't think this question can be answered because size is not really the issue here. A better question would be this: Which dimension transcends and therefore encompasses the other dimension? Wording the question this way, the answer becomes obvious: In your mind, the Holy Spirit's second dimension of light joined with and projected from the first dimension of light both together transcend and encompass the ego's third dimension of darkness and light. Or in other words, the combination of the real world as a reflection of reality and reality itself must transcend the ego and all its illusions. "Nothing real can be threatened. Nothing unreal exists."[286] The unreal world of the ego cannot transcend or encompass anything because it does not exist.

Just as you can project the illusory three-dimensional world and can perceive it as though it is outside the mind, there is a positive form of projection. The perceiving of the light in the second dimension as an outer flat image of shimmering light is a positive variation of the ego's negative projection. It is an attempt of the mind to project outward something positive that is within the mind. In contrast to negative projection that is used to get rid of something in the mind, this positive projection is employed to convince yourself that something good is in your mind by seeing that same something good outside of your mind. Projecting negativity outside the mind does not have the desired effect because instead of getting rid of negative thoughts, it actually keeps your mind focused on negativity and keeps that negativity in your mind. However, this new kind of positive projection does work and proves to you that the light along with its loving content is really within you.

THE CONTENT AND
MEANING OF LIGHT

≈ ∘ ≈

The previous sections discussed the second dimension of light and the first dimension of light, and how these two light dimensions function together. The second dimension of perfect perception is the circle of light expanding infinitely that is projected from the indivisible light of the first dimension. When you see these two dimensions functioning together, you will be seeing the blazing light. The Holy Spirit Who has the content of Light and Love has taken the form of these two dimensions. This section now will discuss the content and meaning of light. Every time this section refers to the term "blazing light," bear in mind that the term is directly referring to seeing the form and awakening the inner content of the second dimension and the first dimension functioning together in the Mind of the Holy Spirit.

The Course uses the word "light" 498 times. Although some might believe that the Course's references to light are only figurative, these references are quite literal. An example is: "He [the Holy Spirit] can therefore perform the function of reinterpreting what the ego makes, not by destruction but by understanding. Understanding is light, and light leads to knowledge. The Holy Spirit is in light because He is in you who are light, but you yourself do not know this. It is therefore the task of the Holy Spirit to reinterpret you on behalf of God."[287] You study the Course to learn that *understanding is light*. And the Holy Spirit Himself is literally light that comes into your mind to bring understanding. The Holy Spirit brings light into your mind to teach you your true nature as light. But you must invite light to come into your darkened private mind. "Ask for light and learn that you *are* light."[288]

The Holy Spirit is both the light of true perception and the Light of knowledge from Heaven. As the light of true perception, the Holy Spirit "is the light in which the forgiven world is perceived; in which the face of Christ alone is seen."[289] You must welcome light into your mind because the darkened private mind you made is a denial of the light that you are. "The Holy Spirit is the light in which Christ stands revealed. And all who would behold Him can see Him, for they have asked for light."[290] You must ask for light since God cannot give you what you have denied and thus do not want. When did you first deny the light? In Heaven where God abides in His Light, you were all light within the Sonship. In order to fall asleep in Heaven at the separation, you had to bring darkness into your mind by denying light for the first time. The light has not gone from your mind since the nature of your mind *is* light. In your creation, God extended His light into you, and even now He continues to extend His light into your mind. The light in your mind can never be extinguished because God, Who loves you eternally, will never stop extending His light into your mind. "God has lit your mind Himself, and keeps your mind lit by His light because His light is what your mind is."[291]

However, your denial of light has made you unaware of the light that is still there. At the separation, you gave yourself an "amnesia pill" that allowed you to forget the light that you are. Normally, amnesia describes the condition of a person who has forgotten who he is because he has forgotten the past. But the amnesia pill you took allowed you to forget who you truly are because you have forgotten the *present*—forgotten the eternal now is where Heaven is. You never really left Heaven and never left the eternal now, but in order to convince yourself that you had left Heaven, you manufactured the illusion of time and an illusory world where time would seem real to you. Ever since then you have allowed your mind to be focused on the past and future without regard to the eternal now where you are in the Light of Heaven.

Since you have denied light and denied the eternal now, you must learn to focus on the present and invite the light you denied. Because your mind has been darkened by focusing on the past, when you invite light into your mind, you are asking for help to let go of the past and accept the present where the light is. When light comes into your mind, it brings understanding and heals your mind, giving you the sight of your brother without his past. "Everyone seen without the past thus brings you nearer to the end of time by bringing healed and healing sight into the darkness, and enabling the world to see. For light must come into the darkened world to make Christ's vision possible even here. Help Him to give His gift of light to all who think they wander in the darkness, and let Him gather them into His quiet sight that makes them one."[292]

Christ's vision is directly related to light in the mind. "Vision depends on light...."[293] Your invitation is essential for light to come into your mind so you can perceive your brother with Christ's vision. "The wish to see calls down the grace of God upon your eyes, and brings the gift of light that makes sight possible."[294] But what exactly is this gift light that comes into your mind as God's grace to you enabling you to have Christ's vision? This light is called "true light." The unified Mind of the Holy Spirit takes the form of the second dimension projected from the first dimension, and both dimensions of light work together. When the light of the two dimensions can be seen *directly*, that light has been referred to as the "blazing light" that brings awakening. But that same light of the two dimensions functioning together is the source of the light that comes into our mind *indirectly*. This light from the Mind of the Holy Spirit is referred to in the Course as "true light." This true light comes into your mind to give you Christ's vision so you can see with it, but it is an indirect light only because it cannot be seen directly as the blazing light is seen. This true light expresses the beneficial content of the Mind of the Holy Spirit that can only perceive light, truth, and love.

> True light that makes true vision possible is not the light the body's eyes behold. It is a state of mind that has become so unified that darkness cannot be perceived at all. And thus what is the same is seen as one, while what is not the same remains unnoticed, for it is not there.
> This is the light that shows no opposites, and vision, being healed, has power to heal. This is the light that brings your peace of mind to other minds, to share it and be glad that they are one with you and with themselves. This is the light that heals because it brings single perception, based upon one frame of reference, from which one meaning comes.
> Here are both giving and receiving seen as different aspects of one Thought whose truth does not depend on which is seen as first, nor which appears to be in second place. Here it is understood that both occur together, that the Thought remain complete.[295]

Workbook Lesson 108, "To give and to receive are one in truth," refers to the "true light" that makes Christ's vision possible. This "true light" is given and is received simultaneously whenever you practice forgiveness, just as the perception of love and holiness is given and received simultaneously.

There is a difference between the experience of light in perception and the experience of light in the knowledge of Heaven. In most cases, when you are studying the Course, it is best to interpret the word "light" literally and to not interpret "light" as a poetic figure of speech. Since references to light in the Course need to be interpreted literally, the light that can be seen in the real world using Christ's vision and performing miracles is indeed light. Yet this light that is seen using Christ's vision is a *symbolic light* because it is the perception of light rather than the direct experience of light as you will experience light in the knowledge of Heaven. In the direct experience of light in Heaven, you will experience *yourself as being the light*. In Heaven you will have the total awareness of knowledge rather than the partial awareness of perception that always involves separation. Thus in Heaven you will experience no separation between you and the light that you are.

But outside of Heaven, the perception of light is always a symbolic experience because you as the perceiver are separate from the light that you perceive. In the perceptual experience of symbolic light, you see light in your brother using Christ's vision. Seeing light in your brother is a helpful reminder to you that this same light must be in you also, although it is not a direct experience of your true nature as light that you will experience in the knowledge of Heaven.

Since light literally comes into your mind enabling you to receive the gift of Christ's vision, you have the potential to see light in your brother as a visual experience. It is possible for you to see light in your mind in meditation with your eyes closed, and it is possible for you to outwardly see light in others and in objects. Workbook Lesson 15 refers to this outward seeing of light, stating that you may see "little edges of light around the same familiar objects which you see now. That is the beginning of real vision. You can be certain that real vision will come quickly when this has occurred."[296]

There are two ways of having a visual experience of the light of the real world: One way is to see light in your mind during meditation. The other way is to see light visually in the outer world. If you see a spiritual light with your eyes open, you are seeing *through* the eyes, but not exclusively *with* the physical eyes. Seeing spiritual light is facilitated by the Holy Spirit in your mind so you can see more than you normally could if you were using only your physical eyes. But the perception of light is both literal and symbolic, as has been explained previously. Workbook Lesson 15 explains the symbolic nature of seeing light, as follows: "As we go along, you may have many 'light episodes.' They may take many different forms, some of them quite unexpected. Do not be afraid of them. They are signs that you are opening your eyes at last. They will not persist, because they merely symbolize true perception, and they are not related to knowledge. These exercises will not reveal knowledge to you. But they will prepare the way to it."[297]

Although it is possible to see the light of the real world as a visual experience of light, that is not the only way to perceive the real world. In fact, the visual experience of the light of the real world is not as common or as important as the perception of the *content* of the real world. The content of the real world is light as spiritual understanding and is love as thoughts of spiritual oneness. The vast majority of spiritual seekers do not have a visual experience of the light of the real world, but anyone can experience the content of light and the content of love in the real world. Those who do have a visual experience of the light of the real world are only enabled to do so because they are at the same time experiencing the content of light and love in the real world. It is more important for you to experience the content of light and love in the real world than to have the visual experience. It is not essential for you to have a visual experience because the visual experience of light is only a *by-product* of experiencing the content of light and love in the real world. Therefore, the visual experience of light is only a secondary consideration and is not the goal of practicing Christ's vision.

The goal of Christ's vision is the content of light and love that can be experienced with or without the by-product of the visual experience of light. The previous quotation states that "light episodes" are experiences that "symbolize true perception." True perceptions are thoughts with the content of light and love, and so seeing light visually is the by-product that symbolizes the content of true perception. The real world is a world of only true perceptions with the content of light and love. But, of course, you can experience the true perceptions of the real world in your mind without the bonus of the visual experience.

Although most seekers do not experience seeing light visually during meditation, they can use their God-given intuition to expand their awareness so they can *feel* the content of light and love in the real world. Similarly, most seekers do not experience the seeing of light visually as they perceive their brothers with Christ's vision, but they can perceive the content of light and love in their brothers because the Holy Spirit's gift of light is coming into their minds. If you think of light coming into the mind as physical light, then you will misunderstand what light coming into the mind means. Light coming into the mind means fearful thoughts in the mind are removed and awareness in the mind is expanded. Light brings forth understanding of spiritual truth and oneness because *light is understanding*, as has been quoted previously: "Understanding is light, and light leads to knowledge."[298] This explains why seeing light visually is only a secondary consideration, and why the primary consideration is the content of understanding that light brings into the mind.

Heaven is filled with light and love since God Himself is Light and Love and you, as His Son, are light and love. The light that makes Christ's vision possible is a symbolic light because it is a reflection of the heavenly light. This reflected light unites you with your brother in the present. "The present offers you your brothers in the light that would unite you with them, and free you from the past. Would you, then, hold the past against them? For if you do, you are choosing to remain in the darkness that is not there, and refusing to accept the light that is offered you."[299] You have learned that a miracle is an exchange of love with your brother, but the miracle is also an exchange of light with your brother in the present. Even if you cannot visually see the light in your mind and even if you cannot feel the light in your mind, you can still use the light in your mind to perform miracles. Thus you can let the light in your mind shine into the minds of your brothers to bring both understanding and healing to them and likewise increase understanding and healing within your own mind.

Jesus reminds you of letting light shine through you when he says in the Course, "Let your mind shine with mine upon their [your brothers'] minds, and by our gratitude to them make them aware of the light in them. This light will shine back upon you and on the whole Sonship, because this is your proper gift to God. He will accept it and give it to the Sonship, because it is acceptable to Him and therefore to His Sons."[300] The light you share comes back to you with gratitude from your brothers in the Sonship. "For the light of perfect vision is freely given as it is freely received, and can be accepted only without limit."[301] Light enables you to see Christ in your brother who in return shines the light upon you in the present. "In this one, still dimension of time [the present] that does not change, and where there is no sight of what you were, you look at Christ and call His witnesses to shine on you *because you called them forth.* And they will not deny the truth in you, because you looked for it in them and found it there."[302]

To perform miracles, you need to accept the Atonement. *"The sole responsibility of the miracle worker is to accept the Atonement for himself."*[303] Accepting the Atonement means accepting perfect love. "Perfect love is the Atonement."[304] When you accept perfect love, you are merely accepting what is already within you. "You have so little faith in yourself because you are unwilling to accept the fact that perfect love is in you."[305] However, love and light always go together, so accepting perfect love and accepting the Atonement also mean accepting the light that is the gift of the Holy Spirit. "The Atonement is entirely unambiguous. It is perfectly clear because it exists in light."[306] If you do not accept the inner light, you will not be able to accept the Atonement and will not be able to perform miracles. "The Atonement can only be accepted within you by releasing the inner light."[307]

You can use prayer to ask for light, or you can rely on meditation to invite the inner light. Your request for light is always made and answered in the present moment. You will always receive light if you ask for it. The Course describes some specific ways of becoming aware of light. For example, Workbook Lesson 67 suggests the possibility of finding the blazing light during your practice of meditation. "Yet perhaps you will succeed in going past that [distracting thoughts], and through the interval of thoughtlessness to the awareness of a blazing light in which you recognize yourself as love created you."[308]

When you have a visual experience of seeing light in your brother using Christ's vision, you are the perceiver, and you are separate from the light that you perceive in your brother. But seeing the blazing light is a much more profound experience of light than the typical way of perceiving light in your brother. When you have your first glimpse of the blazing light, you will initially perceive that you are separate from the blazing light that you see. But the seeing of the blazing light facilitates a deep experience of oneness. It was previously stated that seeing light visually in the outer world is only a secondary and symbolic seeing with true perception that is not related directly to knowledge. However, the seeing of the blazing light is an internal experience and not the same as seeing light visually in the outer world. In fact, seeing the blazing light is necessary to awaken to Heaven.

You can ask God for the blazing light to return the memory of God and enable you to awaken. *"Let me remember that I am Your Son, and opening the door at last, forget illusions in the blazing light of truth, as memory of You returns to me."*[309] Whether you use prayer or practice meditation to invite the awareness of inner light, you must recognize that every gift given to you is not given to you alone. It is meant to be shared through prayer for others, through joining with others in your meditation experience, through the extension of miracles, and through perceiving your brother with Christ's vision.

This sharing is the process of awakening others by recognizing their true nature of light and love that in turn enables you to awaken to the awareness of your own innate light and love. Salvation happens only in the eternal now. "Now is the time of salvation, for now is the release from time. Reach out to all your brothers, and touch them with the touch of Christ. In timeless union with them is your continuity, unbroken because it is wholly shared."[310] You can only share in the light where Christ can be seen now. "God's guiltless Son is only light."[311]

If you see your brother in darkness, you are not seeing him. If you see him in the light, you will see him as he is in Christ. "There is no darkness in him [your brother] anywhere, for he is whole. Call all your brothers to witness to his wholeness, as I am calling you to join with me [Jesus]."[312] When you perceive light using Christ's vision, you recognize that your brother comes from God's Light just as you do. "Each voice [of each brother] has a part in the song of redemption, the hymn of gladness and thanksgiving for the light to the Creator of light. The holy light that shines forth from God's Son is the witness that his light is of his Father."[313]

When you perform a miracle of exchanging light and love with your brother, he becomes a witness to you of your Father. "Shine on your brothers in remembrance of your Creator, for you will remember Him as you call forth the witnesses to His creation. Those whom you heal bear witness to your healing, for in their wholeness you will see your own."[314] Gratitude keeps your heart open to your Father. "And as your hymns of praise and gladness rise to your Creator, He will return your thanks in His clear Answer [the Holy Spirit] to your call. For it can never be that His Son called upon Him and remained unanswered. His Call to you is but your call to Him. And in Him you are answered by His peace."[315]

Light is essential to you, yet you are mostly unaware of the light that you have and are. "Child of Light, you know not that the light is in you. Yet you will find it through its witnesses, for having given light to them they will return it. Each one you see in light brings your light closer to your awareness."[316] The light and love you give in a miracle come back to you as light and love. "Love always leads to love. The sick, who ask for love, are grateful for it, and in their joy they shine with holy thanks. And this they offer you who gave them joy."[317]

If you give joy, you receive joy because "giving *is* receiving."[318] Your brothers whom the Holy Spirit heals through you "are your guides to joy, for having received it of you they would keep it. You have established them as guides to peace, for you have made it manifest in them. And seeing it, its beauty calls you home."[319] You cannot get light from the world of darkness, but you can give light to it. "There is a light that this world cannot give. Yet you can give it, as it was given you. And as you give it, it shines forth to call you from the world and follow it. For this light will attract you as nothing in this world can do."[320]

Just as the real world is a world of only loving thoughts, it is also a world of light. Finding the light in your brother and in yourself, you will release the past and the world of darkness and embrace the real world of light in the eternal now. "And you will lay aside the world and find another. This other world [the real world] is bright with love which you have given it. And here will everything remind you of your Father and His holy Son."[321] Finding the real world will bring you joy that you will share with your brother in light. "Light is unlimited, and spreads across this world [the real world] in quiet joy. All those you brought with you will shine on you, and you will shine on them in gratitude because they brought you here. Your light will join with theirs in power so compelling, that it will draw the others out of darkness as you look on them."[322]

You are attracted to light, and your attraction makes you willing to share your love. "Awaking unto Christ is following the laws of love of your free will, and out of quiet recognition of the truth in them. The attraction of light must draw you willingly, and willingness is signified by giving."[323] While you sleep, the real world is still filled with light and love waiting for you to recognize it. "And yet the laws of love are not suspended because you sleep. And you have followed them through all your nightmares, and have been faithful in your giving, for you were not alone. Even in sleep has Christ protected you, ensuring the real world for you when you awake."[324] Although you are unaware of your true nature, Christ within you is still shining light and love in spite of your limited perception. "In your name He [Christ] has given for you, and given you the gifts He gave. God's Son is still as loving as his Father. Continuous with his Father, he has no past apart from Him."[325] Christ within you is your reminder of the Father and your own true nature.

THE HOLY MEETING PLACE

~ o ~

The blazing light is seen in the second dimension but projected from the first dimension so both dimensions work together to bring about your awakening. These two light dimensions are part of the macrocosm that you perceive outside your body and part of the microcosm that you perceive within your body. It has already been explained that the macrocosm of the world you see outside your body is really within your mind that encompasses the third dimension. The macrocosm of the outer world is a collective dream of the sleeping Son of God. Within this collective dream, the Holy Spirit helps you to become aware of the two light dimensions that overlap and transcend the third dimension.

You are not a body, but the body is the temple of the spirit and the two light dimensions are microcosmically represented within your temple. The Course has many names for the two light dimensions that represent the place of awakening that might be considered the Holy of Holies within your temple. This Holy of Holies within your right mind where God and His Son are joined is called "the holy meeting place." "All this [place of oneness between God and His Son] is safe within you, where the Holy Spirit shines. He shines not in division, but in the meeting place where God, united with His Son, speaks to His Son through Him."[326]

Because of the Holy Spirit, God and His Son dwell in the altar and remain in constant communion, which has not been interrupted by the separation. The Holy Spirit brings your awareness to this holy meeting place so you can accept your true nature as God's Son and you can accept your holy uninterrupted communication with your loving Father. "Communication between what cannot be divided cannot cease. The holy meeting place of the unseparated Father and His Son lies in the Holy Spirit and in you."[327] In this communication, you can recognize that love is your true nature. "All interference in the communication that God Himself wills with His Son is quite impossible here. Unbroken and uninterrupted love flows constantly between the Father and the Son, as Both would have it be. And so it is."[328]

You can avoid bringing your awareness to the holy meeting place by not accepting the Atonement and continuing to invest in your illusions and other false beliefs. Nevertheless, the holy meeting place awaits your recognition of eternal light and love between you and your Father. "Let your mind wander not through darkened corridors, away from light's center. You and your brother may choose to lead yourselves astray, but you can be brought together only by the Guide appointed for you. He will surely lead you to where God and His Son await your recognition."[329] Fulfilling your single purpose of awakening your mind to oneness is the gift the Father and the Son want to give you at the altar of God. God and Christ "are joined in giving you the gift of oneness, before which all separation vanishes."[330]

Where do you awaken to your eternal union with your Father? This full awakening to oneness happens in the holy meeting place. "Unite with what you are. You cannot join with anything except reality. God's glory and His Son's belong to you in truth. They have no opposite, and nothing else can you bestow upon yourself."[331] This holy meeting place is also the home of truth. "There is no substitute for truth. And truth will make this plain to you as you are brought into the place where you must meet with truth. And there you must be led, through gentle understanding which can lead you nowhere else."[332] The Holy of Holies is holy and a meeting place because it to this place that the Holy Spirit is leading you so you will meet God and Christ as your true Self.

Specifically, the greatest significance for you of this meeting place is that here you will inevitably accept the truth about yourself. You will accept who you are as God's Son. You have not lost your knowledge that God gave you in Heaven, but you have obscured your awareness of it. Yet you can never separate yourself from God because you are eternally part of Him and all His power and glory are in you because He shares Himself with you. "Where God is, there are you. Such is the truth. Nothing can change the knowledge, given you by God, into unknowingness."[333] Your knowledge of God is still in you now, and this awareness of union allows you to create your own creations in Heaven. "Everything God created knows its Creator. For this is how creation is accomplished by the Creator and by His creations. In the holy meeting place are joined the Father and His creations, and the creations of His Son with Them together. There is one link that joins Them all together, holding Them in the oneness out of which creation happens."[334]

The link between God and His sleeping Sons seemed to be broken in the separation. However, God instantly created the Holy Spirit to ensure that the eternal link between the Father and His sleeping Sons could never be broken, except in temporary dreams that have the appearance of separation but do not exist in reality. "The link with which the Father joins Himself to those He gives the power to create can never be dissolved. Heaven itself is union with all of creation, and with its one Creator."[335] Although the Holy Spirit is your link to the Father and the Sonship, you cannot hear Him as the Voice for God without your invitation. "The Holy Spirit cannot speak to an unwelcoming host, because He will not be heard."[336] When you welcome the Holy Spirit instead of the ego, you bring the light of understanding into your mind. "Think like Him [the Holy Spirit] ever so slightly, and the little spark becomes a blazing light that fills your mind so that He becomes your only Guest."[337]

God's Will is for you to awaken to your oneness with Him in Heaven. This is God's purpose, the Holy Spirit's purpose, and your purpose. "And Heaven remains the Will of God for you. Lay no gifts other than this upon your altars, for nothing can coexist with it. Here your little offerings are brought together with the gift of God, and only what is worthy of the Father will be accepted by the Son, for whom it is intended."[338] God's Will is for you to accept his gift of awakening to oneness. The gift of oneness God offers you now is the same gift He gave to you when He created you. It is His gift of Himself to you. "To whom God gives Himself, He *is* given. Your little gifts will vanish on the altar, where He has placed His Own."[339]

Just as God has given you the one purpose of awakening, He has given you one place to awaken. This one place is seen from different perspectives because perception always sees things in their parts rather than in their wholeness that the total awareness of knowledge would impart. Although there is only one place for awakening, this place has different names, so let's review those names. This one place is called "the holy meeting place," "the altar of God," "the altar to truth," "the real world," "the vision of the Son of God," "the face of Christ," "the happy dream," "the borderland" and "the bridge" to Heaven.

Also, "the Atonement" is placed on the altar of God, so it is another name for the holy meeting place where your mind is corrected of all unloving thoughts so only the loving thoughts of the real world remain on the altar of God that is the holy meeting place.

> Spiritual vision literally cannot see error, and merely looks for Atonement [on God's altar]. All solutions the physical eye seeks dissolve. Spiritual vision looks within and recognizes immediately that the altar [of God within] has been defiled and needs to be repaired and protected. Perfectly aware of the right defense it passes over all others, looking past error to truth. Because of the strength of its vision, it brings the mind into its service.[340]

You can block your awareness of the purity of God's altar by your false beliefs, or you can accept the Atonement to correct all your mistaken beliefs. By accepting the Atonement, you can accept your oneness in God. "The altar of God where Christ abideth is there [within your mind]. You have defiled [with false beliefs] the altar, but not the world. Yet Christ has placed the Atonement on the altar for you. Bring your perceptions of the world to this altar, for it is the altar to truth."[341] The holy meeting place is the altar of truth. It is also the place in your mind where your vision is transformed into Christ's vision.

There [at the altar of God] you will see your vision changed, and there you will learn to see truly. From this place, where God and His Son dwell in peace and where you are welcome, you will look out in peace and behold the world truly. Yet to find the place, you must relinquish your investment in the world as you project it [with guilt], allowing the Holy Spirit to extend the real world to you from the altar of God.[342]

Another name for the holy meeting place where you awaken is the "borderland," described in this way:

There is a borderland of thought that stands between this world and Heaven. It is not a place, and when you reach it is apart from time. Here is the meeting place where thoughts are brought together; where conflicting values meet and all illusions are laid down beside the truth, where they are judged to be untrue. This borderland is just beyond the gate of Heaven. Here is every thought made pure and wholly simple.[343]

A term not used in the Course to describe this holy meeting place is the Eastern description of the "seventh chakra." This spiritual center is also called "the crown center" because its energy localizes and manifests within and above the crown of the head. This is the center of spiritual awakening associated with divine light and oneness. Although the holy meeting place has many names, there is only one universal experience of awakening that will happen in your acceptance of the blazing light on this altar where God and His Son both abide.

This inner altar is where you can heal your split mind by the sorting process of releasing false and unloving perceptions and accepting only true and loving perceptions. The direct and transcendent experience of wholeness and oneness is inevitable, but the preliminary sorting process of accepting true perceptions and rejecting false perceptions happens gradually as you grow spiritually. Eventually you will give up all of the illusions you have made. "*Wrong-mindedness* listens to the ego and makes illusions."[344] Ultimately you will bring *right-mindedness* to the altar of God and accept only true perceptions there. Yet filling your mind with only true perceptions is only a temporary stage that leads to giving up perception itself. "It cannot be emphasized too often that correcting perception is merely a temporary expedient. It is necessary only because misperception is a block to knowledge, while accurate perception is a steppingstone towards it. The whole value of true perception lies in the inevitable realization that *all* perception is unnecessary."[345] The purpose of God's altar is to serve as this place of transition from perception to knowledge, which is inevitable. "The word 'inevitable' is fearful to the ego, but joyous to the spirit. God is inevitable, and you cannot avoid Him any more than He can avoid you."[346]

THE SPARK AND
THE GREAT RAYS

~ o ~

Let's review some of what has already been said about the blazing light and seeing the face of Christ. On page 63, there is an analogy of looking into a mirror to explain what it is like to see the image of the face of Christ that brings awakening. In this analogy, you look into a mirror and see yourself there. As you look closer, you merge with the two-dimensional mirror and enter into it. Therefore, you become one with the image you see in the mirror. This analogy of merging with an image is similar to the experience of seeing the blazing light that happens when you see the face of Christ because as you see it, you merge with it. There is no separation between you and the blazing light. You become the blazing light. This analogy originally published in another book of mine is more than an analogy. It actually represents what really happens when you see the blazing light and become the light. The face of Christ is only a reflection of the true Christ in Heaven, yet even this reflection as a blazing light has the power to awaken you to the Source of the reflection.

We share one life because we have one Source, a Source from which perfection comes to us, remaining always in the holy minds which He created perfect. As we were, so are we now and will forever be. A sleeping mind must waken, as it sees its own perfection mirroring the Lord of life so perfectly it fades into what is reflected there. And now it is no more a mere reflection. It becomes the thing reflected, and the light which makes reflection possible. No vision now is needed. For the wakened mind is one that knows its Source, its Self, its Holiness.[347]

When you see the face of Christ as the blazing light, you will have the opportunity to realize that you are seeing your divine Self and so you can merge with what you are. In this experience you go past perceptual thinking of separation and experience "the awareness of a blazing light in which you recognize yourself as love created you."[348] God created you literally as a being of light, and by seeing the blazing light you recognize experientially that "you *are* light."[349]

This is the purpose of the face of Christ. It is the gift of God to save His Son. But look on this and you have been forgiven.

How lovely does the world become in just that single instant when you see the truth about yourself reflected there. Now you are sinless and behold your sinlessness. Now you are holy and perceive it so. And now the mind returns to its Creator; the joining of the Father and the Son, the Unity of unities that stands behind all joining but beyond them all. God is not seen but only understood. His Son is not attacked but recognized.[350]

It is possible that you may have a spiritual experience of seeing the blazing light during meditation or in your daily life, but the greatest opportunity you will have to see the blazing light will probably occur at the culmination of your earthly journey as you pass on to the hereafter. If you see the blazing light, you will be seeing the deepest level of the real world, which is the face of Christ that you must see to wake up in Heaven. "*The face of Christ* has to be seen before the memory of God can return."[351] When you ask for and receive Christ's vision to perceive the divine presence in your brother and to perform miracles, your mind is focused on the content of light and love and the visual experience of actually seeing light is only a secondary consideration. But when the previous quotation states that the face of Christ must be seen for you to remember God, it means you have to actually see the blazing light in order for your mind to become so completely filled with love that you experience your eternal oneness with your Father. Seeing the blazing light visually is not a secondary consideration in this case because this experience is a requirement for you to become fully aware of God's Love for you and your love for Him. If you have the opportunity to see the blazing light when your body ceases to function, you will awaken if you embrace this vision. Yet if you are not prepared to embrace this vision, you will be reincarnated. Thus you will have another earthly lifetime to become better prepared to accept this vision of the face of Christ and to awaken to oneness with your Father in Heaven.

In the Course, the blazing light is also called the "Great Rays." The Great Rays are the rays of light within you that are unlimited and reach to God Himself, but in the human condition, access to the awareness of this great light has been obscured. Nevertheless, everyone can access the "spark" of light within. "In many only the spark remains, for the Great Rays are obscured. Yet God has kept the spark alive so that the Rays can never be completely forgotten. If you but see the little spark you will learn of the greater light, for the Rays are there unseen."[352] Saint John of the Cross speaks of experiencing the "living flame of love" during meditation, and this is the experience of the spark of light. You can perceive the spark in yourself and in others to bring healing. "Perceiving the spark will heal, but knowing the light will create."[353]

Thought and light seem to be separate things in your everyday world, but at the spiritual level, they are one. As you identify with the spark of light within you, the darkness of the ego will be replaced by an increased awareness of your true spiritual nature in God's Light.

> You make by projection, but God creates by extension. The cornerstone of God's creation is you, for His thought system is light. Remember the [Great] Rays that are there unseen. The more you approach the center of His thought system, the clearer the light becomes. The closer you come to the foundation of the ego's thought system, the darker and more obscure becomes the way. Yet even the little spark in your mind is enough to lighten it. Bring this light fearlessly with you, and bravely hold it up to the foundation of the ego's thought system.[354]

You can see the Great Rays of blazing light only in the holy instant of the eternal now. "As the ego would limit your perception of your brothers to the body, so would the Holy Spirit release your vision and let you see the Great Rays shining from them, so unlimited that they reach to God. It is this shift to vision that is accomplished in the holy instant."[355] Seeing the blazing light that brings awakening is the same as seeing the Great Rays in the holy instant. "Once you have accepted it [the holy instant] as the only perception you want, it is translated into knowledge by the part that God Himself plays in the Atonement, for it is the only step in it He understands."[356]

In addition to love, there is another very significant common element between perfect perception and knowledge. This common element is light. Perfect perception happens in the holy instant. Then Christ's vision reveals the Great Rays of light in your brothers. In the same way that love in total perception makes the transfer to love in knowledge possible, the perception of the total light of the Great Rays in the holy instant makes the transfer to the light in knowledge possible. "At the altar of God, the holy perception of God's Son becomes so enlightened that light streams into it, and the spirit of God's Son shines in the Mind of the Father and becomes one with it."[357] The Great Rays emanate from you even now, but you are most likely totally unaware of your light. "The Great Light [Rays] always surrounds you and shines out from you."[358] But the spark remains within you and you can put your faith in it. Perceiving the spark opens the mind to the greater light of the Great Rays.

> Yet in the returning the little light [of the spark] must be acknowledged first, for the separation was a descent from magnitude to littleness. But the spark is still as pure as the Great Light, because it is the remaining call of creation. Put all your faith in it, and God Himself will answer you.[359]

First, you will become aware of "the little spark," but it is possible that ultimately "the little spark becomes a blazing light that fills your mind so that He [the Holy Spirit] becomes your only Guest."[360] There are different ways of becoming aware of the little spark so you can open your mind to experiencing the Great Rays of blazing light. One way to experience the spark is meditation and the other way is Christ's vision.

Since the previous quotation states that "the little spark becomes a blazing light that fills your mind," it is obvious that the spark is a point of light that extends outward to manifest the Great Rays. There is an unmistakable parallel between the Great Rays that emanate from the spark and the blazing light of the second dimension likewise emanating from a point of light that is the first dimension. In my opinion, the Great Rays and the blazing light are different terms to describe the same light radiating in the second dimension. Therefore, the terms blazing light and the Great Rays can be used interchangeably to mean the same thing. These terms are symbols of the Light of Heaven, but they are not actually the Light of Heaven. They are only reflections of the light of your true nature in Heaven. Yet these are such perfect reflections that seeing them reminds you that "you *are* light."

Both the blazing light and Great Rays in the second dimension are projections from the first dimension. The source of the Great Rays is the spark in the first dimension, and the source of the blazing light is the point of light in the first dimension. Thus the spark and the center-point of the blazing light are both representatives of your true nature of light in the first dimension. The first dimension is the dimensionless dimension of Heaven. This means the first dimension represents God. The spark is the point of light from God in you that can never be extinguished because it represents your eternal reality, and the light projected from the first dimension to make the blazing light of the second dimension is also the same light from God that is always within you.

Both the Great Rays and the blazing light are seen in the second dimension with your perception and represent your magnitude in God, and they lead to awakening your true nature. Both the Great Rays and the blazing light are the same face of Christ that must be seen before remembering God and waking up in the first dimension. Seeing the face of Christ, as the Great Rays and expanding circle of blazing light, in the second dimension leads to recognizing in the first dimension that you are part of Christ and the whole Christ at the same time. The spark and the point of light come from the first dimension of knowledge where there is no difference between the part-ness and wholeness of Christ. The spark in you emanates outwardly in the second dimension to manifest the awareness of the Great Rays that are always with you but normally unrecognized. The Great Rays coming to your conscious awareness provide a perceptual reminder of your true nature of being part of

Christ and the whole of Christ. This is the same as saying that the circle of blazing light expanding infinitely in the second dimension and the center point of light in the first dimension help you to remember your true nature of being part of Christ and the whole of Christ.

In summary, the Great Rays, the blazing light, and the second dimension, are all related to each other. The spark in the center of the Great Rays and the point of light in the center of the blazing light are the same and both are symbols of the first dimension. The significance of these corresponding relationships is that they describe different aspects of the one process of seeing the face of Christ and awakening to your true nature as the Christ, the Self, the holy Son of God. The partial awareness of perception and the total knowledge of Heaven are mutually exclusive. Therefore, you can either see visions with perception or you can use knowledge to know in the experience of oneness. The Great Rays, the blazing light, and the second dimension can all be seen with perception. This perception of light is not knowledge itself but can lead to knowledge. Similarly, the spark in the center of the Great Rays and the point of light in the center of the blazing light can be perceived. This perception of light brings healing of the perceptual mind. The partial awareness of perceiving light that heals the mind leads directly to the total knowledge of Heaven in which you accept your true nature as light.

The difference between using perception to see the face of Christ and experiencing knowledge to know your true nature can be understood by reviewing the mirror analogy at the beginning of this section. In this analogy, first you saw the image of yourself in the mirror while you were outside of the mirror. Then you actually entered into the mirror itself. So this is a two-part process of externally seeing the mirror and then entering the mirror and becoming one with the reality of yourself. This analogy is just like what really happens when you see the face of Christ. The simplest way to explain this vision of awakening is a two-stage process:

Stage 1: First you see the vision of the Son of God as a blazing circle of light expanding infinitely. But here is a key point that has not been clarified yet: You are seeing only the second dimension in this external seeing and you are not seeing the point of light of the first dimension. Why? Because perception and vision always involve a perceiver who is separate from his object of perception. The object of perception is your vision of the circle of blazing light and your vision of the second dimension. The perceiver is you who are projecting this vision. You are projecting from your spark in the first dimension because the second dimension is always projected from the first dimension. Nevertheless, you are not consciously aware that you are projecting from the first dimension, just as you are not consciously aware that you are still in Heaven and only dreaming of exile from Heaven.

Thus while the vision is occurring as an expression of separation and perception, you can only see the second dimension as a reflection of the first dimension and as a reflection of the knowledge of Heaven. Although seeing the face of Christ will awaken you to the knowledge of Heaven, this seeing starts as an eternal vision. Thus, if it remains only an external vision, this vision cannot awaken knowledge of your true nature.

> True vision is the natural perception of spiritual sight, but it is still a correction rather than a fact. Spiritual sight is symbolic, and therefore not a device for knowing. It is, however, a means of right perception, which brings it into the proper domain of the miracle. A "vision of God" would be a miracle rather than a revelation. The fact that perception is involved at all removes the experience from the realm of knowledge. That is why visions, however holy, do not last.[361]

Since you use perception to see the vision of the face of Christ externally, you must be projecting what you are seeing in your vision. "Projection makes perception."[362] But I said seeing the face of Christ or the vision of the Son of God as a blazing circle of light expanding infinitely is a two-stage process, so here is the second stage:

Stage 2: As you see the vision of blazing light in Stage 1, you will feel you are coming closer and closer to this second-dimension vision. Then in Stage 2, you will feel you are no longer separate from the image of light. *You will feel you are becoming the light you are seeing.* You are in what I call the "gateway" of the first dimension in which you can take one step forward into Heaven or reject awakening. In this crisis of decision, you stand between the world of knowledge and the world of perception. You have no body awareness and experience revelation. "Knowledge is the result of revelation...."[363] You could embrace the total awareness of knowledge imparted in revelation, but you have not yet given up your attachment to consciousness that is the partial awareness of perception. "Revelation unites you directly with God. Miracles unite you directly with your brother. Neither emanates from consciousness [within perception], but both are experienced there."[364] At this gateway, you must give your complete willingness to accept that God's Will is your true will. If you fully accept the union of your will and God's Will, God Himself will take the final step of ushering you into the first dimension that is Heaven where you reclaim your rightful place in the Sonship.

Here is a summary of the stages of awakening: Stage 1 of awakening is using perception to see light in the second dimension. You, as the perceiver, use consciousness to see yourself as separate from the image of light you are seeing. "Consciousness, the level of perception, was the first split introduced into the mind after the separation, making the mind a perceiver rather than a creator."[365] In Stage 2, the sense of separation between you and the image of light you are seeing diminishes. You lose body awareness, and you feel you are joining with the content of the light and becoming the light. You are on the razor's edge in which you can embrace the first dimension or reject awakening. In your crisis of decision, you must choose between fully accepting God's Will as your own will or falling back on the illusion that you have a private will apart from God's Will. After all, God's Will is that you entirely give up your illusion of separation fostered by the ego and that you to awaken to the fact that you never left your true Home in Heaven. But because God has given you free will, the decision to embrace awakening is entirely your choice. "For God Himself has said, 'Your will be done.' And it is done to you accordingly."[366] Inevitably you will make the only choice that will make you eternally happy, and then God will take the final step. "The final step is God's, because it is but God Who could create a perfect Son and share His Fatherhood with him."[367]

Usually Stage 1 of awakening is a slow process of coming closer and closer to the vision of light you are seeing. However, I would like to now clarify that Stage 1 can happen either slowly or suddenly. When Stage 1 happens suddenly, it can be called a "leap." In this case, the second dimension is not seen from a distance. Rather, the second dimension is seen as a flash of light. The seeker jumps through this second dimension of light, similar to jumping through a hoop. In this sudden experience of Stage 1, the second dimension is experienced only as a holy instant so it is not seen as a flat image of light in the second dimension. Here is a quote about the sudden "leap" that can be experienced in Stage 1:

> When the light has come and you have said, "God's Will is mine," you will see such beauty that you will know it is not of you. Out of your joy you will create beauty in His Name, for your joy could no more be contained than His. The bleak little world will vanish into nothingness, and your heart will be so filled with joy that it will leap into Heaven, and into the Presence of God. I cannot tell you what this will be like, for your heart is not ready. Yet I can tell you, and remind you often, that what God wills for Himself He wills for you, and what He wills for you is yours.[368]

The prior quote describes the enlightenment experience as a leap into the Presence of God. Since there is the recognition that "God's Will is mine," God is given permission to take the final step of completing your awakening to Heaven. In Stage 2, you may have a direct experience of God without choosing to fully awaken. The direct experience of God, called "revelation," emanates from the knowledge of Heaven in the first dimension, but is actually experienced in consciousness, which is the level of perception. "Neither [miracles nor revelation] emanates from consciousness [within perception], but both are experienced there."[369]

Revelation induces the response of awe. "Awe should be reserved for revelation, to which it is perfectly and correctly applicable. It is not appropriate for miracles because a state of awe is worshipful, implying that one of a lesser order stands before his Creator. You are a perfect creation, and should experience awe only in the Presence of the Creator of perfection."[370] Awe is the appropriate response of the creature to the Creator. But Jesus says that awe is not the appropriate response to him or any of your brothers, who are your equals.

Yet during revelation, awe for your Creator can be misinterpreted as fear. The Course specifically states that being in the presence of God can be fearful if the proper preparations are not made. Without the necessary preparation, "...awe will be confused with fear, and the experience will be more traumatic than beatific."[371] I had a revelation experience, which I described in my autobiography, *Memory Walk in the Light.* It happened when I was 24 and had not made the preparations of following spiritual practices that would clear my mind of false and unloving perceptions. This was a revelation experience of the blazing light of the face of Christ. At first, this experience was unspeakably wonderful, and I initially felt appropriate awe for my Creator. I had lost all body awareness during this experience, and so I asked myself, "Where is my body?" Then the fear of losing my body entered my mind for the first time. When that single thought of fear occurred, the awe-inspiring experience suddenly changed into a traumatic one. Now the study of the Course is helping me to prepare my mind so hopefully I will not mistake awe for fear in the future when God gives me another opportunity to awaken to His presence, such as when the body ceases to function in the experience called "death," which is the best opportunity for awakening.

The Course also states, "Revelation may occasionally reveal the end to you, but to reach it the means are needed."[5] In other words, even if the end of the road is suddenly shown to you in revelation, you will still have to follow along that road before you are able to return to the divine Presence. You will still have to let the Holy Spirit teach you the lessons of forgiveness and of how to maintain loving relationships. You will still have to set aside quiet time to meditate on the divine within. You will still have to put the spiritual principles you learn into practice in your daily life so you will recognize that God's Will is your true will. Your practices will help you reach the real world, a short step from Heaven. "Your foot has reached the lawns that welcome you to Heaven's gate; the quiet place of peace, where you await with certainty the final step of God. How far are we progressing now from earth! How close are we approaching to our goal! How short the journey still to be pursued!"[372] Then you will be prepared so when God takes the final step of calling you to awaken, you will accept Him and accept His unspeakable Love whole-heartedly without fear.

PART IV

~ ○ ~

THE FACILITATORS
OF AWAKENING

Part IV focuses on the help you have in your journey of awakening. Workbook Lesson 138 states, "Heaven is the decision I must make."

Everyone here has entered darkness, yet no one has entered it alone. Nor need he stay more than an instant. For he has come with Heaven's Help within him, ready to lead him out of darkness into light at any time. The time he chooses can be any time, for help is there, awaiting but his choice. And when he chooses to avail himself of what is given him, then will he see each situation that he thought before was means to justify his anger turned to an event which justifies his love. He will hear plainly that the calls to war he heard before are really calls to peace. He will perceive that where he gave attack is but another altar where he can, with equal ease and far more happiness, bestow forgiveness. And he will reinterpret all temptation as just another chance to bring him joy.[373]

To make the decision for awakening in Heaven requires identifying the alternatives. "Heaven is chosen consciously. The choice cannot be made until alternatives are accurately seen and understood."[374] Your choice requires clarity about the true value of each alternative. "Yet who can fail to make a choice between alternatives when only one is seen as valuable; the other as a wholly worthless thing, but imagined source of guilt and pain? Who hesitates to make a choice like this?"[375] Part IV emphasizes the roles the Holy Spirit and Jesus play in learning what is valuable and what is valueless. But learning to discriminate between the valuable and valueless is not enough. With the help of the Holy Spirit and Jesus, you must also learn to give up your attachment to what is valueless so you can fully invest in what is valuable. Only then will your decision for awakening in Heaven be an easy one to make.

Some spiritual teachings say you must make a sacrifice of your happiness now so that you can experience eternal happiness at a later date in Heaven. But the Course teaches that giving up the goals of the world is not a sacrifice because you are merely releasing what will make you unhappy. "Give up the world! But not to sacrifice. You never wanted it. What happiness have you sought here that did bring you pain? What moment of content has not been bought at fearful price in coins of suffering? Joy has no cost. It is your sacred right, and what you pay for is not happiness."[376]

The Holy Spirit will not ask you to sacrifice happiness now so you can experience happiness later. He offers you the happy dreams now of the real world to replace your nightmares and prepare you for the happiness of Heaven. "Be not content with future happiness."[377] Perhaps you think of salvation as a future event, but the Course maintains, "Salvation is immediate."[378] Once you accept the purpose of awakening, the happy effects of that decision come to you without delay. Your decision for salvation involves using forgiveness as your means of awakening. *"Forgiveness is the key to happiness."*[379] Your decision also includes accepting God's Will. "I share God's Will of happiness."[380]

The Holy Spirit gives you your special function as a part of God's plan of salvation. "Then realize your part is to be happy. Only this is asked of you or anyone who wants to take his place among God's messengers. Think what this means. You have indeed been wrong in your belief that sacrifice is asked."[381] Your purpose is to remove the illusory gap between your brother and you so you can both experience happiness, not just in the future, but also *now*. "The Holy Spirit's purpose now is yours. Should not His happiness be yours as well?"[382] If you lose your peace of mind by throwing it away, I suggest that you mentally say this: "Father, I accept love and happiness now."

Part IV:—The Facilitators of Awakening 105
    The Holy Spirit and Awakening 107
    Jesus and the Holy Relationship 115
    Jesus is the Atonement 117
    The Resurrection and Einstein 121
    Jesus, True Light, and Christ's Vision 123
    The Bridge and the Law of Love 131
    Healing Your Two Major Fears 137
    One Mind and One Will with Jesus 145
    Your Role of Being a Teacher 153
    Recognizing That Truth is True 159
    Happy Learning That Truth is True 169
    Light Dimensions Leading to Heaven 175
    Final Thoughts 185

THE HOLY SPIRIT
AND AWAKENING

≈ o ≈

The most profound spiritual experience is called "samadhi" in yoga philosophy and "enlightenment" in Buddhist philosophy." Saint John of the Cross uses the term "the illumination of glory" to describe the greatest spiritual ecstasy. The Course uses the word "revelation" to refer to the direct experience of God. "Revelation unites you directly with God."[383] No words can adequately convey the depth of this experience. "Revelation is intensely personal and cannot be meaningfully translated. That is why any attempt to describe it in words is impossible."[384] This experience expresses the fullness of God's Love. "Revelation is literally unspeakable because it is an experience of unspeakable love."[385]

The previous described Stage 1 of awaking consists of seeing the light of the second dimension, and this stage can happen slowly or suddenly. The sudden experience of Stage 1 has been called a leap through the second dimension, resulting in immediately entering Stage 2 in which you feel you are merging with the light. This leap is an experience of revelation. Eastern paths of Zen Buddhism and Tantric Yoga teach that through self-effort you can use spiritual practices to directly experience transcendental light and awakening. Thus this experience is brought about similar to the way Olympic athletes seek and attain a gold medal. What's wrong with the belief that only those who are great "spiritual athletes" will be awakened? I had an insight when I participated in a six-day Zen Buddhist retreat that answered the question of what was wrong with the approach of total self-effort to bring about awakening. After sitting in meditation for a long time, this insight came to me right after I had a holy instant in which I disregarded my own pain and had compassion for all my brothers and sisters at the retreat who were also in pain. Below are two paragraphs reprinted from my autobiography:

This holy instant itself was a joining with my brothers for an instant of spontaneous union. Nevertheless, as an aftereffect of this experience, something felt very wrong, and it was not my pain or the pain of others. What felt wrong was the way we, this specific group of fifty or sixty individuals, were each trying to get out of prison, which felt like hell. We were trying to be the Buddha, sitting there to achieve a deep meditative state like the Buddha and as individuals trying to escape this prison by becoming enlightened. It felt like we were spiritual Olympic athletes competing to win the gold medal. It felt wrong that only the strongest spiritual athletes should be able to transcend this world.

I thought: *Why shouldn't we all be enlightened, not by effort, but by free gift?* I reached out to God in my mind and prayed that the doors would be opened for everyone to transcend this world, not just the strongest spiritual athletes. This moment stands out in my mind because it was such a pure moment of compassion, in stark contrast to how selfish I had been all my life.

Unfortunately, after the retreat, I forgot all about that temporary insight of what was wrong and instead invested in the path of self-effort. Later I learned to appreciate a moderate approach that included divine grace. Any approach that leaves out God's Love and His Grace cannot succeed. I have a friend who told me half-jokingly that he was attracted to the Course because of his philosophy of "expending the least effort to get the maximum results." The Course requires your "little willingness" that is multiplied by the help of the Holy Spirit. The Course teaches that God loves His sleeping Son and He will ensure that every sleeping child of God will awaken without being a great spiritual athlete.

Although the direct awakening and union with God can happen spontaneously at any time without great self-effort, the Course firmly states that the experience of revelation is "so rare that it cannot be considered a realistic goal."[386] Even if you do have this experience of revelation, it will be a temporary experience so you end up right back in the world of form. You have not fully awakened because you still have to prepare yourself for your final revelation as the end of your worldly experience. If you do not have to be a great spiritual athlete to fully awaken, what must you do to prepare for returning to your awareness of Heaven? You prepare by building a "bridge" in the second dimension that will enable you to transition to the first dimension of Heaven. This is the typical preparation and slow approach of Stage 1 that provides a solid foundation for preparing to awaken.

There is no gap between your true Self and your ego since only the Self is real, and the ego does not exist. Yet due to your ego identification, you imagine there is a gap between your true Self and what your ego tells you that you are. It is your destiny to build a bridge that would overcome your imagined gap. It is a bridge made of happy dreams that enable you to leave behind your dark illusions of nightmares. Then your bridge of happy dreams will allow you to transition to the acceptance of your true Self. "To your most holy Self all praise is due for what you are, and for what He is Who created you as you are. Sooner or later must everyone bridge the gap he imagines exists between his selves. Each one builds this bridge, which carries him across the gap as soon as he is willing to expend some little effort on behalf of bridging it."[387]

What motivates you to build this bridge and gives you the power to build it? You give your little willingness and make your little efforts to build the bridge. But the Holy Spirit, the Christ, and God magnify your efforts, enabling the bridge to be built so you can awaken to your true Self awaiting you on the other side of the bridge. "His little efforts are powerfully supplemented by the strength of Heaven, and by the united will of all who make Heaven what it is, being joined within it. And so the one who would cross over is literally transported there."[388]

You seem to yourself to be building a weak bridge, but it is so much reinforced by Heaven that it will surely transport you to the other side. "Your bridge is built stronger than you think, and your foot is planted firmly on it."[389] The power of Heaven ensures that your awakening is inevitable. "Have no fear that the attraction of those who stand on the other side and wait for you will not draw you safely across. For you will come where you would be, and where your Self awaits you."[390]

> Some of the later steps in this course, however, involve a more direct approach to God Himself. It would be unwise to start on these steps without careful preparation, or awe will be confused with fear, and the experience will be more traumatic than beatific. Healing is of God in the end. The means are being carefully explained to you. Revelation may occasionally reveal the end to you, but to reach it the means are needed.[391]

The last sentence above states "the means are needed." This refers to means used by the Holy Spirit to bring about correction of the split mind that entertains both loving and unloving perceptions, both true and false perceptions, without distinguishing between them. Knowledge cannot heal perception. It transcends perception and is not at the level in which correction of perception is needed within the split mind. In the Course Jesus says, "As a man I did not attempt to counteract error with knowledge, but to correct error from the bottom up."[392] In other words, the errors of the ego must be corrected at the level of perception, where they occur. "The Holy Spirit has the task of undoing what the ego has made. He undoes it at the same level on which the ego operates, or the mind would be unable to understand the change."[393] Instead of seeking the lofty experience of revelation and the total knowledge that comes with it, the Course recommends setting the more attainable goal of performing miracles that change perception and that produce results in the world. The reason is that miracles "are more useful [than revelation] because of their interpersonal nature."[394]

Unlike the type of revelation that can temporarily occur in your daily life, this final step of awakening is revelation as a *permanent condition* in which there are no more illusions of separation from God. Although everyone will eventually experience this final revelation and awaken in Heaven, the Course focuses on realistic spiritual goals that can be accomplished right now in your current ego-based condition as your means of healing your split mind.

Before being ready to awaken directly to God in Heaven, you must first prepare by learning how to remove the blocks to your awareness of love, such as fear, anger, guilt, and the other tools of the ego. To help you prepare for the direct experience of Heaven, the Holy Spirit offers you *indirect* experiences of Heaven that help you remove your inner blocks. Just as the ego has tools to block your awareness, the Holy Spirit has tools that open your awareness.

A split mind sees ideas as distinctly separate and perceives ideas only in the duality of light and darkness, truth and falsehood, and love and hate rather than oneness. The split mind is confused because it cannot see the true nature of oneness and reality. "The mind is therefore confused, because only One-mindedness can be without confusion. A separated or divided mind *must* be confused."[395] Since your split mind defines terms only by their differences, the Holy Spirit communicates to you by using different terms to describe what He perceives as oneness in order to lead you to the acceptance of sameness behind what appears to be differences. The Holy Spirit is leading you to replace your split mind with the natural wholeness of the mind

> Joining with Him in seeing is the way in which you learn to share with Him the interpretation of perception that leads to knowledge. You cannot see alone. Sharing perception with Him Whom God has given you teaches you how to recognize what you see. It is the recognition that nothing you see means anything alone. Seeing with Him will show you that all meaning, including yours, comes not from double vision, but from the gentle fusing of *everything* into *one* meaning, *one* emotion and *one* purpose. God has one purpose which He shares with you.[396]

The Holy Spirit has *one* meaning—the meaning of light. The Holy Spirit has *one* emotion—the emotion of love. The Holy Spirit has *one* purpose—the purpose of oneness awakening you. The Holy Spirit wants you to recognize that you are part of Christ and the whole Christ. But your split mind wants to see only differences that separate and cannot see wholeness that unites. Thus the Holy Spirit and the Course present the various means of awakening as separate activities. But the Holy Spirit wants you to perceive the wholeness in each apparently separate activity. Previously I stated that the seven elevators in the analogy of the hospital were the Holy Spirit's tools used as your means of healing your mind. Then later, I mentioned that there is only one elevator and the Atonement is that one elevator that contains all the others. Let's go further in our understanding by saying that excluding the Atonement, the other six elevators are part of the six and the whole of the six, just as you are part of Christ and the whole of Christ.

Excluding the Atonement, forgiveness is one elevator or tool of the Holy Spirit that contains the other five. Forgiveness overlooks bodies and judgments, and it sees others with Christ's eyes so it includes Christ's vision. Forgiveness overlooks differences in your brother and allows you to join with him in the common purpose of seeing holiness in each other so it contains the holy relationship. Forgiveness overlooks past guilt and future punishment and looks for the timelessness of now so it contains the holy instant. Forgiveness overlooks grievances and looks for expressions of love so it contains miracles. Forgiveness is a way of focusing your mind on divine thought and letting go of stray thoughts so it is an outer form of the inner process of meditation.

Similarly, Christ's vision is a part and the whole of the other six tools. Christ's vision overlooks all guilt and looks for the divine in others so it contains forgiveness. Christ's vision enables you to see your brother with the eyes of holiness that allows you to accept the common purpose of seeing holiness in each other, so it contains the holy relationship. Christ's vision can only see your brother without his past or future and only see him as he is now so it contains the holy instant. Christ's vision allows you to overlook the outer appearance of your brother and see his love nature so it contains the loving expression of miracles. Christ's vision is a single-minded focus on thoughts of the divine and overlooks stray thoughts so it contains an outer form of meditation.

The holy relationship is a part and the whole of the other six tools. The holy relationship is your best means of joining in the common purpose of seeing holiness in your brother so it contains forgiveness. The holy relationship is your best means of joining in the common purpose of using Christ's eyes to see the divine in each other and overlooking guilt so it contains Christ's vision. The holy relationship is your best means of joining in the common purpose of seeing your brother without his past and future and instead accepting his divine nature now so it contains the holy instant. The holy relationship is your means of joining in the common purpose of expressing love and releasing grievances so it contains miracles. The holy relationship requires only one partner to go within for prayer and receive perfect love, and this love goes to the other partner so it contains the inward focusing on love of meditation.

By this time, you are getting the idea, so there is no need to spell it all out in as much detail as shown above. The holy instant contains all the others because they all rely on letting go of the past and future and rely on accepting the eternal now. Likewise, miracles contain all the others because they all express love that is the function of miracles. Meditation contains all the others because they all rely on the ability to focus the mind inwardly or outwardly on the divine and require letting go of stray thoughts as all meditation practices do. In summary, just as every part of Christ contains the whole of Christ, every part of the six tools of the Holy Spirit contains the whole of the six tools. They all use the same process of looking for the real and overlooking all else that was never real.

Let's consider the practice of accepting the Atonement in relation to the other six practices. Forgiveness overlooks guilt and looks for healing and correction so it contains the practice of accepting the Atonement. Christ's vision overlooks all appearances of sickness and sees your brother with true perception by inviting light into the mind so it contains the practice of accepting the Atonement that only happens by releasing the inner light. The holy relationship requires that only one partner accept the Atonement, and then both partners are healed, so it contains the correction and healing of the Atonement. The acceptance of the Atonement can only be done in the holy instant of the eternal now. Miracles express love and the practice of the Atonement is the acceptance of perfect love. The practice of accepting the Atonement requires the practice of meditation that is the focusing of the mind to accept truth and let go of stray thoughts.

In order to fully accept the Atonement, you must use all of the other six tools. But why does the Atonement encompass the other six tools in a unique way? The six tools are practices. Likewise, the Atonement is a practice of accepting the divine and releasing everything else, but it is more than just a practice. The uniqueness of the Atonement is that it is the plan of God for your salvation and has His power. In addition to the practice of accepting the Atonement, the other six practices are the means of carrying out God's plan of the Atonement. "This is not a course in philosophical speculation, nor is it concerned with precise terminology. It is concerned only with Atonement, or the correction of perception. The means of the Atonement is forgiveness."[397]

In addition to forgiveness, Christ's vision is a very important means of fulfilling God's plan of the Atonement. "The single vision which the Holy Spirit offers you will bring this oneness to your mind with clarity and brightness so intense you could not wish, for all the world, not to accept what God would have you have."[398] In this quotation, the words "single vision," refer to Christ's vision that is given to you by the Holy Spirit, bringing true light into your mind. This single vision shows you the face of Christ that "will bring oneness to your mind with clarity and brightness" because you will be seeing the blazing light. This blazing light is in the form of a circle of light expanding infinitely. It is the form of the second dimension of reflected light coming from the indivisible light of the first dimension. But what will you really be seeing that will awaken you in seeing the blazing light, the second dimension, and the face of Christ? You will actually be seeing the Mind of the Holy Spirit that has taken the form of the blazing light, the face of Christ, and the second dimension, which is projected from the first dimension.

The following quotation has already been shared: "The Holy Spirit is the Mind of the Atonement. He represents a state of mind close enough to One-mindedness that transfer to it is at last possible."[399] What are the implications of the Holy Spirit being the Mind of the Atonement? Since the Holy Spirit has taken the form of the circle of blazing light, the face of Christ, and the second dimension, the content of Atonement must have also taken this form as the "circle of Atonement." In all the visions of the second dimension, you are seeing the same form of the Holy Spirit and that single form represents the content of the Atonement that brings healing and correction to every split mind.

What if there was a doctor who had one pill that he could give to every sick person who came to him and that person would be cured? Wouldn't that simplify his job as a doctor? The Holy Spirit is your Doctor, and He has one "pill" for you that heals you. This one pill is the Atonement, God's plan of salvation, that heals every mistake and all the effects of every mistake. The Atonement heals all your problems, you have only one problem. What is your only problem?

Perhaps you think you have many problems that you must solve in order to accept your Christ nature now. "A long series of different problems seems to confront you, and as one is settled the next one and the next arise. There seems to be no end to them. There is no time in which you feel completely free of problems and at peace."[400] However, all your problems can be solved now because the truth is that you have only one problem. "Everyone in this world seems to have his own special problems. Yet they are all the same, and must be recognized as one if the one solution that solves them all is to be accepted."[401] What is the one problem that has one solution? "The problem of separation, which is really the only problem, has already been solved. Yet the solution is not recognized because the problem is not recognized."[402] The problem of separation has already been solved for you and so all you have to do is accept this solution. But if you do not know what the problem is, you cannot accept the solution that is given to you and awaiting your acceptance. "A problem cannot be solved if you do not know what it is. Even if it is really solved already you will still have the problem, because you will not recognize that it has been solved. This is the situation of the world."[403]

To awaken, you must recognize that your only problem is the ego's false perception of separation. "It is possible to do this [accept Christ now] all at once because there is but one shift in perception that is necessary, for you made but one mistake [the detour from union to separation]. It seems like many, but it is all the same. For though the ego takes many forms, it is always the same idea [of separation]."[404] Your only problem of separation has already been solved. "Your only problem has been solved!"[405] Through accepting the Atonement, you recognize the solution that brings union and thus corrects all your mistakes that were based on the one problem of separation. But will you accept that separation is your only problem and will you receive the gift of union to acknowledge that your only problem has already been solved? The solution is merely awaiting your acceptance of this gift. Will you accept the gift of the Atonement that brings union and releases you from false and unloving thoughts of separation?

> The Atonement was established as the means of restoring guiltlessness to minds that have denied it, and thus denied Heaven to themselves. Atonement teaches you the true condition of the Son of God. It does not teach you what you are, or what your Father is. The Holy Spirit, Who remembers this for you, merely teaches you how to remove the blocks that stand between you and what you know. His memory is yours. If you remember what you have made, you are remembering nothing. Remembrance of reality is in Him, and therefore in you.[406]

I have repeatedly emphasized that if you accept perfect love into your mind, you are accepting the Atonement because "Perfect love is the Atonement."[407] Now I would like to offer you another option. Since the "Holy Spirit is the Mind of the Atonement,"[408] you can accept the full awareness of the Holy Spirit into your mind, and you will be accepting the Atonement. After all, the "Voice of the Holy Spirit is the Call to Atonement" that heals your split mind.

> The Holy Spirit is the Christ Mind which is aware of the knowledge that lies beyond perception. He came into being with the separation as a protection, inspiring the Atonement principle at the same time. Before that there was no need for healing, for no one was comfortless. The Voice of the Holy Spirit is the Call to Atonement, or the restoration of the integrity of the mind. When the Atonement is complete and the whole Sonship is healed there will be no Call to return. But what God creates is eternal. The Holy Spirit will remain with the Sons of God, to bless their creations and keep them in the light of joy.[409]

JESUS AND THE
HOLY RELATIONSHIP

~ o ~

You can decide to join with any brother in a holy relationship with the common purpose of seeing holiness in your partner. There is one specific brother who is asking you to form a holy relationship with him. He is your "elder brother," who is Jesus. He asks you to join him in the common purpose of seeing holiness and facilitating the awakening of the entire Sonship. He calls you to fulfill your special function in the Atonement, which is a form of forgiveness assigned to you.

Because Jesus is calling you to be his holy relationship partner and join in the common purpose of facilitating awakening, you will have to consider if you are willing to change your current relationship with him. You are aware of what you consider to be your relationship with Jesus, but are you aware of his relationship with you? For example, if you already have a long-term relationship with one other person, the Holy Spirit entered that relationship the instant it was formed, and then Jesus entered with him. When you truly join with one brother, you join with the whole Sonship, including Jesus.

> Forgive me your illusions, and release me from punishment for what I have not done. So will you learn the freedom that I taught by teaching freedom to your brother, and so releasing me. I am within your holy relationship, yet you would imprison me behind the obstacles you raise to freedom, and bar my way to you. Yet it is not possible to keep away One Who is there already. And in Him it *is* possible that our communion, where we are joined already, will be the focus of the new perception that will bring light to all the world, contained in you.[410]

As far as Jesus is concerned, he is always already joined with you, even if you do not recognize his presence. However, if you place your faith in him, he will be able to help you even more than he is already helping you. The Holy Spirit sets the goal of seeing holiness in your holy relationship partner because He has faith in you, and Jesus also has faith in you to fulfill your common purpose of holiness. But you must learn to increase your faith in your holy relationship partner, and also increase your faith in Jesus.

Only what *you* have not given can be lacking in any situation. But remember this; the goal of holiness was set for your relationship, and not by you. You did not set it because holiness cannot be seen except through faith, and your relationship was not holy because your faith in your brother was so limited and little. Your faith must grow to meet the goal that has been set. The goal's reality will call this forth, for you will see that peace and faith will not come separately. What situation can you be in without faith, and remain faithful to your brother?[411]

Some seekers turn to metaphysics because they have given up on Jesus due to limited religious ideas about him imposed upon them during their childhood. But Jesus humbly asks you to forgive him for the idols men have mistakenly made of him. He asks you to forgive him because how you perceive him is how you perceive yourself. If you forgive Jesus your illusions and judgments about him, you will forgive your illusions and judgments about yourself. If you perceive guilt in yourself, Jesus must be guilty also, since you are joined in one Sonship that must be seen as either guilty or guiltless. You can mistakenly perceive yourself as separate from Jesus, but he never sees himself as separate from you.

Let me be to you the symbol of the end of guilt, and look upon your brother as you would look on me. Forgive me all the sins you think the Son of God committed. And in the light of your forgiveness he will remember who he is, and forget what never was. I ask for your forgiveness, for if you are guilty, so must I be. But if I surmounted guilt and overcame the world, you were with me. Would you see in me the symbol of guilt or of the end of guilt, remembering that what I signify to you you see within yourself?[412]

In contrast to those who have undervalued Jesus and his role, others have overvalued him and his role. These seekers have elevated Jesus to an unreachable lofty status and they devalue themselves. In the Course, Jesus reminds you of his equality with you.

God gave your will its power, which I can only acknowledge in honor of His. If you want to be like me I will help you, knowing that we are alike. If you want to be different, I will wait until you change your mind. I can teach you, but only you can choose to listen to my teaching. How else can it be, if God's Kingdom is freedom? Freedom cannot be learned by tyranny of any kind, and the perfect equality of all God's Sons cannot be recognized through the dominion of one mind over another. God's Sons are equal in will, all being the Will of their Father. This is the only lesson I came to teach.[413]

JESUS IS THE ATONEMENT

~ • ~

Many seekers read the Course and understand Jesus as its author but fail to understand the role that Jesus has played and continues to play in God's plan for their awakening. To understand the role of Jesus in God's plan of the Atonement, it is helpful to first review the Holy Spirit's role in the Atonement. When the Holy Spirit was created by God as the instant Answer to the separation, the Atonement was already the principle of love. However, the Atonement itself as it is now had not yet been established. "The Atonement *principle* was in effect long before the Atonement began. The principle was love...."[414]

Although the Atonement is the principle of love or God's law of love that existed in Heaven, after the separation the sleeping Son of God rejected this law of love. God's law of love was replaced by what became known as the law of karma. Karma was even considered to be a universal divine law, but karma is not a universal divine law. There is the law of cause and effect that happens simultaneously in the present, which is a divine law. But karma depends upon past events producing future rewards or punishments. Karma is a human construct, which is supported only by human belief in it. Karma is a self-imposed system of self-judgment, which consists of rewarding one's self for past "good" deeds and punishing one's self for past "bad" deeds. This belief system is based on the belief in guilt that deserves punishment. The principle of Atonement could overcome the false belief in karma based on guilt, but only if this principle of love could be "built into the space-time belief to set a limit on the need for the belief itself, and ultimately to make learning complete."[415] Because after the separation the Atonement had not yet been established within the space-time belief, the Holy Spirit needed one part of the Sonship to help Him manifest the Atonement at the level of space-time. Since the Atonement is the principle of love, an act of love was needed to establish the Atonement within the space-time belief.

> The principle was love and the Atonement was an *act* of love. Acts were not necessary before the separation, because belief in space and time did not exist. It was only after the separation that the Atonement and the conditions necessary for its fulfillment were planned.[416]

Jesus was the one part of the Sonship who volunteered to perform the act of love that would establish the Atonement. Because of the oneness of the Sonship, if any part of the Sonship expresses love or any other ability, that expression is shared by every other part of the Sonship. After Jesus established the Atonement, his act of pure love became available for acceptance by every other part of the Sonship. Therefore, if you accept the Atonement, you invite the law of love and the truth that only perfect love exists. Thus you will replace the false belief in karma with the law of love. This acceptance of the Atonement automatically corrects all errors by accepting that lack of love does not exist, so there is no reason to believe in the illusions of karma, guilt, and self-punishment.

Many followers of Jesus feel they have been saved by the crucifixion. But the resurrection was actually the "act of love" that Jesus manifested to establish the Atonement and make it available to everyone.

> The crucifixion did not establish the Atonement; the resurrection did. Many sincere Christians have misunderstood this. No one who is free of the belief in scarcity could possibly make this mistake. If the crucifixion is seen from an upside-down point of view, it does appear as if God permitted and even encouraged one of His Sons to suffer because he was good. This particularly unfortunate interpretation, which arose out of projection, has led many people to be bitterly afraid of God. Such anti-religious concepts enter into many religions. Yet the real Christian should pause and ask, "How could this be?" Is it likely that God Himself would be capable of the kind of thinking which His Own words have clearly stated is unworthy of His Son?[417]

God did not ask Jesus to die for Him. He asked Jesus for "an act of love," which was the resurrection, clearly demonstrating that death is an illusion and love is the only reality. The resurrection of Jesus is your resurrection. "I am *your* resurrection and *your* life. You live in me because you live in God. And everyone lives in you, as you live in everyone."[418] When Jesus was fully awakened, you were also awakened, but you must accept the Atonement to realize you have been resurrected with him.

> Your resurrection is your reawakening. I am the model for rebirth, but rebirth itself is merely the dawning on your mind of what is already in it. God placed it there Himself, and so it is true forever. I believed in it, and therefore accepted it as true for me.[419]

In addition to establishing the Atonement, Jesus joined his will with God's Will to bring about the resurrection. "I have also made it clear that the resurrection was the means for the return to knowledge, which was accomplished by the union of my will with the Father's."[420] Thus Jesus became the Christ by accepting both his part-ness and wholeness in Christ. This is why he is the model for your acceptance of both your part-ness and wholeness in Christ.

In his complete identification with the Christ—the perfect Son of God, His one creation and His happiness, forever like Himself and One with Him—Jesus became what all of you must be. He led the way for you to follow him. He leads you back to God because he saw the road before him, and he followed it. He made a clear distinction, still obscure to you, between the false and true. He offered you a final demonstration that it is impossible to kill God's Son; nor can his life in any way be changed by sin and evil, malice, fear or death.[421]

As was previously stated, if you accept perfect love, you will be accepting the Atonement. Also, if you accept the Holy Spirit, you will be accepting the Atonement. Jesus is your model of accepting your own Christ nature. Jesus states, "I am the Atonement."[422] Thus fully accepting Jesus also means you are accepting the Atonement. Jesus established the Atonement so it could be available for acceptance by all parts of the Sonship. Also, Jesus made it possible for every part of the Sonship to accept and hear the Holy Spirit. Jesus made the Voice for God available because he listened only to the Holy Spirit and became the embodiment of Him. "I am the manifestation of the Holy Spirit, and when you see me it will be because you have invited Him."[423]

Jesus is the manifestation of the *Holy Spirit*, Whom he called down upon the earth after he ascended into Heaven, or became completely identified with the Christ, the Son of God as He created Him. The Holy Spirit, being a creation of the one Creator, creating with Him and in His likeness or spirit, is eternal and has never changed. He was "called down upon the earth" in the sense that it was now possible to accept Him and to hear His Voice. His is the Voice for God, and has therefore taken form. This form is not His reality, which God alone knows along with Christ, His real Son, Who is part of Him.[424]

Because the Atonement was "built into the space-time belief,"[425] the question may be reasonably asked: How and where did Jesus, as the manifestation of the Holy Spirit, establish the Atonement? The answer to this question is not explicitly stated in the Course, but I would like to offer you my theory to answer this question. I have previously stated that the Holy Spirit has taken the form of the real world manifesting as the blazing light. There are many names used for this form of the Holy Spirit in the real world. The content of the real world consists of all loving thoughts, but the form of the real world is the image within the second dimension that can be seen. This image that can be seen is described in the Course as "the face of Christ" and "the vision of the Son of God" that is an infinitely expanding circle of light. I feel this circle in the real world is also the "circle of Atonement."

All three of these names of the image of the real world represent the form the Holy Spirit has taken. The previous quotation states: "Jesus is the manifestation of the *Holy Spirit...*" Then later in the quotation it states: "His [the Holy Spirit] is the Voice for God, and has therefore taken form." In his earthly life, Jesus embodied the manifested form of the Holy Spirit, but I believe Jesus is currently still manifesting the form of the Holy Spirit as the image of the real world. Thus Jesus has manifested the single image of the circle of infinitely expanding light, which has been given the three different names of the face of Christ, the vision of the Son of God, and the circle of Atonement.

Now let's return to the previous question: How and where did Jesus, as the manifestation of the Holy Spirit, establish the Atonement? To answer this question, it is necessary to explain how Jesus was able to manifest the form of the Holy Spirit as the circle of infinitely expanding light? The answer goes back to the resurrection since the Course states that this "act of love" established the Atonement in the space-time belief. But when was the holy instant in which the resurrection happened? The crucified body of Jesus, presumably covered with the Shroud of Turin, was located within a sealed tomb. The spirit of Jesus reanimated his body. This unseen event was the instant of the resurrection, but there is no description of this in the Course.

Yet the Shroud of Turin is a record of the event of the resurrection because scientists believe the image on this cloth appears to be caused by radiation. There are no possible credible alternatives. With the power of God and the Holy Spirit, the spirit of Jesus Christ returned to the physical body and converted all the mass of the body to infinite energy as blazing light in the second dimension and so left behind a radiation imprint on the Shroud of Turin. But is there a scientific explanation for how all of the mass of the body of Jesus could have been converted to pure energy as light? The answer is in the next section.

If Jesus had the power to convert his physical body into pure infinite energy at the resurrection itself in the tomb, he also had the power to reverse that process. Therefore, he was able to present to his followers a resurrected body by converting pure infinite energy back into a finite form of a transformed body. This glorified body could pass through walls as energy but also could be seen eating and performing other physical functions of a normal body. After the Ascension, he returned the glorified body back to pure energy as blazing light in the second dimension. This two-dimensional face of Christ is only an image that is a reflection of the reality of Christ Who resides in Heaven.

THE RESURRECTION
AND EINSTEIN

~ o ~

Jesus knew that an image of blazing light in the real world would be such a pure reflection of Christ in Heaven that seeing it would awaken any sleeping Son of God. "Yet what is true in God's creation cannot enter here until it is reflected in some form the world can understand."[426] In order to make this image that would return the memory of God, Jesus converted the entire mass of his body into the pure energy of blazing light. Jesus could do this because he had awakened to his own Christ Identity and so he was functioning under God's law of love, the principle of Atonement. He was not under the physical laws of the world, yet I would like to share a scientific interpretation of how Jesus could convert all of his physical body into a blazing circle of light in the real world of the second dimension.

Let's review Einstein's thought experiment of a rocketship described on pages 66 and 67. If a rocketship travels at the speed of light, it will shorten from front to back until it becomes entirely flat, and its width will expand to form a circle. Although the physical laws of this world state that a rocketship could never reach the speed of light, I believe that Jesus accelerated his physical body to the speed of light. Like the rocketship at the speed of light, the matter of his physical body was entirely converted into energy in the form of light. Also, an expanding circle of light was formed in the second dimension, which is the real world. This circle of light retained the content of divine love.

This expanding circle of light is the "vision of the Son of God," and it symbolizes the resurrection of Jesus Christ. It is not the reality of Jesus Christ. But it is an image so close to the reality that it awakens the reality that it represents. Here is the "face of Christ" that is actually the face of Jesus and *your face* because you are part of him and you were resurrected with him. Just as Jesus is part of Christ and the whole of Christ, seeing this face will remind you that you are part of Christ and the whole Christ. When you see this image, you will remember the love of Christ that you are and then remember the love of your Father.

The face of Christ is looked upon before the Father is remembered. For He must be unremembered till His Son has reached beyond forgiveness to the Love of God. Yet is the Love of Christ accepted first. And then will come the knowledge They are One.[427]

There is no order of difficulty in miracles since they all have the full power of God behind them, so no miracle is harder to perform than any other. Thus Jesus had no problem accelerating the mass of his body to the speed of light and converting it all into the energy of light itself. Although miracles transcend physical laws, this acceleration of mass can be explained by Einstein's formula $E = mc^2$. This formula states that accelerating mass (m) to the speed of light squared (c^2) would result in converting all of the mass into (one-dimensional) energy (E).

This formula can be interpreted in relation to the three dimensions. In this interpretation, E equals a *relatively tiny* amount of Light from the infinite first dimension that was needed to make the second and third dimensions. Let's reconfigure Einstein's formula $E = mc^2$ so the new configuration is $E / c = mc$. Notice that E / c is the Light or Energy from the first dimension divided by the speed of light, 186,282 miles per second. Was the Light of the first dimension "slowed down"? Because the Light of the first dimension is everywhere, it is not moving at all so it cannot be slowed down. It is more correct to say that this infinite Light was "extracted" from the first dimension. The result of this extraction was that part of the infinite Light of the first dimension was changed into the second dimension (E / c). Here in this second dimension, the infinite Light of the first dimension was limited to the two-dimensional shape of an expanding circle of light. Christ's vision enables you to see this two-dimensional light that is a limited reflection of the infinite and transcendental Light of Heaven existing in the first dimension.

The other side of Einstein's reconfigured formula is matter multiplied times the speed of light ($E / c = mc$). This acceleration of matter (mc) is the idea of Einstein's previously described thought experiment of the rocketship moving toward the speed of light. It is also the idea of the resurrected Jesus accelerating his physical body to the speed of light. Unlike the rocketship that would be limited by Newton's laws of physics, Jesus was able to succeed in accelerating his body so it traveled at the speed of light, 186,282 miles per second. Jesus was able to transcend the third dimension and reach the second dimension where the matter of his body became the face of Christ, which is the circle of blazing light expanding toward infinity. Matter, as *frozen light*, multiplied by the speed of light became *unfrozen light* ($m \times c = E / c$). From the second dimension, Jesus was lifted into Heaven by God. But Jesus left behind for you the face of Christ in the second dimension as your bridge to awakening in Heaven. After you see the blazing light of the face of Christ, God will take the final step of accelerating you from real world of the second dimension to the first dimension of Heaven. In summary, the light extracted from Heaven can be decelerated by 186,282 miles per second (E / c) into the blazing light of the second dimension. Also, the matter of the third dimension can be accelerated by the speed of light (mc) so it becomes the same blazing light.

JESUS, TRUE LIGHT, AND CHRIST'S VISION

≈ • ≈

Three-dimensional physical light travels at 186,282 miles per second *in a vacuum*. Since the physical universe is not a vacuum, the physical light that can be seen with the physical eyes is slowed down slightly as it interacts with matter and the gravitational forces of the physical world of three dimensions. More important than the speed of physical light is the fact that physical light can only be seen by interactions with physical eyes when photons enter the eyes and contact the photoreceptors in the eyes. Your eyes detect light being reflected from objects, and chemical and electrical impulses in your brain are converted into images. You are not seeing objects, such as bodies, cars, and trees outside of your body. You are seeing visual symbols of objects. All these representations are merely images of thoughts within your mind. "It is because the thoughts you think you think appear as images that you do not recognize them as nothing. You think you think them, and so you think you see them. This is how your 'seeing' was made. This is the function you have given your body's eyes. It is not seeing. It is image making. It takes the place of seeing, replacing vision with illusions."[428]

Your physical eyes by themselves cannot see light traveling on a flat plane in only two dimensions. However, when you receive the gift of Christ's vision, you will be able to see the blazing light traveling in two dimensions. But there are different levels of seeing the blazing light. At the deepest level of the real world, you will see the perfect image of the face of Christ that will lead directly to awakening. Yet with Christ's vision, you can look at any brother and see light in him that is a lesser version of the same blazing light of the second dimension.

> Christ's vision is the miracle in which all miracles are born. It is their source, remaining with each miracle you give, and yet remaining yours. It is the bond by which the giver and receiver are united in extension here on earth, as they are one in Heaven. Christ beholds no sin in anyone. And in His sight the sinless are as one. Their holiness was given by His Father and Himself.[429]

The light coming into your mind that makes Christ's vision possible is called "true light," and it comes as an expression of the blazing light of the second dimension. This light is not physical light that is seen by the physical eyes. "True light that makes true vision possible is not the light the body's eyes behold."[430]

> True light is strength, and strength is sinlessness. If you remain as God created you, you must be strong and light must be in you. He Who ensured your sinlessness must be the guarantee of strength and light as well. You are as God created you. Darkness cannot obscure the glory of God's Son. You stand in light, strong in the sinlessness in which you were created, and in which you will remain throughout eternity.[431]

Christ's vision is used to practice forgiveness as you see holiness in your brother and overlook the ego's illusory symbols of the body and guilt. Christ's vision is facilitated by an inner light. "The wish to see calls down the grace of God upon your eyes, and brings the gift of light that makes sight possible."[432] Christ's vision and the true light that makes it possible are a single gift, but what is the source of this gift? The Course says the Holy Spirit gives the gift of Christ's vision if you ask for this ability to see the real world. "This [true vision] is the Holy Spirit's single gift; the treasure house to which you can appeal with perfect certainty for all the things that can contribute to your happiness."[433]

> Correction is for all who cannot see. To open the eyes of the blind is the Holy Spirit's mission, for He knows that they have not lost their vision, but merely sleep. He would awaken them from the sleep of forgetting to the remembering of God. Christ's eyes are open, and He will look upon whatever you see with love if you accept His vision as yours. The Holy Spirit keeps the vision of Christ for every Son of God who sleeps. In His sight the Son of God is perfect, and He longs to share His vision with you. He will show you the real world because God gave you Heaven. Through Him your Father calls His Son to remember. The awakening of His Son begins with his investment in the real world, and by this he will learn to re-invest in himself. For reality is one with the Father and the Son, and the Holy Spirit blesses the real world in Their Name.[434]

The Holy Spirit gives the gift of Christ's vision, but it is not called the "Holy Spirit's vision." Because vision of the real world in the second dimension is called "Christ's vision," it must be Christ's gift to you. The wholeness of Christ is in Heaven so He has only the total awareness of knowledge, and He does not have any of the limited awareness of perception. Since Christ's vision is a perceptual gift, Christ in Heaven cannot possibly be the giver of the gift of real vision in which true light comes into the mind. Nevertheless, there is another way Christ's vision can be the gift of Christ. Christ's vision is the gift of Jesus Christ. Since

Jesus has accepted his true nature, he has awakened the awareness of his part-ness in Christ and wholeness in Christ. Because Jesus is the manifestation of the Holy Spirit, he has both perception and knowledge just as the Holy Spirit does. Because he has retained perception, he can give the perceptual gift of Christ's vision.

Jesus gives you the gift of Christ's vision to help your brother and you awaken to your true nature. Jesus wants you to see Christ in your brother. "The only gift I [Jesus] can accept of you is the gift I gave to you."[435] Your gift to Jesus is accepting his gift of perceiving your brother as Christ that releases you from your self-imposed limitations. "What other gift can you offer me, when only this I choose to offer you?"[436] The gift of Jesus is union in the holy instant and in Christ's vision, enabling you to see Christ in everyone. In return, you can give back to Jesus the same gift of union in Christ's vision that he gave to you. Thus you see your brothers as the Christ and encourage them to see as the Christ. You offer to everyone the gift of union in Christ's vision that is the same gift Jesus gave to you. "And to see me is to see me in everyone, and offer everyone the gift [of union in Christ's vision] you offer me."[437]

When you receive this gift yourself from Jesus and share this gift of Christ's vision with your brothers, you are giving Jesus the return gift that he wants from you. This return gift you give to Jesus is union and release for you and your brothers. Jesus always sees you with Christ's vision, so he always sees your holiness. Jesus has remained with you in your world of perception in order to show you with Christ's vision how to free yourself as you free your brothers with him.

> Jesus has led the way. Why would you not be grateful to him? He has asked for love, but only that he might give it to you. You do not love yourself. But in his eyes your loveliness is so complete and flawless that he sees in it an image of his Father. You become the symbol of his Father here on earth. To you he looks for hope, because in you he sees no limit and no stain to mar your beautiful perfection. In his eyes Christ's vision shines in perfect constancy. He has remained with you. Would you not learn the lesson of salvation through his learning? Why would you choose to start again, when he has made the journey for you?[438]

When you receive the gift of Christ's vision from Jesus, you can see the beauty of Christ in your brothers that Jesus sees in you. Also, your ability to see Christ in your brothers enables them to accept the gift of Christ's vision and see Christ in you. Thus you give to others the same gift Jesus gave to you, and this is the gift you give to Jesus because Jesus does not see himself as separate from any part of the one Christ. What you give to your brothers you give to Jesus.

Jesus wants you to follow his example, but that does not mean you have to have his same experiences. "You are not asked to be crucified, which was part of my own teaching contribution. You are merely asked to follow my example in the face of much less extreme temptations to misperceive, and not to accept them as false justifications for anger."[439] In order to give Jesus the gift of union by accepting Christ's vision, he does not require you to sacrifice anything. You do have to give up your attraction to guilt, but that kind of "sacrifice" is not really the letting go of anything you want. "I [Jesus] am as incapable of receiving sacrifice as God is, and every sacrifice you ask of yourself you ask of me."[440]

The ego defines sacrifice as the giving up of something you want in order to get something that you want more. To the ego, sacrifice is always a trade that involves giving only to get in return. If you give without getting, then the ego tells you that you are losing. The ego always wants to give away something of lesser value to get something of greater value and thus "win" the bargain. Sacrifice is always the ego's calculation of deciding how to get and how to get *more*.

> To the ego, to give anything implies that you will have to do without it. When you associate giving with sacrifice, you give only because you believe that you are somehow getting something better, and can therefore do without the thing you give. "Giving to get" is an inescapable law of the ego, which always evaluates itself in relation to other egos. It is therefore continually preoccupied with the belief in scarcity that gave rise to it.[441]

But if you focus entirely on giving as God, the Holy Spirit, and Jesus give, the getting mechanism of sacrifice has no meaning. True love is always giving so there is no need to calculate how you can get or how you can get more. This giving attitude makes sacrifice meaningless. When you give love, you are keeping love in your mind. It is a law of God that "giving is receiving." Giving love is gaining love and not the loss of anything. "Learn now that sacrifice of any kind is nothing but a limitation imposed on giving. And by this limitation you have limited acceptance of the gift I offer you [of union in Christ's vision]."[442]

Giving is receiving in your real relationships because there is no real separation between the giver and the receiver, who are united with each other. For example, Jesus and you are united in the Sonship, so what he gives to you, you give to him. What you give to him, you receive from him. Your relationship with Jesus is a relationship based entirely on giving without thought of getting, so there is no guilt in the relationship if you can accept the reality of your union. "We [Jesus and you] who are one cannot give separately. When you are willing to accept our relationship as real, guilt will hold no attraction for you."[443]

In addition to the benefit of letting go of guilt by uniting your mind with the mind of Jesus, your real relationship also enables you to lessen your identification with the ego and accept the unlimited power of the

Son of God. "There is no limit to the power of a Son of God, but he can limit the expression of his power as much as he chooses. Your mind and mine can unite in shining your ego away, releasing the strength of God into everything you think and do."[444]

What is the ego? The Course states that you are not the ego, but the ego is part of your whole mind that is unreal. "The ego's voice is an hallucination. You cannot expect it to say 'I am not real.' Fortunately, you are not asked to dispel your hallucinations alone. You are merely asked to evaluate them in terms of their results to you. If you do not want them on the basis of loss of peace, they will be removed from your mind for you."[445]

The ego represents the tiny unreal part of your mind that is unwilling to awaken to the reality and wholeness of knowledge in Heaven. The ego cannot be destroyed because it is part of your mind, but it can be undone. Your whole mind is like a rope. The ego is like a knot in the rope. If you use a knife to cut out the knot, a part of the rope would be missing. However, if you untie the knot, it is still the same whole rope. In this analogy, untying the knot is like undoing the ego. But you need help to undo the ego because the ego is unwilling to be undone without resistance. You might convince yourself mentally that you are totally committed to awakening, but even so, there is a part of your mind that remains unwilling and resistant to awakening. When you find that you have lost your peace of mind over something in the world, you might foolishly imagine you are a victim of a person or an event. But this is not possible. "The secret of salvation is but this: that you are doing this unto yourself."[446] Everything that occurs in your life is an expression of your will, either in accord or not in accord with God's Will. *"And everything that seems to happen to me I ask for, and receive as I have asked."*[447]

Instead of projecting blame onto others for the unhappy experiences of life, it is helpful to look within and say to yourself, "This must be the ego-based part of my mind that does not want to wake up." After acknowledging this unwillingness, don't stop there or blame yourself. Although you are likely to have some lingering unwillingness in your mind, the Course states that you only need a "little willingness," not "completed willingness" because you have help from the Holy Spirit.

> He [the Holy Spirit] needs only your willingness to share His perspective to give it to you completely. And your willingness need not be complete because His is perfect. It is His task to atone for your unwillingness by His perfect faith, and it is His faith you share with Him there. Out of your recognition of your unwillingness for your release, His perfect willingness is given you. Call upon Him, for Heaven is at His Call. And let Him call on Heaven for you.[448]

Along with the Holy Spirit, Jesus is your ideal helper because he has overcome the unwillingness of the ego that is still in your mind. Jesus is confident you will choose to unite your mind with his. "I do not attack your ego. I do work with your higher mind, the home of the Holy Spirit, whether you are asleep or awake, just as your ego does with your lower mind, which is its home. I am your vigilance in this, because you are too confused to recognize your own hope. I am not mistaken. Your mind will elect to join with mine, and together we are invincible."[449]

In order to accomplish the goal of uniting your mind with the mind of Jesus, you must observe the ego-based thoughts of your mind that would block this union.

> Watch your mind carefully for any beliefs that hinder its [the goal of uniting your mind with the mind of Jesus] accomplishment, and step away from them. Judge how well you have done this by your own feelings, for this is the one right use of judgment. Judgment, like any other defense, can be used to attack or protect; to hurt or to heal. The ego *should* be brought to judgment and found wanting there. Without your own allegiance, protection and love, the ego cannot exist. Let it be judged truly and you must withdraw allegiance, protection and love from it.[450]

When you understand your relationship of union with Jesus, you will understand that you are united with every part of the Sonship, with no one excluded from your union of love. "For in our union [of Jesus and you] you will accept all of our brothers."[451] The gift Jesus gave you and wants you to give to him is union that releases you from all sense of separation based on the ego. If you give the gift of union to Jesus, you will keep the gift of union that you have given. "The gift of union is the only gift that I was born to give. Give it to me, that you may have it."[452] The gift of union that you receive from Christ is your freedom from the limitations of the ego. By accepting this gift from Christ, you offer the gift of freedom to every brother you encounter. Thus you use Christ's vision to see your brother as the guiltless Son of God. Your true perception of your brother using Christ's vision encourages him to be a host to God and no longer be a hostage to the ego and its limitations. "The time of Christ is the time appointed for the gift of freedom, offered to everyone. And by your acceptance of it, you offer it to everyone."[453]

Instead of seeing with physical eyes that would show you only the outer forms of objects and people, Christ's vision shows you the inner content of holiness in the world and the transparency of what at first seems so solid. Christ's vision is possible because of the true light that comes into our mind, but notice in the following quotation that Christ's vision enables you to perceive the inner light shining within objects and people that is hidden from seeing with your physical eyes alone.

Christ's vision is the bridge between the worlds. And in its power can you safely trust to carry you from this world into one made holy by forgiveness. Things which seem quite solid here are merely shadows there; transparent, faintly seen, at times forgot, and never able to obscure the light that shines beyond them. Holiness has been restored to vision, and the blind can see.[454]

Notice the first sentence of the above quotation: "Christ's vision is the bridge between the worlds." I do not interpret this as the bridge between the world of three dimensions and the real world of two dimensions. The section heading titled "The Bridge to the Real World,"[455] implies that the bridge is not another name for the real world. But all the headings were inserted by Ken Wapnick during editing and were not the scribed words of Jesus. The scribed words do refer to the "bridge to Heaven,"[456] and state, "The bridge that He would carry you across lifts you from time into eternity. Waken from time, and answer fearlessly the Call of Him Who gave eternity to you in your creation. On this side of the bridge to timelessness you understand nothing."[457] These scribed words imply that the bridge is another name for the real world, which offers a transition to Heaven. The bridge is consistently described as a "transition," which supports the idea that the bridge is another name for the real world. "The bridge itself is nothing more than a transition in the perspective of reality."[458] I believe this transition bridges the gap between Heaven in the first dimension and the nightmares of the third dimension. This bridge has already been discussed as the second dimension, but what is the nature of the bridge, and who built it as it is right now?

Any bridge allows for travel from one side to another. But because this particular bridge connects different dimensions, changes happen when there is a movement from one dimension to another. Specifically, the nature of light changes when it moves from one dimension to another. These dimensional changes are expressed in reconfiguring Einstein's formula of $E = mc^2$ as was identified in the previous section for your consideration.

Now it would be helpful to consider a simple analogy. A concise summary of this analogy states that light is like water, chemically H_2O, that has the three different states of gas, liquid, and solid. Steam has the fastest moving atoms of H_2O, water has slower moving atoms, and ice has the slowest moving atoms. Likewise, light is different in each dimension because it has different speeds with different qualities. Before being extracted from Heaven, Light is infinitely expansive motionless light, similar to steam being the most expansive form of H_2O as a gas. Just as water is the medium speed form of H_2O, the blazing light of the real world in the second dimension is the medium speed form of light. Just as ice is the slowest moving H_2O, the light of the three-dimensional world is the slowest form of light. This slowest form of light is what is known as "matter" because light has been so condensed that it no longer appears as light. Energy being converted into the solid form of matter and matter being converted into energy is what Einstein proved by his formula $E = mc^2$. The idea of light being "frozen" into matter ($E / c^2 = m$) and the idea of matter being "unfrozen" back into light ($m \times c = E / c$) are merely my reconfigured variations of Einstein's formula.

There is a relationship between the changing of light in dimensions and the previous question: What is the nature of the bridge, and who built it? The real world is called a world of only loving thoughts, but it is also a world of only light. In order to understand the bridge function of the real world, it is necessary to understand that the real world is the transition place from the slowest form of light, called matter, to the blazing light of the second dimension and on to the Light of Heaven. The real world is a "world of light" and a "circle of brightness."

> This world of light, this circle of brightness is the real world, where guilt meets with forgiveness. Here the world outside is seen anew, without the shadow of guilt upon it. Here are you forgiven, for here you have forgiven everyone. Here is the new perception, where everything is bright and shining with innocence, washed in the waters of forgiveness, and cleansed of every evil thought you laid upon it. Here there is no attack upon the Son of God, and you are welcome. Here is your innocence, waiting to clothe you and protect you, and make you ready for the final step in the journey inward. Here are the dark and heavy garments of guilt laid by, and gently replaced by purity and love.[459]

Consequently, the real world of both pure light and pure love is your bridge to awakening. You made an unhappy three-dimensional dream world of darkness and light. But the Holy Spirit offers you the alternative of the real world of happy dreams to replace your unhappy dreams. "The Holy Spirit, ever practical in His wisdom, accepts your dreams and uses them as means for waking. You would have used them to remain asleep. I said before that the first change, before dreams disappear, is that your dreams of fear are changed to happy dreams."[460]

All dreams, even the happy dreams of the real world, are perceptions, meaning limited awareness. But the content of light and love in the happy dreams of the real world is so much like the light and love of Heaven that the real world becomes the bridge to awakening. All perception has a form, and the form of the real world of light is a single circle of blazing light expanding infinitely, but given different names. This single circular form of blazing light and its inner content of love are inseparable. The real world as a bridge of both light and love is obvious, but who built this bridge as it is now? The next section will answer this question.

THE BRIDGE AND
THE LAW OF LOVE

~ ∘ ~

Most Course interpreters agree that at the instant of the separation the Holy Spirit as the Maker of the world made the real world as the bridge to awakening in Heaven. The following is one of three Course references that provide the clarity that "the Holy Spirit is the Bridge":

> The way to recognize your brother is by recognizing the Holy Spirit in him. I have already said that the Holy Spirit is the Bridge for the transfer of perception to knowledge, so we can use the terms as if they were related, because in His Mind they are. This relationship must be in His Mind because, unless it were, the separation between the two ways of thinking would not be open to healing. He is part of the Holy Trinity, because His Mind is partly yours and also partly God's. This needs clarification, not in statement but in experience.[461]

To the typical idea of the Holy Spirit building the real world, this book adds the ideas that the real world is in the second dimension and has been projected from the first dimension in order to make a bridge where the transfer from perception to knowledge can be made. But the original real world that the Holy Spirit built at the instant of the Big Bang was actually *functionally only half of a bridge*. The side of the bridge that was built was the connection of light and love from the first dimension where it originated to the second dimension. At this point, the Atonement was the principle of love, but the Atonement itself had not been established within the space-time belief. The bridge was functionally only half a bridge because the bridge did not extend into the three-dimensional world to bring about the Atonement that would be able to correct all errors in perception. Errors needed to be corrected where they occurred within the minds of the sleeping children of God who were locked into dreams of three-dimensional awareness. What good is a bridge if the people who need to use it cannot even reach that bridge?

The Holy Spirit would have to bring the law of love into the third dimension in order to have the Atonement become established. The law of love was needed to replace what is commonly called the "law of karma." The Course never mentions the word "karma," but it does talk about "cause and effect." God did establish the fundamental law of cause and effect. The Holy Spirit maintains that cause and effect happen at the same time in the present. "Cause and effect are one, not separate."[462] The Holy Spirit's interpretation of time emphasizes only the present. However, there is no past karma and no future karma. The Holy Spirit supports the idea that there is only present karma, which is cause and effect that always occurs only now. "Thinking and its results are really simultaneous, for cause and effect are never separate."[463] Whatever you are currently carrying in your mind you will be experiencing now. The decisions you make stay in effect in your mind in every instant until you change your mind and make a new decision that will stay in effect until you change it. If you carry beliefs about guilt from past events in your mind now, you are experiencing the effect of carrying guilt in your mind now. But you can decide to release that guilt right now and experience the freedom now of a guiltless mind. The act of releasing guilt becomes the cause that produces the effect now of freedom and acceptance of the innocence God gave you in your creation. Since the idea of past karma and future karma are illusions, you can let go of these illusions in the present simply by realizing they are illusions.

The belief in past karma causing future punishment or reward is a human construct that only seems to work because of the belief that past guilt deserves future punishment. Before the Atonement was established, the belief in the law of karma was so widespread that the idea of the law of love was inconceivable. The Holy Spirit's difficulty in bringing the law of love into the three-dimensional world was that the sleeping Son of God was invariably not hearing His Voice that speaks for God and for God's Love. Of course, a small number of spiritual seekers did hear the Voice for God. But a single act of extraordinary love was needed to open the human condition to hear the Voice for God and to build the other half of the bridge that would enable the sleeping Son of God to have access to the real world of the second dimension.

> The Atonement *principle* was in effect long before the Atonement began. The principle was love and the Atonement was an *act* of love. Acts were not necessary before the separation, because belief in space and time did not exist. It was only after the separation that the Atonement and the conditions necessary for its fulfillment were planned.[464]

Although the Voice for God was not being heard, Jesus was the extraordinary exception. He manifested the act of love that was the Atonement and that built the other half of the bridge that was needed. The following quotation refers to the Bible reference of bringing the Holy Spirit down into the space-time belief because beforehand He was not being heard because the Voice for God had not yet taken form.

Jesus is the manifestation of the *Holy Spirit*, Whom he called down upon the earth after he ascended into Heaven, or became completely identified with the Christ, the Son of God as He created Him. The Holy Spirit, being a creation of the one Creator, creating with Him and in His likeness or spirit, is eternal and has never changed. He was "called down upon the earth" in the sense that it was now possible to accept Him and to hear His Voice. His is the Voice for God, and has therefore taken form. This form is not His reality, which God alone knows along with Christ, His real Son, Who is part of Him.[465]

By this act of love that was the resurrection, Jesus enabled the Holy Spirit to be accepted and heard, as is indicated in the above sentence, "He [the Holy Spirit] was 'called down upon the earth' in the sense that it was now possible to accept Him and to hear His Voice." Why couldn't the Holy Spirit be accepted, and why couldn't His Voice be heard before the resurrection? God put the Holy Spirit in the mind of every part of the Sonship who had fallen asleep by closing off communication with God. Thus if it was not possible to accept the Holy Spirit and hear the Voice for God, it must have been unwillingness to communicate, with the exception of a few seekers who were willing to hear the divine within. One overlooked factor is that the three-dimensional world is a collective dream that was made as an escape from God. The sleeping children of God believed in the law of karma. Believing in guilt, they thought they would be punished by God for their act of leaving Heaven, and so it seemed necessary to close off communication in order to hide from God and His expected punishment. The dream world was made to escape from God, but the sleeping Son of God built into the dream of the world the belief in death as the ultimate punishment for guilt.

In this context, the sleeping Son of God could not conceive of a law of love that would tell them they are still guiltless and beloved by God. Thus the Holy Spirit as the Bridge would be ineffective until one part of the sleeping portion of the Sonship reestablished perfect communication through perfect alignment with God's Will of Love. The belief in death itself would have to be overcome in order to open the mind of the sleeping Son of God. *"Death is illusion; life, eternal truth. There is no opposition to Your Will. There is no conflict, for my will is Yours."*[466] An act of love was needed to usher in the law of love and to overcome the false belief in the law of karma that said death is deserved for rebellion against God. Jesus brought in the law of love and accomplished the Atonement with the act of love that was the resurrection.

Very simply, the resurrection is the overcoming or surmounting of death. It is a reawakening or a rebirth; a change of mind about the meaning of the world. It is the acceptance of the Holy

Spirit's interpretation of the world's purpose; the acceptance of the Atonement for oneself. It is the end of dreams of misery, and the glad awareness of the Holy Spirit's final dream. It is the recognition of the gifts of God.[467]

Accepting the resurrection means accepting the Atonement since they are both the same one act of love correcting all errors. Although the Atonement is within the world of dreams, it is the means provided by Jesus and the Holy Spirit for releasing all illusions. If you accept the Atonement, you will use the body only for communication. "It (the acceptance of the Atonement) is the dream in which the body functions perfectly, having no function except communication."[468] The acceptance of the Atonement is the only lesson you need to welcome your awakening. "It (the acceptance of the Atonement) is the lesson in which learning ends, for it is consummated and surpassed with this. It is the invitation to God to take His final step [of awakening you]."[469]

Through love and desire, Jesus was able to manifest the resurrection and establish the Atonement. The single-minded desire of Jesus was to fully awaken to His Father and enable all parts of the Sonship to awaken. Jesus had no other desire than his purpose of aligning the will of the Son and the Will of the Father. Thus he paved the way for the Holy Spirit to likewise be accepted and be heard by the sleeping parts of the Sonship. "It (the acceptance of the Atonement) is the relinquishment of all other purposes, all other interests, all other wishes and all other concerns. It is the single desire of the Son for the Father."[470]

Previously, I said that Jesus resurrected his body and accelerated it to the speed of light so it changed into the circle of blazing light expanding infinitely in the second dimension. I also said that at the separation, the Holy Spirit made this same circle of blazing light expanding infinitely in the second dimension as a visual image and as a perfect reflection of the reality of the wholeness of Christ in Heaven. There is no contradiction here because both the Holy Spirit and Jesus brought in the one circle of light expanding infinitely in the second dimension. The union of these two circles became the vision of one circle as the completion of the two halves of the bridge—the half made by the Holy Spirit connecting the second dimension to the first dimension at the separation and the half manifested by Jesus establishing communication between the second and third dimension with the act of love of the resurrection.

It is not a great stretch of the imagination to believe that before the earthly ministry of Jesus, he had already experienced seeing the vision of the blazing light manifested by the Holy Spirit, and through this vision he had remembered God. This was for him the ultimate experience of revelation as a direct experience of His Father. Therefore, when Jesus resurrected his body and changed it into blazing light, it would be only natural for him to allow his transformed body of blazing light to assume the same form of the circle of blazing light that would bring back the memory of God to anyone who saw it. This is also reasonable because the resurrected Jesus had fully accepted his own dual nature of part-ness and wholeness in Christ so he could rightly be called "Jesus Christ." Thus it was altogether appropriate for his former concrete body to be transformed into an image of blazing light called "the face of Christ" and "the vision of the Son of God," as well as the circle of Atonement.

Jesus could have completely ascended to His Father and into the first dimension of Heaven, but it was God's Will and his own will to join with the Mind of the Holy Spirit and have the dual awareness of perception in the second dimension and knowledge in the first dimension. The Holy Spirit is the Mind of the Atonement and the Christ Mind so Jesus was chosen to lead the Atonement. Jesus says, "I am the Atonement."[471] If you call on perfect love to accept the Atonement, you are knowingly or unknowingly calling on Jesus. "The name of Jesus Christ as such is but a symbol. But it stands for love that is not of this world."[472] The Course also says of Jesus, "So has his name become the Name of God, for he no longer sees himself as separate from Him."[473] Jesus plays the central role in the Holy Spirit's plan of Atonement. "Everyone has a special part to play in the Atonement, but the message given to each one is always the same; *God's Son is guiltless.*"[474]

The Course's visual image of the circle of Atonement helps you visualize your function of forgiveness. Jesus, who is inside this circle of holiness, welcomes everyone to come inside. "In guiltlessness we know Him, as He knows us guiltless. I [Jesus] stand within the circle, calling you to peace. Teach peace with me, and stand with me on holy ground."[475] Jesus asks you to join him in forgiving everyone. Thus you invite everyone to come inside the circle. Your brothers who stand outside the circle imagine that they are guilty. If you see guilt in any brother outside the circle, you will believe you are guilty, and you will join your brother outside the circle. The circle of Atonement is a helpful reminder to forgive and heal your brother of his mistaken belief in guilt and thus heal your mind of your own belief in guilt. Forgiveness is an enlightened form of self-interest because it enables you to claim your holiness by seeing guiltlessness in everyone.

> Each one you see you place within the holy circle of Atonement or leave outside, judging him fit for crucifixion or for redemption. If you bring him into the circle of purity, you will rest there with him. If you leave him without, you join him there. Judge not except in quietness which is not of you. Refuse to accept anyone as without the blessing of Atonement, and bring him into it by blessing him.[476]

With your permission, Jesus and the Holy Spirit will guide you to accept the Atonement, practice forgiveness, use Christ's vision, join in holy relationships, experience the holy instant, practice meditation, and perform miracles as your various means of taking the journey across the bridge to the real world. Although the Holy Spirit and Jesus built the universal bridge that is the transition place from this world to Heaven, you participate actively in building your own experience of crossing this bridge. You have God beside you as your Self while you build this bridge and your creations in Heaven beckon you to cross over to knowledge in your true Home. Your building of your bridge always involves the process of accepting on truth and letting go of the illusions you have made, but which you realize you do not want.

> The bridge that leads to union in yourself *must* lead to knowledge, for it was built with God beside you, and will lead you straight to Him where your completion rests, wholly compatible with His. Every illusion you accept into your mind by judging it to be attainable removes your own sense of completion, and thus denies the Wholeness of your Father. Every fantasy, be it of love or hate, deprives you of knowledge for fantasies are the veil behind which truth is hidden. To lift the veil that seems so dark and heavy, it is only needful to value truth beyond all fantasy, and to be entirely unwilling to settle for illusion in place of truth.[477]

By building this bridge with God, you are seeking your completion in which you recognize your part-ness and wholeness in Christ and your oneness with God and your creations. One major obstacle can be clinging to special love relationships that offer you only the illusion of love. Yet only real love in your real relationships will ever satisfy you and bring you your completion in your Father and in the Sonship. Jesus will help you make this journey to your awakening if you let him by joining your mind with his.

> If special relationships of any kind would hinder God's completion, can they have any value to you? What would interfere with God must interfere with you. Only in time does interference in God's completion seem to be possible. The bridge that He would carry you across lifts you from time into eternity. Waken from time, and answer fearlessly the Call of Him Who gave eternity to you in your creation. On this side of the bridge to timelessness you understand nothing. But as you step lightly across it, upheld *by* timelessness, you are directed straight to the Heart of God. At its center, and only there, you are safe forever, because you are complete forever. There is no veil the Love of God in us together cannot lift. The way to truth is open. Follow it with me.[478]

HEALING YOUR TWO
MAJOR FEARS

~ • ~

You have two major related fears: One is the fear of God's Will. You will believe that God's Will is fearful when you identify with the illusions of this world, especially with the illusion of the ego itself. Since reality offers only truth, it would dissolve illusions the same way light dispels darkness. Attachment to illusions and especially clinging to the ego-based illusion of yourself encourages you to fearfully perceive reality as your "enemy." "Reality cannot 'threaten' anything except illusions, because reality can only uphold truth. The very fact that the Will of God, which is what you are, is perceived as fearful, demonstrates that you *are* afraid of what you are. It is not, then, the Will of God of which you are afraid, but yours."[479] When you disown your own will and own reality in God, you will make the mistake of seeking to find safety in the ego. "Your will is not the ego's, and that is why the ego is against you. What seems to be the fear of God is really the fear of your own reality."[480]

When you are afraid of your true reality, you do not know that you really want to accept reality and accept your will as God's Will. The Holy Spirit as your trustworthy Guide knows your reality and knows what you want that will truly make you happy. "The purpose of this Guide is merely to remind you of what you want. He is not attempting to force an alien will upon you. He is merely making every possible effort, within the limits you impose on Him, to re-establish your own will in your awareness."[481] The Holy Spirit "has the power to look into what you have hidden and recognize the Will of God there. His recognition of this Will can make it real to you because He is in your mind, and therefore He is your reality. If, then, His perception of your mind brings its reality to you, He *is* helping you to remember what you are."[482]

Since you believe your will is different than God's Will, you believe you must sacrifice your will if you accept God's Will. The Holy Spirit never asks you to sacrifice your will or anything you truly want, because He wants to preserve your will. "There is no difference between your will and God's. If you did not have a split mind, you would recognize that willing is salvation because it is communication."[483] Since your mind is split, you cannot communicate effectively because your mind is confused about what you truly want. "How sensible can your messages be, when you ask for what you do not want? Yet as long as you are afraid of your will, that is precisely what you are asking for."[484] Inevitably you will learn that your true will is God's Will. "Ultimately everyone must remember the Will of God, because ultimately everyone must recognize himself. This recognition is the recognition that his will and God's are one."[485]

To awaken your true will, the first step you can take is to ask for an increase of your awareness of God and His Love. "God is Love and you do want Him. This *is* your will. Ask for this and you will be answered, because you will be asking only for what belongs to you."[486] Asking in prayer for an increase in your awareness of love is the most important step you can take in learning to understand and accept that God's Will is your true will. Why? The reason is that God's Will is the will of Love. If you increase your awareness of the infinite love already within you, you will realize that you only want to exert your will for the purpose of expressing the love that you are. In this case, you would recognize that your will and God's Will are perfectly united in the one purpose of expressing love. With the awareness that love is your true nature and true purpose, it would never occur to you to oppose God's Will because doing so would oppose the expression of love. Having found your single purpose of expressing love, you would understand and accept that God's Will of love is your own true will of love.

The Holy Spirit always answers your prayers for an increase in the awareness of love, but He cannot answer your prayers if you ask for what will hurt you or for anything He knows you do not really want. "When you ask the Holy Spirit for what would hurt you He cannot answer because nothing can hurt you, and so you are asking for nothing. Any wish that stems from the ego is a wish for nothing, and to ask for it is not a request. It is merely a denial in the form of a request. The Holy Spirit is not concerned with form, being aware only of meaning."[487]

In addition to the first step of asking for an increased awareness of love in order to understand and accept your true will as God's Will, a second step you can take is to commit yourself to seeking the truth instead of illusions. "In the presence of truth, there are no unbelievers and no sacrifices. In the security of reality, fear is totally meaningless. To deny what is can only *seem* to be fearful. Fear cannot be real without a cause, and God is the only Cause."[488] In order to awaken your true will as God's Will, a third step you can take is to recognize that you have been in denial about the truth. Accepting responsibility for hiding the truth does not mean accepting guilt for your denial. But accepting this responsibility does mean you realize that you can change your decision to be in denial. Therefore, you can invite the Holy Spirit to help you let go of denial and open your mind to truth.

Your illusions require you to believe in them because your belief is necessary for you to invest in them. But reality is a fact, whether you believe in it or not. Thus reality requires your acceptance not your belief.

"The fact that God is Love does not require belief, but it does require acceptance. It is possible for you to deny facts, although it is impossible for you to change them."[489] To accept reality you must stop investing in the denial of reality. "If you hold your hands over your eyes, you will not see because you are interfering with the laws of seeing. If you deny love, you will not know it because your cooperation is the law of its being."[490] Denial of reality results in fear because it is a denial of yourself. "Any attempt to deny what is must be fearful, and if the attempt is strong it will induce panic. Willing against reality, though impossible, can be made into a very persistent goal even though you do not want it."[491] When you devote your mind to illusions that you do not truly want, you will make yourself unhappy. "God in His devotion to you created you devoted to everything, and gave you what you are devoted to. Otherwise you would not have been created perfect. Reality is everything, and you have everything because you are real."[492]

You cannot devote yourself to the impossible task of opposing God's Will without also bringing illusions of fear into your mind. "Remember, then, that God's Will is already possible, and nothing else will ever be. This is the simple acceptance of reality, because only that is real. You cannot distort reality and know what it is. And if you do distort reality you will experience anxiety, depression and ultimately panic, because you are trying to make yourself unreal."[493] To help you dispel illusions and accept reality, one option to consider is to remind yourself that Christ is within you by saying to yourself: *"Christ is in me, and where He is God must be, for Christ is part of Him."*[494]

The fear of God's Will has been described as one of your two major fears that must be recognized and overcome, but it is only your second greatest fear. Your greatest fear is your *fear of redemption*. Just as your fear of God is the fear of His Love, your fear of redemption is the fear of being swallowed up by God's Love. You are mostly unaware of your fears. Because of your unconscious fears, you are not fully committed to removing attack thoughts from your mind. "We have said that no one will countenance fear if he recognizes it. Yet in your disordered state of mind you are not afraid of fear. You do not like it, but it is not your desire to attack that really frightens you."[495] You are also not committed to removing anger from your mind. "You are not seriously disturbed by your hostility. You keep it hidden because you are more afraid of what it covers."[496] The reason why you are not committed to releasing attack thoughts and hostility is that these hide your greatest fear. "You could look even upon the ego's darkest cornerstone without fear if you did not believe that, without the ego, you would find within yourself something you fear even more. You are not really afraid of crucifixion. Your real terror is of redemption."[497]

Your fear of redemption is terrifying because you are influenced by the ego's fear of bringing back the memory of God. "Under the ego's dark foundation is the memory of God, and it is of this that you are really afraid. For this memory would instantly restore you to your proper place, and it is this place that you have sought to leave."[498] You are afraid of your attack thoughts, but much more afraid of love. "Your fear of attack is nothing compared to your fear of love. You would be willing to look even upon your savage wish to kill God's Son, if you did not believe that it saves you from love."[499] Your fear of love is so intense because it goes back to the separation when you first became afraid of your Father's Love. "For this wish [to reject your Father's Love] caused the separation, and you have protected it because you do not want the separation healed. You realize that, by removing the dark cloud that obscures it, your love for your Father would impel you to answer His Call and leap into Heaven. You believe that attack is salvation because it would prevent you from this."[500] In addition to your fear of God's Love, you are even more afraid of your own intense love for your Father. "For still deeper than the ego's foundation, and much stronger than it will ever be, is your intense and burning love of God, and His for you. This is what you really want to hide."[501]

Do you find it hard to express love verbally? "In honesty, is it not harder for you to say 'I love' than 'I hate'? You associate love with weakness and hatred with strength, and your own real power seems to you as your real weakness."[502] But what if you have learned in your spiritual seeking that your real power is in your love nature? In that case, perhaps you believe that the section of the Course titled "The Fear of Redemption" does not apply to you because you consider yourself to be a loving person who loves God. Many spiritual seekers will read this section and say initially that they do not fear redemption and do not fear God's Love. However, it is important to take into account that the fear of God's all-encompassing Love is in the part of your mind that is not in your conscious awareness because of denial.

Let's consider the following analogy: Imagine that you are an artist, and you are having a large exhibit that will display all of your best paintings. Your exhibit is open only to those whom you invite. Now imagine that you hear from a very reliable source that if you invite one particular guest, he will come to your exhibit and use a knife to destroy every one of your paintings. Knowing that this specific person would destroy all your life's work, would you invite this person to your exhibit? No, you would not invite him since you would be inviting destruction. In this analogy, who is this destructive guest whom you would not invite to the exhibit of your life's work? He is God! Your Father is reality. His divine Love dissolves all illusions just as light dispels darkness. Your Father only creates reality like Himself. Other than your extensions of love, everything you have "made" (not "created" with love) in this world is an illusion. Yet you love your illusions and are attached to them. You are afraid your illusory world that you have made will be destroyed by awakening in God's presence.

This analogy of you as an artist fearing the destruction of his art work explains the theme of this section about the fear of redemption. Your art work that God's Love would destroy is your whole idea of yourself— the idea that you are a body, that you are a mind limited by the size of your brain, and that you are an ego, a separate worldly person. God's Love would dispel all that you have made of yourself. What would be left is what He created that had been hidden from your awareness by what you made. God's Love would reveal that you are a formless spirit because your entire world of form would evaporate in His presence. What a vast gap there is between what you made in form and time and what you are in spirit and eternity! No matter how blissful you will be in your redemption in Heaven, it is not surprising that you are now afraid of the unknown as you cling to the world of very familiar appearances that you made. As a spiritual seeker, it is true that you consciously want Heaven at some future date, but right now you are afraid of the cost of losing everything you made and possess in time and space.

You are not only afraid of God's Love, but also afraid of your love for God. You are attached to what you made and are afraid of giving it up by recognizing your love for God that would dissolve the illusions you have made in your private mind. Your ego-based thought system is your means of denying both God's Love for you and your love for God.

> For you could not control your joyous response to the call of love if you heard it, and the whole world you thought you made would vanish. The Holy Spirit, then, seems to be attacking your fortress, for you would shut out God, and He does not will to be excluded.
>
> You have built your whole insane belief system because you think you would be helpless in God's Presence, and you would save yourself from His Love because you think it would crush you into nothingness. You are afraid it would sweep you away from yourself and make you little, because you believe that magnitude lies in defiance, and that attack is grandeur.[503]

You are afraid that you would abandon the world you made if you opened your awareness to God's all-encompassing Love for you.

> You think you have made a world God would destroy; and by loving Him, which you do, you would throw this world away, which you *would*. Therefore, you have used the world to cover your love, and the deeper you go into the blackness of the ego's foundation, the closer you come to the Love that is hidden there. *And it is this that frightens you.*[504]

Pride is a factor in your refusal to accept your true love nature that God gave you. Your pride makes you believe what you made is more valuable to you than what God created.

> You can accept insanity because you made it, but you cannot accept love because you did not. You would rather be a slave of the crucifixion than a Son of God in redemption. Your individual death seems more valuable than your living oneness, for what is given you is not so dear as what you made. You are more afraid of God than of the ego, and love cannot enter where it is not welcome. But hatred can, for it enters of its own volition and cares not for yours.[505]

Why might your fear of redemption prevent you from accepting the Atonement? You will want to accept the Atonement if you realize it will release you from guilt and the unsatisfying offerings of the ego. Yet you may decide to not accept the Atonement if you are afraid of salvation.

> The Atonement has always been interpreted as the release from guilt, and this is correct if it is understood. Yet even when I [Jesus] interpret it for you, you may reject it and do not accept it for yourself. You have perhaps recognized the futility of the ego and its offerings, but though you do not want them, you may not yet look upon the alternative with gladness. In the extreme, you are afraid of redemption and you believe it will kill you. Make no mistake about the depth of this fear. For you believe that, in the presence of truth, you might turn on yourself and destroy yourself.[506]

Why would you be afraid of redemption? Your most secret form of guilt goes back to the original separation when you first experienced guilt. That original guilt was the belief that you had attacked God and killed the perfect nature of the Christ, and so you are afraid of this secret being revealed. You are afraid that redemption attended by the return of God's Light would bring your "guilty secret" out into the open and you would be destroyed by the revealing of the darkness in your mind. But your fear of redemption is unwarranted because God's Light will release you to the freedom to accept what you already are as the invulnerable Christ. "Your 'guilty secret' is nothing, and if you will but bring it to the light, the light will dispel it. And then no dark cloud will remain between you and the remembrance of your Father, for you will remember His guiltless Son, who did not die because he is immortal."[507]

Although you might fear redemption, you have actually already been redeemed because Christ has never lost His awareness of the Father. In spite of being fearful of your attack on God being revealed, you have not really attacked God or the Christ in Heaven because God and His Son cannot be successfully attacked. "You have not attacked God and you do love Him. Can you change your reality? No one can will to destroy himself. When you think you are attacking yourself, it is a sure sign that you hate what you *think* you are."[508] You can hate what you imagine you are in this world of illusions, but that self-hate has not in any way changed your true nature as the invulnerable holy Son of God.

Jesus overcame the illusion of death, and his redemption was your redemption. "And you will see that you were redeemed with him [Jesus], and have never been separated from him. In this understanding lies your remembering, for it is the recognition of love without fear."[509] When you have fully recognized that Jesus has been redeemed, you will simultaneously recognize that you have been redeemed with him. "There will be great joy in Heaven on your homecoming, and the joy will be yours. For the redeemed son of man is the guiltless Son of God, and to recognize him *is* our redemption."[510]

How can you accept your redemption that Jesus has given to you with his redemption? The sign of redemption that Jesus has given you is the resurrection. This was an event in time that Jesus manifested to prove that he is still alive and death is an illusion. Also, the resurrection of Jesus established the Atonement. The way to accept your redemption given to you by Jesus is to accept the Atonement that corrects every error you have ever made and all the effects of all your errors.

One of the most powerful errors you have made is to believe that you are guilty. Guilt is self-hate that says you do not deserve love and do deserve punishment. If you invest in guilt, you will not believe that love is your true nature that cannot be lost by whatever mistakes you make in the world. "You have so little faith in yourself because you are unwilling to accept the fact that perfect love is in you."[511] If you find it difficult to trust in the perfect love already within you, then turn to the perfect love of God that Jesus offers to you. The resurrected Jesus invites you to abandon the self-hate of guilt by accepting the perfect love of the Atonement. You can also join your mind with the mind of Jesus as is described in the next section.

In addition to Jesus, the Holy Spirit can help you overcome your fear of redemption. Your fear of redemption means you are afraid of God's Love and afraid of your love for God. Many of your fears have been denied. You can heal what has been denied by bringing it out of hiding so the Holy Spirit can heal it. To bring healing to your mind, you must trade your self-made illusions for the reality of God's Love. "You must look upon your illusions and not keep them hidden, because they do not rest on their own foundation. In concealment they appear to do so, and thus they seem to be self-sustained. This is the fundamental illusion on which the others rest."[512] You must uncover your "loving mind" that is hidden by the illusions you made. "For beneath them [illusions], and concealed as long as they are hidden, is the loving mind that thought it made them in anger."[513] Your loving mind is in pain and needs healing. "And the pain in this mind is so apparent, when it is uncovered, that its need of healing cannot be denied. Not all the tricks and games you offer it can heal it, for here is the real crucifixion of God's Son."[514]

You normally think of the crucifixion of God's Son as being related only to Jesus, but the previous quotation states that your loving mind is continually being crucified by the thought that you have made what you had intended to be an angry attack directed toward your Father. This is the place of pain in your loving mind where you experience self-condemnation for your attack on God. It is the same place where healing happens. "Here is both his pain and his healing, for the Holy Spirit's vision is merciful and His remedy is quick. Do not hide suffering from His sight, but bring it gladly to Him. Lay before His eternal sanity all your hurt, and let Him heal you."[515] If you want to heal, you need to give your pain to the Holy Spirit and let Him heal it for you. "Do not leave any spot of pain hidden from His light, and search your mind carefully for any thoughts you may fear to uncover. For He will heal every little thought you have kept to hurt you and cleanse it of its littleness, restoring it to the magnitude of God."[516]

In the place in your mind where your pain is the greatest, there is also your "call for help." "Beneath all the grandiosity you hold so dear is your real call for help. For you call for love to your Father as your Father calls you to Himself. In that place which you have hidden, you will only to unite with the Father, in loving remembrance of Him."[517] How can you find the place in your mind where the "call for love" is? "You will find this place of truth as you see it in your brothers, for though they may deceive themselves, like you they long for the grandeur that is in them. And perceiving it you will welcome it, and it will be yours."[518] You will not be satisfied until you awaken to your true reality that is hidden by your illusions. "For grandeur is the right of God's Son, and no illusions can satisfy him or save him from what he is. Only his love is real, and he will be content only with his reality."[519]

By seeing the divine in your brother, you can become his savior, helping him release his illusions. "Save him from his illusions that you may accept the magnitude of your Father in peace and joy."[520] However, you cannot be selective with your love, which must be extended to everyone in order to truly be love. "But exempt no one from your love, or you will be hiding a dark place in your mind where the Holy Spirit is not welcome."[521] If you limit your love, you will limit your healing. "And thus you will exempt yourself from His healing power, for by not offering total love you will not be healed completely. Healing must be as complete as fear, for love cannot enter where there is one spot of fear to mar its welcome."[522]

ONE MIND AND ONE WILL WITH JESUS

~ o ~

Because Jesus became of one mind with the Holy Spirit, he can "bring the Holy Spirit down to you" if you invite this intervention:

> I have said already that I can reach up and bring the Holy Spirit down to you, but I can bring Him to you only at your own invitation. The Holy Spirit is in your right mind, as He was in mine. The Bible says, "May the mind be in you that was also in Christ Jesus," and uses this as a blessing. It is the blessing of miracle-mindedness. It asks that you may think as I thought, joining with me in Christ thinking.[523]

You can ask Jesus or the Holy Spirit to be your guide for navigating through this world and for awakening. Whichever one of these two you invite to be your guide, you can be certain that both of them will be included in your awakening process because Jesus and the Holy Spirit are of one Mind, one purpose, and one Will, joined with God the Father. Jesus offers you many options for you to allow him to help you to awaken from your dream of separation. "If you are willing to renounce the role of guardian of your thought system and open it to me [Jesus], I will correct it very gently and lead you back to God."[524] Jesus will teach you and live with you if you think with him. But you must not perceive him as merely a "larger ego," which would only engender fear in you. Every good teacher, such as Jesus, has the goal of "giving his students so much of his own learning that they will one day no longer need him."[525] Good teachers are patient and repeat their lessons until they are learned. Jesus says he is an "elder brother," who "can be entrusted with your body and your ego only because this enables you to not be concerned with them,"[526] so he can teach you their unimportance. Jesus wants you to be at peace and trust him. *"In this world you need not have tribulation because I [Jesus] have overcome the world."*[527] Since Jesus woke up from the dream of this world, he is in a unique position to help you awaken from your dream with the Holy Spirit's help.

In the first chapter of the Course, Jesus describes his relationship with you: "An elder brother [Jesus himself] is entitled to respect for his greater experience, and obedience for his greater wisdom. He is also entitled to love because he is a brother, and to devotion if he is devoted. It is only my devotion that entitles me to yours."[528] Since Jesus is your elder brother, he sees you as his equal in God and as having an equal potential for awakening from your illusions just as he did, "There is nothing about me that you cannot attain. I have nothing that does not come from God. The difference between us now is that I have nothing else. This leaves me in a state which is only potential in you."[529]

The role of Jesus in your awakening is to assist you because without him you could not bridge the current communication gap between you and God. "You stand below me and I stand below God. In the process of 'rising up,' I am higher because without me the distance between God and man would be too great for you to encompass. I bridge the distance as an elder brother to you on the one hand, and as a Son of God on the other. My devotion to my brothers has placed me in charge of the Sonship, which I render complete because I share it."[530]

Jesus says, "I am the Atonement. You have a role in the Atonement, which I will dictate to you."[531] Accepting the Atonement corrects all errors and their effects for the benefit of your awakening, but Jesus has a specific part to play in the Atonement that will be important to you.

> I am in charge of the process of Atonement, which I undertook to begin. When you offer a miracle to any of my brothers, you do it to *yourself* and me. The reason you come before me is that I do not need miracles for my own Atonement, but I stand at the end in case you fail temporarily. My part in the Atonement is the cancelling out of all errors that you could not otherwise correct. When you have been restored to the recognition of your original state, you naturally become part of the Atonement yourself.[532]

Jesus plays a crucial part in your awakening by fulfilling his unique role of "cancelling out all the errors you could not otherwise correct." Presumably, if Jesus did not play this vital role, you would be unable to awaken. Regardless of whatever relationship or lack of relationship you have had with Jesus in the past, the Course offers you an opportunity for looking at him differently. If you change your perception of Jesus, you may want to consider establishing a new and more meaningful relationship with him as your elder brother and personal guide.

Jesus helps you by walking with you on your journey of awakening. His companionship can be experienced literally by those who have faith in his presence and those who call upon his help and guidance. "In me [Jesus] you have already overcome every temptation that would hold you back. We walk together on the way to quietness that is the gift of God. Hold me dear, for what except your brothers can you need?"[533] You must find salvation by joining with your brother. "We will restore to you the peace of mind that we must find together. The Holy Spirit will teach you to awaken unto us and to yourself. This is the only real need to be fulfilled in time. Salvation from the world lies only here."[534]

Jesus needs your help to fulfill his role. "We cannot sing redemption's hymn alone. My task is not completed until I have lifted every voice with mine. And yet it is not mine, for as it is my gift to you, so was it the Father's gift to me, given me through His Spirit."[535] Singing the song of redemption together "will banish sorrow from the mind of God's most holy Son, where it cannot abide. Healing in time is needed, for joy cannot establish its eternal reign where sorrow dwells."[536] You seem to be in the world, but you really are asleep in Heaven right now while you dream of exile from your everlasting home. "You dwell not here, but in eternity. You travel but in dreams, while safe at home. Give thanks to every part of you that you have taught how to remember you. Thus does the Son of God give thanks unto his Father for his purity."[537]

Your strength is in your dependence upon God, just as the strength of Jesus relies upon his dependence upon God. "Of yourself you can do nothing, because of yourself you *are* nothing. I am nothing without the Father and you are nothing without me, because by denying the Father you deny yourself."[538] God is reality and life. Without God you would have no life and so you would not exist and literally be nothing. Also, your strength comes from your oneness with the entire Sonship. The ego-based belief in a separate mind and a separate will have weakened your mind and will. To correct this, Jesus wants to share his Mind with you. "Yet I do want to share my mind with you because we are of one Mind, and that Mind is ours. See only this Mind everywhere, because only this is everywhere and in everything."[539] This Mind you share with Jesus is the Mind of God. "Alone we can do nothing, but together our minds fuse into something whose power is far beyond the power of its separate parts. By not being separate, the Mind of God is established in ours and as ours. This Mind is invincible because it is undivided."[540] This Mind of God is the Mind of the Sonship expressing the undivided Will of God. Your will is the same as God's Will and the will of Jesus.

> The recognition of God is the recognition of yourself. There is no separation of God and His creation. You will realize this when you understand that there is no separation between your will and mine. Let the Love of God shine upon you by your acceptance of me. My reality is yours and His. By joining your mind with mine you are signifying your awareness that the Will of God is One.[541]

If you deny that your will is joined with the will of Jesus, you will be denying your own will since both your will and the will of Jesus are God's Will. "By the belief that your will is separate from mine, you are exempting yourself from the Will of God which *is* yourself."[542] Because you have imprisoned your will, you may be confused in your daily life about what choices to make that would be truly loving. You can ask the Holy Spirit to guide you to express God's Will, which is the wisest and most loving choice you would make yourself if you were aware of all the wisdom and love of your true nature in God. But in addition to receiving guidance from the Holy Spirit, you can also ask Jesus to guide you to do God's Will because he knows God's Will for you. "He has revealed it [God's Will for you] to me because I [Jesus] asked it of Him, and learned of what He had already given."[543] Thus a benefit of joining your mind with Jesus is that he will help you accept and express God's Will and not be confused by the ego. In particular, Jesus will show you the nature of your specific assignment in accomplishing the Atonement, and Jesus will show you what miracles to perform.

You and Jesus share your oneness with each other because you are both joined in the Oneness of God. "God's Oneness and ours are not separate, because His Oneness encompasses ours. To join with me is to restore His power to you because we are sharing it."[544] Jesus is aware of God's power within himself, so he makes you aware of God's power within you when you join with him. "I offer you only the recognition of His power in you, but in that lies all truth. As we unite, we unite with Him. Glory be to the union of God and His holy Sons! All glory lies in Them *because* They are united."[545] The joint will of the Sonship, which relies on the power of God, is your power that you draw upon as you join with Jesus. Joining with Jesus helps you to perform miracles together. "The miracles we do bear witness to the Will of the Father for His Son, and to our joy in uniting with His Will for us."[546]

If you join your mind and will with the mind and will of Jesus, the divine light of Jesus shines from his mind into your mind. His divine light shines away the darkness in your mind and awakens your awareness of your own divine light that is always with you. "Your mind is so powerful a light that you can look into theirs [your brothers' minds] and enlighten them, as I [Jesus] can enlighten yours."[547] By joining in the same divine light with Jesus, you can perform miracles of love in which you shine light into the minds of your brothers in whom you see holiness. "Your right mind sees only brothers, because it sees only in its own light. God has lit your mind Himself, and keeps your mind lit by His light because His light is what your mind is."[548] The light in which Jesus and you are joined is the divine Light of God Himself shining through you to others. "Then let the Holy One shine on you in peace, knowing that this and only this must be. His Mind shone on you in your creation and brought your mind into being. His Mind still shines on you and must shine through you. Your ego cannot prevent Him from shining on you, but it can prevent you from letting Him shine through you."[549]

It's difficult to release attachment to the ego, but joining with Jesus helps you release your ego-based identification. "When you unite with me you are uniting without the ego, because I have renounced the ego in myself and therefore cannot unite with yours. Our union is therefore the way to renounce the ego in you."[550] Jesus is perfectly aware of the truth within himself and within you. The ego cannot prevail against the truth and against your will that is joined with God's Will. "The truth in both of us is beyond the ego. Our success in transcending the ego is guaranteed by God, and I share this confidence for both of us and all of us. I bring God's peace back to all His children because I received it of Him for us all. Nothing can prevail against our united wills because nothing can prevail against God's."[551]

The ego will actively resist your union with Jesus. For example, if you experience fear, it is a sign that the ego is trying to interfere with your union with Jesus. "On this journey [with Jesus back to God] you have chosen me as your companion *instead* of the ego. Do not attempt to hold on to both, or you will try to go in different directions and will lose the way."[552] The ego doesn't have the power to prevent your union and journey with Jesus unless you give it that power. "Never accord the ego the power to interfere with the journey. It has none, because the journey is the way to what is true. Leave all illusions behind, and reach beyond all attempts of the ego to hold you back."[553] Jesus has totally overcome the ego so he can help you overcome the ego. "Reach, therefore, for my hand because you want to transcend the ego. My strength will never be wanting, and if you choose to share it you will do so. I give it willingly and gladly, because I need you as much as you need me."[554]

If you are considering welcoming Jesus into your awareness as your partner on your journey back to God, perhaps the most important thing to remember is that he loves you. "I [Jesus] love you for the truth in you, as God does. Your deceptions may deceive you, but they cannot deceive me. Knowing what you are, I cannot doubt you. I hear only the Holy Spirit in you, Who speaks to me through you."[555] Jesus is your elder brother, but he knows you are his equal in God's eyes even if you are unaware of your equality with him. "I have made it perfectly clear that I am like you and you are like me, but our fundamental equality can be demonstrated only through joint decision."[556] Jesus wants you to keep the focus of your identity on what comes to you from God as your Creator. This includes valuing and identifying with the expressions of love that you manifest with God's Love flowing through you. Jesus also teaches you to let go of the illusions you have made by yourself apart from God's Love. The purpose of Jesus is to help you return you to the full awareness of your true nature and true function as the holy Son of God and co-creator with God.

The world tempts you to believe you are alone. Jesus helps you to know that you can never be alone. The world is "an illusion of isolation, maintained by fear of the same loneliness that *is* its illusion"[557] because this world represents a denial of reality. Workbook Lesson 61 is "I am the light of the world." It may be easy to accept that Jesus is the light of the world, but Jesus wants to remind you that you are also united with him as the light of the world. As the light of the world, Jesus remains with you until the end of the world. "If I am with you in the loneliness of the world, the loneliness is gone. You cannot maintain the illusion of loneliness if you are not alone."[558] Jesus as "the light of the world" is not merely a metaphor. The truth that Jesus is light is not surprising when you consider that you share your true Identity with Jesus and, in fact, "you are light."[559] You are not fully aware of your true nature as light, but Jesus is fully aware of himself as being light.

The light of Jesus actually shines into your mind if you welcome him into your mind dispelling the darkness of misperceptions and loneliness. "Light does not attack darkness, but it does shine it away. If my light goes with you everywhere, you shine it away with me. The light becomes ours, and you cannot abide in darkness any more than darkness can abide wherever you go."[560] Light and love are two sides of the same coin, so inviting the light of Jesus into your mind is the same as inviting his love into your mind. The most effective time to invite the light and love of Jesus into your mind is during prayer and meditation. This quiet time of heightened awareness enables you to focus your mind and your will upon your desire to join with Jesus, who is a part of you just as you are a part of him. Jesus wants you to remember him not as a historical figure in the past, but rather as he is now in his true Identity. The reason why Jesus wants you to remember him is that doing so enables you to accept your own true nature that he shares with you because you are the Son of God. "The remembrance of me [Jesus] is the remembrance of yourself, and of Him Who sent me to you."[561]

You have forgotten your wholeness as the one Christ that you share equally with all your brothers and sisters. Jesus is part of the one Christ and the whole of the one Christ, just as you are. The difference between Jesus and you is that he is completely aware of his Christ nature and his sameness and equality with you. This perfect awareness is why he is the savior. His role is to help you restore the awareness of your Christ nature. Jesus helps you restore this awareness since his resurrection restored this awareness to his own mind and made this complete awareness available to every part of the whole Sonship.

With his resurrection, Jesus was the first part of the Sonship that joined perfectly with God's Will. "You were in darkness until God's Will was done completely by any part of the Sonship. When this was done, it was perfectly accomplished by all."[562] It is easy to believe that Jesus overcame the world, but it is hard to understand how his union with God's Will was "perfectly accomplished by all," including by you. You perfectly overcame the world with Jesus because you are already one with him, whether you realize it or not. "One brother is all brothers. Every mind contains all minds, for every mind is one."[563]

Since the overcoming of the world by Jesus is your achievement as well as his, why haven't you already awakened to your true nature just as he has? Though Jesus accomplished the perfect union of the Sonship with God's Will, you can still refuse to accept his gift of perfect love. Although Jesus has overcome the world on the behalf of the whole Sonship, his mission is still salvation because you have yet to join your will with his will, which is God's Will just as your true will is God's Will. "My mission was simply to unite the will of the Sonship with the Will of the Father by being aware of the Father's Will myself. This is the awareness I came to give you, and your problem in accepting it is the problem of this world."[564] Salvation is dispelling the illusory idea that your will is different than God's Will. "Dispelling it [your problem of accepting God's Will as your will] is salvation, and in this sense I *am* the salvation of the world."[565] Jesus is your savior because he embodies the union of the will of the Sonship with the Will of God. Welcoming the mind of Jesus into your mind means you want to accept God's Will as your will. "If you will accept the fact that I am with you, you are denying the world and accepting God. My will is His, and your decision to hear me is the decision to hear His Voice and abide in His Will."[566]

Your will is as powerful as the will of Jesus. "God's Sons are equal in will, all being the Will of their Father. This is the only lesson I came to teach."[567] But if you listen to the ego and exert your will in the illusory attempt to oppose God's Will, you will imprison your will and imprison yourself by denying your true nature. Jesus can't oppose your decision to imprison your will. "Your will is as free as mine, and God Himself would not go against it. I cannot will what God does not will. I can offer my strength to make yours invincible, but I cannot oppose your decision without competing with it and thereby violating God's Will for you."[568] Jesus offers you his strength as you participate with him in the Atonement. "I have said before that I am in charge of the Atonement. This is only because I completed my part in it as a man, and can now complete it through others. My chosen channels cannot fail, because I will lend them my strength as long as theirs is wanting."[569]

Jesus, who knows who he is as the Christ, always remembers you to help you remember who you are as the Christ. "I will always remember you, and in my remembrance of you lies your remembrance of yourself. In our remembrance of each other lies our remembrance of God. And in this remembrance lies your freedom because your freedom is in Him."[570] Jesus asks you to join with his gratitude. "Join, then, with me in praise of Him and you whom He created. This is our gift of gratitude to Him, which He will share with all His creations, to whom He gives equally whatever is acceptable to Him. Because it is acceptable to Him it is the gift of freedom, which is His Will for all His Sons. By offering freedom you will be free."[571] God does not need your gratitude for

Himself, but your gratitude opens your mind to your love for Him and your love for every part of the Sonship.

You will find your freedom as you offer freedom to every brother. "Freedom is the only gift you can offer to God's Sons, being an acknowledgment of what they are and what He is. Freedom is creation, because it is love."[572] Since freedom is love, if you don't offer freedom, you don't offer love. Thus you deny your own freedom and love nature. "Therefore, when you seek to imprison anyone, including yourself, you do not love him and you cannot identify with him. If you imprison yourself you are losing sight of your true identification with me and with the Father."[573] Your identity is in both God and the Sonship. "Your identification is with the Father *and* the Son. It cannot be with One and not the Other. If you are part of One you must be part of the Other, because They are One."[574] You are part of the Holy Trinity's oneness. "The Holy Trinity is holy *because* It is One. If you exclude yourself from this union, you are perceiving the Holy Trinity as separated. You must be included in It, because It is everything."[575] Because the Holy Trinity is everything, you must be included. "Unless you take your place in It and fulfill your function as part of It, the Holy Trinity is as bereft as you are. No part of It can be imprisoned if Its truth is to be known."[576]

To have the peace and union that Jesus offers, you must help others find peace and union. "As God sent me to you so will I send you to others. And I will go to them with you, so we can teach them peace and union."[577] To have peace, you must give peace and become a healer just as Jesus is a healer. Jesus teaches that "healing is a collaborative venture."[578] Jesus asks you to join him in healing. "Healing reflects our joint will."[579] Healing requires union. "Healing is the way in which the separation is overcome. Separation is overcome by union. It cannot be overcome by separating."[580] You must be definite about your decision to join. "The decision to unite must be unequivocal, or the mind itself is divided and not whole. Your mind is the means by which you determine your own condition, because mind is the mechanism of decision. It is the power by which you separate or join, and experience pain or joy accordingly."[581] Jesus calls you to be a teacher of God.

> Blessed are you who teach with me. Our power comes not of us, but of our Father. In guiltlessness we know Him, as He knows us guiltless. I stand within the circle [of Atonement], calling you to peace. Teach peace with me, and stand with me on holy ground. Remember for everyone your Father's power that He has given him. Believe not that you cannot teach His perfect peace. Stand not outside, but join with me within. Fail not the only purpose to which my teaching calls you. Restore to God His Son as He created him, by teaching him his innocence.[582]

YOUR ROLE OF
BEING A TEACHER

~ • ~

The previous sections emphasized the Holy Spirit and Jesus for their ability to teach you, but now let's consider another teacher whom you may not have noticed. Before discussing this unrecognized teacher, here is a question for you to ask yourself: *Do I have two selves in conflict with each other?* The most common answer to this question is: *Yes, one self is the false self of the ego, and the other self is my true Self.* At first glance, this seems to be the teaching of the Course, but that is not true. You only seem to be a true Self in conflict with a false self called the "ego." If you were two selves, it would mean that both selves would have to be real. But you are only one Self. The other idea of yourself is not real. What you call your "ego" or little "self" is not part of God, and so does not exist. The self that does not exist cannot be in conflict with anything that is real. "You are not two selves in conflict. What is beyond God? If you who hold Him and whom He holds are the universe, all else must be outside, where nothing is."[583] Your true Self is the whole Christ as well as your part-ness of Christ in the Sonship.

So, who is your teacher whom you may not have recognized? Your Self, Whom you share with the entire Sonship, has been your unknown teacher. Since you are this Self, you have been teaching yourself. As the wholeness of Christ with all of His parts, you have taught that only God and what is part of God is real and all else is unreal. Your whole Self has taught parts of Christ, and these parts are your witnesses to your teaching of what is real and what is unreal. "You [as the whole Christ] have taught this, and from far off in the universe, yet not beyond yourself, the witnesses to your teaching have gathered to help you learn. Their gratitude has joined with yours and God's to strengthen your faith in what you taught."[584] In your true nature as the Self, you have taught the truth, but in your current ego identification, you have now rejected what you taught. "For what you [as the Self] taught is true. Alone, you [identified with your ego] stand outside your teaching and apart from it."[585] But with the witnesses to what you taught as the whole Christ, you must learn that the whole Christ has been teaching you to accept your true Self. "But with them [the witnesses to your teaching] you must learn that you but taught yourself, and learned from the conviction you shared with them."[586]

Based on the idea that your true Self has been your teacher all along, you have not learned as much as you, as your true Self, have taught. Thus you haven't received the reward of your teaching that would bring peace and joy to your mind. The Course section called "The Reward of Teaching" recommends that you learn what you, as your true Self, have taught and gain the benefits of teaching and learning. "This year you will begin to learn, and make learning commensurate with teaching. You have chosen this by your own willingness to teach. Though you seemed to suffer for it, the joy of teaching will yet be yours."[587] You, as your true Self, teach yourself. It is appropriate for you, as the learner of your own teaching, to offer gratitude and joy back to yourself for your teaching of yourself. "For the joy of teaching is in the learner, who offers it to the teacher in gratitude, and shares it with him."[588]

When you in your ego identification learn more about your true Self as your teacher, you will become grateful for your true Self. "As you learn, your gratitude to your Self, Who teaches you what He is, will grow and help you honor Him."[589] As you increase your recognition of your true Self and feel more gratitude to Him, you will learn to trust in Him and His God-given strengths. "And you will learn His power and strength and purity, and love Him as His Father does. His Kingdom has no limits and no end, and there is nothing in Him that is not perfect and eternal."[590] The Self, including His Kingdom, is who you are now, although now unrecognized. "All this is *you*, and nothing outside of this *is* you."[591] You can learn to trust in the power of the Self Who will help you to reach the bridge of the real world and to then proceed to your Home in Heaven. "Have no fear that the attraction of those who stand on the other side and wait for you will not draw you safely across. For you will come where you would be, and where your Self awaits you."[592]

In addition to your unknown teacher as your Self, you are always teaching by the example of how you live your life. Also, when you learn to apply spiritual principles in your daily life, Jesus in the center of the circle of Atonement calls you to join him by accepting your guiltlessness. Jesus also asks you to be a teacher of God. As a teacher of God, your function is to see your brother's holiness and welcome him to join you within the circle of Atonement where you can give him your embrace of love. As you give the blessing of the Atonement, you will simultaneously receive the blessing of Atonement, which is an experience of sharing and union in the perfect Love of God.

A teacher of God who shares the Course principles is anyone who chooses to be one. His choice implies he has already read the Text and Manual for Teachers and also completed the one year of Workbook lessons. He expresses his understanding by making a deliberate choice to join with another in a holy relationship. The choice of being a teacher of God invariably requires the perceiving of common interests and a common purpose, which is the basis for all holy relationships.

A teacher of God is anyone who chooses to be one. His qualifications consist solely in this; somehow, somewhere he has made a deliberate choice in which he did not see his interests as apart from someone else's.[593]

The teacher of God improves his ability to make decisions through giving up judgment. By giving up his reliance on his own judgment, he increases his ability to listen to the Voice for God, the Holy Spirit. The teacher of God always turns to the Holy Spirit and asks Him to decide for God for him and trusts in His answer to every question. Then he follows the Holy Spirit's guidance in all his actions.

As the teacher of God advances in his training, he learns one lesson with increasing thoroughness. He does not make his own decisions; he asks his Teacher for His answer, and it is this he follows as his guide for action. This becomes easier and easier, as the teacher of God learns to give up his own judgment. The giving up of judgment, the obvious prerequisite for hearing God's Voice, is usually a fairly slow process, not because it is difficult, but because it is apt to be perceived as personally insulting.[594]

The teacher of God knows he must learn to give up his judgment because he realizes why judgments by him cannot be relied upon for accuracy. He remembers the many times in the past when his judgments were totally wrong. The teacher of God knows that judgments based on his own personal viewpoint, coming from his ego perspective, are merely illusions. When he gives up making his own judgments, he is honestly seeing the illusory nature of his own limited ego. He does not judge even those who are judging him, since he sees the judgments of others as a call for love, and he gives them the love they are calling for instead of his judgment. The teacher of God accepts that no one can have the all-encompassing awareness that would be required to always make judgments that are correct and fair to everyone.

The teacher of God knows that accurate judgment is impossible for him and only the Holy Spirit is qualified to make totally accurate judgments. "Recognizing that judgment was always impossible for him, he no longer attempts it. This is no sacrifice. On the contrary, he puts himself in a position where judgment *through* him rather than *by* him can occur."[595] Judgment that happens *through* the teacher of God is inspired by Holy Spirit. This judgment affirms that false beliefs in sin and guilt have never changed the perfect holiness of the Son of God.

The aim of our curriculum, unlike the goal of the world's learning, is the recognition that judgment in the usual sense is impossible. This is not an opinion but a fact. In order to judge anything rightly, one would have to be fully aware of an inconceivably wide range of things; past, present and to come. One would have to recognize in advance all the effects of his judgments on everyone and everything involved in them in any way. And one would have to be certain there is no distortion in his perception, so that his judgment would be wholly fair to everyone on whom it rests now and in the future. Who is in a position to do this? Who except in grandiose fantasies would claim this for himself?[596]

The teacher of God puts the Course principles into practice as he completes the one year of structured daily Workbook lessons. This is his solid foundation for future less structured daily practice. The Manual recommends that the teacher of God has quiet times every morning and evening to connect with God. The term "quiet times" is another term for meditation practices that usually focus on one thought of God. As was learned in Workbook lessons, the teacher of God sits erect for meditation practices and does not lie down, which can induce drowsiness. "Perhaps the one generalization that can be made is this; as soon as possible after waking take your quiet time, continuing a minute or two after you begin to find it difficult."[597] The Course recommends two daily quiet times for the teacher of God.

If possible, however, just before going to sleep is a desirable time to devote to God. It sets your mind into a pattern of rest, and orients you away from fear. If it is expedient to spend this time earlier, at least be sure that you do not forget a brief period,— not more than a moment will do,— in which you close your eyes and think of God.[598]

Before the teacher of God can allow healing to happen through him, he needs to focus on healing his own mind. When he experiences the least bit of irritation, it is helpful for the teacher of God to realize he has made an incorrect interpretation originating from his ego. Then he needs to ask the Holy Spirit for guidance and allow His judgment to replace the false judgment he had previously made. This enables his mind to be healed. When the mind of the teacher of God is healed, the mind of his pupil is automatically healed at the same time.

In order to heal, it thus becomes essential for the teacher of God to let all his own mistakes be corrected. If he senses even the faintest hint of irritation in himself as he responds to anyone, let him instantly realize that he has made an interpretation that is not true. Then let him turn within to his eternal Guide, and let Him judge what the response should be. So is he healed, and in his healing is his pupil healed with him.[599]

To be a healer, meaning a miracle worker, the teacher of God has the one required responsibility of accepting the Atonement for himself. By accepting the Atonement, the teacher of God allows his own mistakes to be forgiven, and he releases inner self-condemnation. The forgiveness he receives and his loss of self-condemnation are passed along to his pupil through the action of the Holy Spirit, Who unites all the minds of the sleeping Sons of God. Accepting the Atonement is the only function of a teacher of God. At first, the teacher of God will bring healing to a few others and accept the Atonement only in some situations. "The offer of Atonement is universal. It is equally applicable to all individuals in all circumstances."[600] As the teacher of God makes progress, he applies the acceptance of Atonement for himself to more and more situations. Finally, he will generalize his learning to apply the acceptance of the Atonement for himself to every single situation and problem at all times.

The progress of the teacher of God may be slow or rapid, depending on whether he recognizes the Atonement's inclusiveness, or for a time excludes some problem areas from it. In some cases, there is a sudden and complete awareness of the perfect applicability of the lesson of the Atonement to all situations, but this is comparatively rare. The teacher of God may have accepted the function God has given him long before he has learned all that his acceptance holds out to him. It is only the end that is certain. Anywhere along the way, the necessary realization of inclusiveness may reach him.[601]

To make progress, the teacher of God needs to learn that forgiveness is healing. "That forgiveness is healing needs to be understood, if the teacher of God is to make progress."[602] The teacher of God knows that every sick person has made a decision to be sick, while not being consciously aware of that decision. But analyzing the ego that made the choice for sickness is not the job of the healer. To heal others the teacher of God must know for certain who is in need of healing. The ego is not this "who" since the ego is nothing but an illusion that does not have any reality. The "who" that needs healing is the sleeping Son of God. In order to facilitate healing through the Holy Spirit, the teacher of God overlooks what is not the Son of God and looks for the Son of God. The process of overlooking and looking is forgiveness. The body and the part of the mind ruled by the ego are overlooked. Looking for the Son of God is accomplished by seeing only the face of Christ, which is identical to accepting the Atonement. Welcoming the face of Christ and inviting the Atonement are exactly the same because they both bring the same result of correcting all errors and healing all perception.

> He [the teacher of God] overlooks the mind *and* body [of the person needing healing], seeing only the face of Christ shining in front of him, correcting all mistakes and healing all perception. Healing is the result of the recognition, by God's teacher, of who it is that is in need of healing. This recognition has no special reference. It is true of all things that God created. In it are all illusions healed.[603]

The teacher of God's most important characteristic is trust. Here are stages of learning trust that prepare him to awaken in Heaven:

1. A Period of Undoing — This is a time of change in which the teacher of God may experience the pain of giving up things that seem worthwhile, but are not really valuable. There is the recognition that changes are always helpful.

2. A Period of Sorting Out — The teacher of God makes difficult decisions based on whether choices increase or hinder helpfulness.

3. A Period of Relinquishment — This stage starts with the teacher of God feeling conflicted because he is giving up things while mistakenly thinking he is making a sacrifice. Later in this stage, he finds out his apparent sacrifices were really blessings in disguise.

4. A Period of Settling Down — This is a relatively peaceful time of respite in which the teacher of God consolidates his learning. He increases his ability to generalize his learning to new situations and relationships.

5. A Period of Unsettling — This is a period of reassessment in which he finds out he did not really know what was valuable and valueless. He must ask for only what is truly valuable and learn to give up all judgment.

6. A Period of Achievement — In this stage, there is peace of mind because learning has been consolidated. Here the teacher of God maintains consistency of thought and has learned to generalize his learning to all situations and all relationships. His mind has become a reflection of Heaven, and so he has successfully prepared his mind for the final step of awakening in his Home in the Arms of God.

RECOGNIZING THAT
TRUTH IS TRUE

≈ ● ≈

Using your physical eyes, you perceive only the three-dimensional world where you encounter truth and illusion, and both appear to be equally real. If you can open your mind to a world of true perceptions and no false perceptions, you will be able to perceive the real world. The full acceptance of only truth that rejects all beliefs in illusions is the condition of reality. The perception of the real world is a preparation for meeting the condition of awakening to the reality of Heaven, where there are no illusions. "The real world can actually be perceived. All that is necessary is a willingness to perceive nothing else. For if you perceive both good and evil, you are accepting both the false and the true and making no distinction between them."[604]

If you do perceive the real world, you will not be accepting the ego's perception because the ego cannot perceive only good without evil and only truth without illusion. "The ego may see some good, but never only good. That is why its perceptions are so variable. It does not reject goodness entirely, for that you could not accept. But it always adds something that is not real to the real, thus confusing illusion and reality."[605] Perceptions can't be partly true and partly false, because truth can't also be untrue. "Truth must be all-inclusive, if it be the truth at all. Accept no opposites and no exceptions, for to do so is to contradict the truth entirely."[606] The combination of the true and false does not contain the wholeness that is characteristic of truth. If you try to add an illusion to the truth, you will lose the awareness of the integrity of truth being entirely truthful. "For perceptions cannot be partly true. If you believe in truth and illusion, you cannot tell which is true."[607]

The separation from the awareness of Heaven was caused by your desire to be self-sufficient by creating without God and unlike God and therefore unlike your own true nature. It is impossible to create without God since God is present within everything that is real. Excluding God is excluding reality. But your separation succeeded only in making (not creating) illusions that are self-deceptive, producing a world that does not exist except in your imagination. Everything God creates is loving. What you made is sometimes loving and sometimes unloving. Because you have made and value a combination of unreal illusions and loving expressions of truth that reflect reality, you can't tell the basic difference between illusions and the truth. "To establish your personal autonomy you tried to create unlike your Father, believing that what you made is capable of being unlike Him. Yet everything true *is* like Him."[608]

The significance of the real world is that it stands between Heaven having only truth and your world of combining illusions and truth. In this very unique position, the real world is your bridge to Heaven. "Perceiving only the real world will lead you to the real Heaven, because it will make you capable of understanding it."[609]

Before you can accept the reality of Heaven and fully embrace the reality of God as your Father, the condition you must meet is that you learn that you can deny the opposite of good and deny the opposite of truth. Thus you can recognize the condition in which there are, in fact, no opposites. This condition in which there are not opposites is the real world of only loving thoughts and true perceptions and no opposing unloving thoughts or false perceptions. Illusions are not the opposite of truth or reality, because illusions do not exist. The only power illusions have is to deny that truth has no opposite and reality has no opposite. "The perception of goodness is not knowledge, but the denial of the opposite of goodness enables you to recognize a condition in which opposites do not exist. And this *is* the condition of knowledge."[610]

The condition of being aware of reality is the same as the condition of knowledge, which is the awareness of no opposites. "Without this awareness [of no opposites] you have not met its conditions, and until you do you will not know it is yours already."[611] You still have the inner awareness of no opposites in your whole mind that never left Heaven because the separation was merely an illusion of separation maintained only by your false belief you have separated yourself from God. Only a small part of your whole mind in Heaven is devoted to the ego that persists in believing in opposites. "You have made many ideas that you have placed between yourself and your Creator, and these beliefs are the world as you perceive it. Truth is not absent here, but it is obscure. You do not know the difference between what you have made and what God created, and so you do not know the difference between what you have made and what *you* have created."[612]

In the Course, the word "make" refers to your fabricating of illusions that are untrue, unreal, and unloving. The word "create" refers to your true perceptions that accurately reflect the truth, reality, and love of Heaven. You cannot distinguish between the illusions you make without truth and love and the true perceptions you create with love. But your confusion is replaced by clarity when you perceive the real world that consists of only loving thoughts and true perceptions you have created. The real world has no perceptions you have made without God. "To believe that you can perceive the real world is to believe that you can know yourself. You can know God because it is His Will to be known."[613] The Holy Spirit has preserved the real world so you can perceive it as your steppingstone to awakening in Heaven to realize you have never left. "The real world is all that the Holy Spirit has saved for you out of what you have made, and to perceive only this is salvation, because it is the recognition that reality is only what is true."[614]

The real world is a place of transition from sleeping in the illusions of the world and to awakening in Heaven. Two stages of the process of awakening related to the real world have been described previously. Stage 1 involves seeing the blazing light from a distance. Stage 2 is merging with the blazing light being seen at close range. The image of the blazing can be perceived in four different ways. If it is called the face of Christ, it is perceived as love and as the symbol of forgiveness. If it is called the vision of the Son of God, it is perceived as light. If it is called the circle of Atonement, it is perceived as error corrected and truth revealed. If it is perceived as the resurrection of the body of Jesus transformed into blazing light, it is perceived as life.

The face of Christ, the circle of Atonement, the vision of the Son of God, and the resurrected body of Jesus transformed into blazing light are four names for the single image that must be seen for the memory of God to return. This single image contains all four qualities of love, light, truth, and life, but only as reflections of these qualities as they exist in the reality of Heaven. Love, Light, Truth, and Life are the qualities of God, so the reflections of these qualities call to mind the memory of God Himself to anyone who sees the single image of blazing light in the second dimension.

In the illusory three-dimensional world, love seems to have fear as its equally believable opposite. Light seems to have darkness as its equally believable opposite. Truth appears to have illusions based on false perception as its equally believable opposite. Life seems to have death as its equally believable opposite.

In contrast to the third dimension, the qualities of love, light, truth, and life all have one outstanding aspect that is the reason why they are all reflections of God and Heaven. Their one common characteristic is that they have no opposites. Thus the love, light, truth, and life of the second dimension are so much like the Love, Light, Truth, and Life of Heaven that the transfer from these reflections to reality can be made. Then God can take the final step of awakening His Beloved Son in whom He is well pleased even in his dream of exile.

I have already explained that it is appropriate to be in awe when you have a direct experience of God in revelation. But you must make the necessary preparations beforehand so that awe is not mistaken for fear in which case seeing the blazing light could be traumatic. I shared that I had such a traumatic experience. Also, there is a friend of mine who told me that he had a similar experience. The next paragraph is a reprint from my autobiography, *Memory Walk in the Light*:

The first day there [at the Zen center], I met Joel, who invited me to move into a house near the center, where he and five other members lived. Joel told me that one day while traveling in Mexico, he was meditating facing a wall with his eyes partially opened (one way to practice Zen meditation). "Suddenly," he said, "a large swirling mass of light appeared in front of me and moved toward me. I was thrown into a state of panic, and the light disappeared. For a while I was afraid to meditate again. That's why I came here. I decided that I needed to find a qualified roshi, instead of trying to do it all on my own."[615]

Joel's experience is an example of the fear of redemption that is also the fear of God's Will and of His Love. The Course recommends preparation before having a direct experience of God in revelation. That means that there must be necessary preparation for seeing the blazing light of the real world that leads to the direct experience of God. This preparation involves various ways of overcoming the fear of God by opening to receive and to express His Love. Through living a life of practicing the principles of the Course, you will be prepared for the moment of truth in which you will make the single worthy choice that will bring your awakening. It will be your choice of truth instead of illusions. This is an easy choice because having practiced the Course, you will understand that truth really has no opposite.

> Complexity is not of God. How could it be, when all He knows is One? He knows of one creation, one reality, one truth and but one Son. Nothing conflicts with oneness. How, then, could there be complexity in Him? What is there to decide? For it is conflict that makes choice possible. The truth is simple; it is one, without an opposite. And how could strife enter in its simple presence and bring complexity where oneness is? The truth makes no decisions, for there is nothing to decide. And only if there were could choosing be a necessary step in the advance toward oneness. What is everything leaves room for nothing else. Yet is this magnitude beyond the scope of this curriculum. Nor is it necessary we dwell on anything that cannot be immediately grasped.[616]

In this world, you only see illusions and so you occupy your mind with the meaningless choosing between valueless illusions. Yet, as you enter the real world, you will make the inevitable and meaningful choice of truth instead of illusion. The real world is not a place in the usual sense. The real world is a region of thought where truth and illusion are seen side by side so that you can accept truth and release illusion.

The real world is also called the "forgiven world" that lets you release the illusion of the past, where fear, sin, and guilt seem to be. "Forgiveness is the great release from time. It is the key to learning that the past is over."[617] When you enter this forgiven world, your mind alternates between focusing on the past and experiencing the present. "Now you are shifting back and forth between the past and present. Sometimes the past seems real, as if it *were* the present."[618] Entering the real world, you hear the shadow voices of the past, yet you question their messages of guilt. "Voices from the past are heard and then are doubted. You are like to one who still hallucinates, but lacks conviction in what he perceives."[619] In the real world, you make the transition from darkness to light, from fear to love, and from guilt to guiltlessness. "This is the borderland between the worlds, the bridge between the past and present. Here the shadow of the past remains, but still a present light is dimly recognized. Once it is seen, this light can never be forgotten. It must draw you from the past into the present, where you really are."[620] This "present light" it the blazing light of the face of Christ.

At this region of transition, called the real world, the borderland, or the bridge, you will be able to see truth and illusions right next to each other, when you are accustomed to seeing only illusions next to each other in the three-dimensional world. Deciding between equally unreal choices is so familiar to you that choosing between truth and illusions in the real world at first will bring a period of confusion. Before seeing the image of the real world in Stage 1 and before merging with the light in Stage 2 to remember God, you will probably experience a time of disorientation in the real world. This temporary disorientation is related to your attachment to body identification before being ready to cross the bridge. "For a time the body is still seen, but not exclusively, as it is seen here. The little spark that holds the Great Rays within it is also visible, and this spark cannot be limited long to littleness."[621]

After you cross the bridge, you will see the blazing light of the Great Rays as you perceive the image of the face of Christ at a distance during Stage 1 of awakening. During Stage 2 of awakening, you will merge with the Great Rays of blazing light, and your body awareness will entirely disappear. "For in seeing them [the Great Rays] the body would disappear, because its value would be lost. And so your whole investment in seeing it [body identification] would be withdrawn from it."[622] Your preoccupation with body identification is briefly challenging and disorienting before crossing the bridge, but this attachment to the body is resolved after crossing the bridge. "Once you have crossed the bridge, the value of the body is so diminished in your sight that you will see no need at all to magnify it. For you will realize that the only value the body has is to enable you to bring your brothers to the bridge with you, and to be released together there."[623]

Fortunately, the period of disorientation before crossing the bridge is only a very temporary time. During this confusing time, you are giving up your old frame of reference based on ego-based worldly thinking and opening your mind to the Holy Spirit's frame of reference that will bring truth to your mind. You will especially be challenged by the need to let go of your former investment in the illusion of specialness and your former special relationships. But you will make a new investment in divine love based on true union with God and the Sonship.

> In the transition there is a period of confusion, in which a sense of actual disorientation may occur. But fear it not, for it means only that you have been willing to let go your hold on the distorted frame of reference that seemed to hold your world together. This frame of reference is built around the special relationship. Without this illusion there could be no meaning you would still seek here.[624]

God is gracious, so you will not see the image of the blazing light prematurely before you are fully prepared to embrace God and His Love. Thus you will be given the time you need in the real world to make the adjustment in your mind that will allow you to overcome your disorientation.

> Fear not that you will be abruptly lifted up and hurled into reality. Time is kind, and if you use it on behalf of reality, it will keep gentle pace with you in your transition. The urgency is only in dislodging your mind from its fixed position here. This will not leave you homeless and without a frame of reference. The period of disorientation, which precedes the actual transition, is far shorter than the time it took to fix your mind so firmly on illusions. Delay will hurt you now more than before, only because you realize it *is* delay, and that escape from pain is really possible. Find hope and comfort, rather than despair, in this: You could not long find even the illusion of love in any special relationship here. For you are no longer wholly insane, and you would soon recognize the guilt of self-betrayal for what it is.[625]

This world is the first part of the hallucination of time and death, and the real world is the second part of this hallucination. "The real world is the second part of the hallucination time and death are real, and have existence that can be perceived."[626] The real world is not real, but it is an illusion that perfectly reflects reality. This illusory reflection of Heaven offers you salvation from all illusions. The real world reflects Heaven because it contains *total perception* of only perceptions of love, light, truth, and life, without perceptions of fear, darkness, falsehood, and death. Here in the real world, total perception meets knowledge. Here perception ceases at the gateway of Heaven and the total awareness of knowledge remains in Heaven, as it has always been while it was hidden from your awareness.

This is the journey's end. We have referred to it as the real world. And yet there is a contradiction here, in that the words imply a limited reality, a partial truth, a segment of the universe made true. This is because knowledge makes no attack upon perception. They are brought together, and only one continues past the gate where oneness is. Salvation is a borderland where place and time and choice have meaning still, and yet it can be seen that they are temporary, out of place, and every choice has been already made. [627]

To pass through the borderland, which is the real world, and to awaken in Heaven, you must decide for truth and against illusion. But can you really choose between what exists and what does not exist? "The truth makes no decisions, for there is nothing to decide between." [628] Your *apparent* decision can only be the "re"-"cognition" of your true nature that has always been true and the acceptance of the unreality of the ego that has never been true. "To recognize means to 'know again,' implying that you knew before." [629]

> Nothing the Son of God believes can be destroyed. But what is truth to him must be brought to the last comparison that he will ever make; the last evaluation that will be possible, the final judgment upon this world. It is the judgment of the truth upon illusion, of knowledge on perception: "It has no meaning, and does not exist." This is not your decision. It is but a simple statement of a simple fact. But in this world there are no simple facts, because what is the same and what is different remain unclear. The one essential thing to make a choice at all is this distinction. And herein lies the difference between the worlds. In this one, choice is made impossible. In the real world is choosing simplified. [630]

Preparation has been emphasized as necessary prior to accessing the real world and seeing the blazing light of the second dimension. The Course is designed to provide this preparation by teaching you to identify the difference between the real and the unreal. "This difference is the learning goal this course has set." [631] In fact, the introduction to the Course sets you off on the right track with what might be called its theme: "*This course can therefore be summed up very simply in this way: Nothing real can be threatened. Nothing unreal exists.*" [632]

The idea that "truth is true, and nothing else is true" seems much too obvious to devote to learning. Yet if you consider what happened in the separation, you can see why "truth is true" is not so obvious. In the separation, the sleeping parts of the Son of God made a dream world where they could not just reject God but also reject the fact that "truth is true" and the fact that "reality is reality." Actually there are three dream worlds. The first dream world is the collective dream of all the sleeping parts of the Sonship, symbolic of what is left of the oneness of mind they had in Heaven. The second dream world is the personal dream of each person's thought system based on the individual's responses to other people and the outer world. The third dream world is the nighttime sleeping dream world where individual fantasies are completely private. All three dream worlds are a way of attempting to create a fabricated reality where truth and reality become what you want them to be. All three dreams worlds are one illusion with various degrees of investment in separation. You seem to not have conscious control over these three dream worlds, but you actually write the script for how they play out, and you are the main actor in each of your dream plays.

Thus your dream worlds are places of manufactured false truth that only have the appearance of truth and the appearance of reality. This three-dimensional world hides truth and reality behind illusions. Truth in Heaven has no opposite, and reality has no opposite. However, in the illusory world, true perceptions are pitted against false perceptions, and both can seem to be real. Because illusions appear to be different and opposed to each other, you spend most of your time choosing between equally unreal illusions, while imagining them to be real.

Your devotion to illusions has happened because you have lost your access to the heavenly awareness of knowledge, which is the total awareness of Truth only. This absolute level of Truth is a mystery to those who fell asleep, replacing knowledge with the partial awareness of perception. With knowledge in Heaven, there is the creative will to extend love, but there is no choice to make about truth since everything is Truth. Therefore, Truth in Heaven is impossible to misunderstand or misinterpret since there is nothing else to choose. Perception in this world brings a choice of truth or untruth or a choice of one form of untruth and another. Thus the nature of truth as the only reality seems not so obvious. Devotion to illusions makes it difficult to recognize that "truth is true, and nothing else is true," as is expressed below:

> You need to be reminded that you think a thousand choices are confronting you, when there is really only one to make. And even this but seems to be a choice. Do not confuse yourself with all the doubts that myriad decisions would induce. You make but one. And when that one is made, you will perceive it was no choice at all. For truth is true, and nothing else is true. There is no opposite to choose instead. There is no contradiction to the truth.
>
> Choosing depends on learning. And the truth cannot be learned, but only recognized. In recognition its acceptance lies, and as it is accepted it is known. But knowledge is beyond the goals we seek to teach within the framework of this course.[633]

The Course can't teach you knowledge but can teach you to change your perceptions in order to lead you to accept knowledge, which you have not lost, but have hidden from your awareness. You are being taught to accept that only true perceptions are true. Thus the Course uses various different terms to teach you the importance of accepting that truth is true and of letting go of all forms of nonexistent untruth. In order to increase your awareness that "truth is true and nothing else is true," the Course recommends that you use the following sequence: You make progress from understanding truth, to appreciating truth, to believing in truth, to applying truth, to having a conviction in truth, to having faith in truth, and finally to using truth for your final healing of accepting the Atonement. This final healing is salvation in which all of the partial awareness of perception is completely replaced by the total awareness of knowledge, and you awaken to Truth in Heaven.

A major difference between Truth in Heaven and truth in this world is that knowledge of Truth in Heaven includes only thought and not action. Perceiving truth in this world involves both thought and action. This necessary action is the *correction of perception*. "Perception is a continual process of accepting and rejecting."[634] Thus the correction of perception, which is the *correction of error*, involves accepting only what is true and rejecting what is untrue. All seven tools of the Holy Spirit described in the Course are your means of accepting that "truth is true, and nothing else is true." They are the seven different but interrelated *means* used for the correction of perception in which false perceptions are rejected and replaced by true perceptions. They are also ways of opening to God's Love and His gift of redemption.

Each of the seven instruments of the Holy Spirit looks for the divine truth and overlooks everything else. Thus each of the tools listed below accepts that truth is true in a specific way and rejects its illusory opposite, seeing it is not true and so does not exist:

1. Forgiveness affirms the truth of your brother's guiltlessness and affirms that projections of guilt are not true and do not exist. The result is that forgiveness removes the blocks to the awareness of God's Love and removes the perception of separation.

2. Christ's vision affirms the truth of your brother's Christ nature and his inner light while simultaneously releasing all limiting judgments that are not true and do not exist. This enables you to see God's Love in your brother and accept His Love must be in you as well.

3. The holy relationship accepts the truth of your oneness with your brother by joining with him in a common purpose and rejects illusions of differences and separateness that are not true and do not exist. The result is that partners see holiness and God's Love in each other and then generalize their perception to see His Love in everyone and everything that exists.

4. The holy instant affirms the truth of the timelessness of now and rejects the illusory beliefs in the past and future that are not true and do not exist. The result is that you express God's Love by communicating perfectly with Him and the whole Sonship in the eternal now.

5. Miracles express the truth that God's Love flows through you and reject illusory beliefs in unworthiness and littleness because illusions are not true and do not exist. Because God's Love is exchanged, miracles result in healing and increase the awareness of His love in both the one who gives and the one who receives the miracle.

6. Meditation affirms the truth of the ever-present Divine Presence and rejects mental distractions and inner grievances that are not true and do not exist. Through the practice of meditation, which the Course calls "prayer," the awareness of God's Love is received directly. Daily meditation has been very helpful for me in regard to opening to God's Love. Gradually, my heart has opened as I have practiced meditation in which I focus on feeling God's Love for me and extending His Love to everyone. The true spirit of meditation is that it is an experience of the holy instant of sharing God's Love with the whole Sonship.

7. Atonement is the most direct way of accepting that "truth is true, and nothing else is true." The Atonement accepts the truth that you are the guiltless Son of God and you are totally worthy of God's Love, healing, and the correction of error. The Atonement rejects the illusory belief that you must pay a karmic debt for mistakes since karmic debt does not exist. The sole responsibility of the miracle worker is to accept perfect love for himself. This removes fear and guilt, and the result is healing. The seven tools of the Holy Spirit enable you to increasingly remove the fear of redemption and help prepare you to see the face of Christ and wholeheartedly welcome God's Love as you awaken.

The terms "healing" and "salvation" are *results* of perception being corrected and not the means. When a correction of error is made, the mind is partially healed. In your final healing at the end of time, you will fully accept the Atonement, which provides the correction of all errors and their effects. Your final healing is your final self-evaluation, called your "Last Judgment," in which you accept your expressions of love and truth and discard all your unloving and untrue miscreations. By accepting that truth is true, you will wake up in Heaven.

> Salvation is the recognition that the truth is true, and nothing else is true. This you have heard before, but may not yet accept both parts of it. Without the first, the second has no meaning. But without the second, is the first no longer true. Truth cannot have an opposite. This can not be too often said and thought about. For if what is not true is true as well as what is true, then part of truth is false. And truth has lost its meaning. Nothing but the truth is true, and what is false is false.[635]

HAPPY LEARNING
THAT TRUTH IS TRUE

~ o ~

The ego's first law of chaos is "truth is different for everyone."[636] The Holy Spirit teaches that the truth is simple because it is the same for everyone. The idea that truth is true is "the simplest of distinctions, yet the most obscure."[637] If you listen to the ego, the obvious nature of truth being truth is obscured and "concealed behind a vast array of choices that do not appear to be entirely your own."[638] Yet if you listen to your true Teacher, the Holy Spirit, you will become a happy learner of the truth. The Holy Spirit teaches through contrast. "The Holy Spirit needs a happy learner, in whom His mission can be happily accomplished. You who are steadfastly devoted to misery must first recognize that you are miserable and not happy. The Holy Spirit cannot teach without this contrast, for you believe that misery *is* happiness."[639] The ego will tell you that your goal is happiness, and then it will lead you to seek your happiness in ways that ensure you will only find misery. This is why listening to the ego fosters the belief that "misery *is* happiness." You will be an unhappy learner if you attempt to teach yourself how to be happy by listening to the ego instead of the Holy Spirit. The unhappy learner practices the basic doctrine of the ego: "Seek but do not find."[640]

When you follow the ego's guidance, you will devote yourself to learning to value illusions, which means you will be devoted to what will make you miserable while you consciously seek happiness. Your seeking of happiness in illusions where it cannot be found "has so confused you that you have undertaken to learn to do what you can never do, believing that unless you learn it you will not be happy."[641] Since your futile search is based on motivation from the ego, "You do not realize that the foundation [the ego] on which this most peculiar learning goal depends means absolutely nothing. Yet it may still make sense to you. Have faith in nothing and you will find the 'treasure' that you seek."[642] When you invest in illusions, you value what has no meaning. You cannot find purpose in what is meaningless. "Yet you will add another burden to your already burdened mind. You will believe that nothing is of value, and will value it."[643] It doesn't matter what varieties of illusions that you value because they are all equally meaningless. "A little piece of glass, a speck of dust, a body or a war are one to you. For if you value one thing made of nothing, you have believed that nothing can be precious, and that you *can* learn how to make the untrue true."[644]

Your ego guides the unhappy learner to think he can find truth and find reality in illusions. The Holy Spirit teaches through the contrast between truth and illusions. The Holy Spirit guides you to simply accept what is true as true and what is real as real.

> The Holy Spirit, seeing where you are [lost in the world of illusions] but knowing you are elsewhere [asleep in Heaven], begins His lesson in simplicity with the fundamental teaching that *truth is true*. This is the hardest lesson you will ever learn, and in the end the only one.[645]

Why is "truth is true" your hardest lesson? Your mind has denied light, love, and truth. What has been denied cannot be seen, even when it is quite obvious to an unclouded mind. The unhappy learner has decided that illusions are real, and this is the same as believing what is untrue is true. The unhappy learner clouds his mind, but the happy learner has an unclouded mind. Therefore, the happy learner possesses simplicity. His simplicity enables him to see that "truth is true" so he does not make the mistake of believing that illusions are real. You can only see what your mind is open to seeing.

> Simplicity is very difficult for twisted minds. Consider all the distortions you have made of nothing; all the strange forms and feelings and actions and reactions that you have woven out of it. Nothing is so alien to you as the simple truth, and nothing are you less inclined to listen to. The contrast between what is true and what is not is perfectly apparent, yet you do not see it. The simple and the obvious are not apparent to those who would make palaces and royal robes of nothing, believing they are kings with golden crowns because of them.[646]

The Holy Spirit teaches you to give up being an unhappy learner who foolishly attempts to find happiness through devoting himself to illusions. "All this [devotions to illusions that are nothing] the Holy Spirit sees, and teaches, simply, that all this is not true." The Holy Spirit also teaches you to become a happy learner by accepting only what is true as true. The Holy Spirit knows you cannot distinguish between illusions and reality, but He asks you to let Him be your Guide and make this distinction for you. The Holy Spirit wants you to replace your faith in nothingness with faith in Him.

> To those unhappy learners who would teach themselves nothing, and delude themselves into believing that it is not nothing, the Holy Spirit says, with steadfast quietness: *The truth is true. Nothing else matters, nothing else is real, and everything*

beside it is not there. Let Me make the one distinction for you that you cannot make, but need to learn. Your faith in nothing is deceiving you. Offer your faith to Me, and I will place it gently in the holy place where it belongs. You will find no deception there, but only the simple truth. And you will love it because you will understand it.[647]

Faith in the Holy Spirit opens your mind to understanding, inviting His gift of light and dispelling your illusion of darkness. "Like you, the Holy Spirit did not make truth. Like God, He knows it to be true. He brings the light of truth into the darkness, and lets it shine on you."[648] You become a happy learner when you accept His light into your mind. Your brother will see the light in you and provide testimony to you of your light. "And as it [the light in you] shines your brothers see it, and realizing that this light is not what you have made, they see in you more than you see. They will be happy learners of the lesson this light brings to them, because it teaches them release from nothing and from all the works of nothing."[649]

When you express love by extending light from your mind to your brother, the result is a change in perception. Your gift of light enables your brother to realize that he has been foolishly wasting his time by being devoted to nothing and to the unhappiness that illusions bring. "The heavy chains that seem to bind them [your brothers] to despair they do not see as nothing, until you bring the light to them. And then they see the chains have disappeared, and so they *must* have been nothing."[650] You learn indirectly from your brother that the light must be in you because you sent it to your brother who returns it to you in gratitude. "And you will see it [light] with them. Because you taught them gladness and release, they will become your teachers in release and gladness."[651] You are saved by learning to be a savior for your brother as you exchange light with him, manifesting true forgiveness resulting in healing. The healing light and love you give to your brother you immediately receive. "Salvation is a better gift than this. And true forgiveness, as the means by which it is attained, must heal the mind that gives, for giving is receiving."[652]

You can learn that truth is true by teaching this to others and then you and your brother both become happy learners. "When you teach anyone that truth is true, you learn it with him. And so you learn that what seemed hardest was the easiest. Learn to be a happy learner."[653] A happy learner remembers what previously made him an unhappy learner. "You will never learn how to make nothing everything. Yet see that this has been your goal, and recognize how foolish it has been."[654] To become a happy learner, it is necessary to realize how much time you have wasted in being an unhappy learner of nothingness. "Be glad it is undone, for when you look at it in simple honesty, it *is* undone. I said before, 'Be not content with nothing,' for you have believed that nothing could content you. *It is not so.*"[655]

Becoming a happy learner requires that you make a decision to let go of what you have foolishly taught yourself by giving your previous learning to the Holy Spirit. "If you would be a happy learner, you must give everything you have learned to the Holy Spirit, to be unlearned for you."[656] You need to unlearn whatever thoughts that are based on nothing. How do you understand whether you have invested in nothing or not? Whenever you have invested in nothing, it is because you have taught yourself with the guidance of the ego. Thinking with the ego means you are not thinking with God. The ego encourages you to believe the following teachings of nothingness:

You are alone. You are a body separate from other bodies. You are in the world. You are not loved. You can be hurt. If you are attacked, you are justified in attacking in return. You have sinned. You are guilty and deserve punishment.

If you believe any of the previous ideas or similar ideas, you must give them to the Holy Spirit for correction. The Holy Spirit teaches you through subtraction and then addition. What you have taught yourself must be subtracted as a process of unlearning guided by the Holy Spirit. Then your unlearning will make way for the addition of the new ideas that you have learned from the Holy Spirit. When you subtract the old ego-based ideas and add the new ideas from the Holy Spirit, you are thinking with God. Here are some examples of thinking with God:

You are never alone because you are always joined in oneness with God, the Holy Spirit, and the entire Sonship. You are a spirit joined with all other spirits in reality. You are in Heaven, dreaming of exile in an illusory world of separation. You are loved unceasingly. You can never be hurt because you are God's Son. You cannot be attacked by others, and any attack you make on others is never justified. You have not sinned, but you have made mistakes that can be corrected. You can never be guilty, and you deserve only love.

You can trust the Holy Spirit because His teachings are founded on the Truth of God Himself. After giving your old learning to the Holy Spirit, "then begin to learn the joyous lessons that come quickly on the firm foundation that truth is true. For what is built there *is* true, and built on truth. The universe of learning will open up before you in all its gracious simplicity. With truth before you, you will not look back."[657] Learning how to be a happy learner is your willingness to stop investing in your illusions and willingness to let the Holy Spirit show you what is true. "The happy learner meets the conditions of learning here, as he meets the conditions of knowledge in the Kingdom. All this lies in the Holy Spirit's plan to free you from the past, and open up the way to freedom for you."[658] Accepting the Holy Spirit's plan by accepting His guidance shows you the truth. "For truth *is* true. What else could ever be, or ever was?"[659]

The acceptance of truth unclouded by illusions is the fundamental lesson that "holds the key to the dark door that you believe is locked forever. You made this door of nothing, and behind it *is* nothing."[660] The Holy Spirit and the Mind of Christ give you the key to awakening to the knowledge of Heaven, and this key is literally the gift of light coming into your mind. "Understanding is light, and light leads to knowledge."[661] Yet this key element does not come to you for you alone and just for your salvation. You are given this light so you can then share it with others for it is the nature of light and love to be shared. The way to keep light and love in your mind is not to hold onto them, but to share them. Sharing your light and love with your brother will bring awakening to him. Likewise, your brother will gratefully return light and love to you bringing awakening to your mind. Thus you become the savior for your brother, and your brother becomes the savior for you. "The key is only the light that shines away the shapes and forms and fears of nothing. Accept this key to freedom from the hands of Christ Who gives it to you, that you may join Him in the holy task of bringing light. For, like your brothers, you do not realize the light has come and freed you from the sleep of darkness."[662]

The gift of light will awaken you because you will use it to heal and awaken your brothers and your brothers will help you to heal and awaken. "Behold your brothers in their freedom, and learn of them how to be free of darkness. The light in you will waken them, and they will not leave you asleep."[663] The happy learner will be guided by the Holy Spirit to use Christ's vision to let go of perceiving guilt in others and to instead perceive the divine presence in everyone. The Holy Spirit's gift of light makes Christ's vision possible so you can see light, love, truth, and holiness in all of your brothers. "The vision of Christ is given the very instant that it is perceived. Where everything is clear, it is all holy. The quietness of its simplicity is so compelling that you will realize it is impossible to deny the simple truth."[664] Light in your mind helps you perceive that "truth is true and nothing else is true." "For there is nothing else"[665] other than the reality of light, love, and truth in God. "God is everywhere, and His Son is in Him with everything. Can he [the happy learner] sing the dirge of sorrow when this is true?"[666]

Perhaps you have studied the Course and learned the importance of investing only in what it true and letting go of illusions that do not exist. "The decision whether or not to listen to this course and follow it is but the choice between truth and illusion."[667] But you may have become so accustomed to accepting illusions and believing they are real that you cannot rely entirely on your own evaluation of what is true and what is illusion. Nevertheless, you can fully rely on the Holy Spirit's judgment because that is His function, not your function. The Holy Spirit acts like a filter for what is real and true in your mind and what is not real and not true because you have combined your true loving thoughts of love and your untrue unloving thoughts. You believe both your true loving thoughts and your untrue unloving thoughts are real since you made them both. Although you have deceived yourself by believing illusions, the Holy Spirit knows that only your true loving thoughts are real. Thus He brings all your true loving thoughts into the real world saving them for you as your bridge to awakening in Heaven. "We said before that the Holy Spirit is evaluative, and must be. He sorts out the true from the false in your mind, and teaches you to judge every thought you allow to enter it in the light of what God put there. Whatever is in accord with this light He retains, to strengthen the Kingdom in you. What is partly in accord with it He accepts and purifies. But what is out of accord entirely He rejects by judging against."[668]

If you trust in the judgment of the Holy Spirit, you will "make the easiest decision that ever confronted you, and also the only one. You will cross the bridge into reality simply because you will recognize that God is on the other side, and nothing at all is here. It is impossible not to make the natural decision as this is realized."[669]

You will awaken when you are prepared to accept reality and when nothing else will hold value for you. The "Last Judgment" is not God's evaluation. It is your final judgment of yourself guided by the Holy Spirit that allows you to accept that "truth is true, and nothing else is true." In this final self-evaluation, you will apply the test of truth "to everything you have made, and retain in your memory only what is creative and good. This is what your right-mindedness cannot but dictate. The purpose of time is solely to 'give you time' to achieve this judgment. It is your own perfect judgment of your own perfect creations. When everything you retain is lovable, there is no reason for fear to remain with you. This is your part in the Atonement."[670] When your mind contains only love, light, and truth, God will quickly take the last step because you are ready to embrace Him Who is Love, Light, and Truth.

> The stars will disappear in light, and the sun that opened up the world to beauty will vanish. Perception will be meaningless when it has been perfected, for everything that has been used for learning will have no function. Nothing will ever change; no shifts nor shadings, no differences, no variations that made perception possible will still occur. The perception of the real world will be so short that you will barely have time to thank God for it. For God will take the last step swiftly, when you have reached the real world and have been made ready for Him.[671]

LIGHT DIMENSIONS
LEADING TO HEAVEN

~ o ~

This section of this book is a review of the light dimensions with new information about the nature of light in each dimension and how light changes as your awareness shifts from one dimension to another. Let's start with the first dimension and the nature of light in Heaven. God's Home and your Home is Heaven, and God is reality and Divine Abstraction.

God, Who encompasses all being, created beings who have everything individually, but who want to share it to increase their joy. Nothing real can be increased except by sharing. That is why God created you. Divine Abstraction takes joy in sharing. That is what creation means.[672]

Heaven in the first dimension is hard to describe because the partial knowledge of perception cannot fully grasp the wholeness of knowledge in Heaven. The first dimension is a state of complete abstraction that is natural for your heavenly mind, but not for your limited perception that sees everything in parts without seeing the wholeness that would give them meaning.

Complete abstraction is the natural condition of the mind. But part of it is now unnatural. It does not look on everything as one. It sees instead but fragments of the whole, for only thus could it invent the partial world you see. The purpose of all seeing is to show you what you wish to see. All hearing but brings to your mind the sounds it wants to hear.[673]

One brother is all brothers. Every mind contains all minds, for every mind is one. Such is the truth. Yet do these thoughts make clear the meaning of creation? Do these words bring perfect clarity with them to you? What can they seem to be but empty sounds; pretty, perhaps, correct in sentiment, yet fundamentally not understood nor understandable. The mind that taught itself to think specifically can no longer grasp abstraction in the sense that it is all-encompassing.[674]

Although divine abstraction is natural for your mind in the reality of Heaven, "part of it [your mind] is now unnatural." Part of your mind has become concrete and so focuses only on the specific. Nevertheless, in spite of the limited awareness of perception, there are some general ideas about the nature of Heaven that can make sense to you. But you must realize that what you picture in your mind cannot encompass the reality of the first dimension. Reality is the realm of eternity, but eternity does not mean an endless past and endless present and an endless future. Eternity is only an endless *now* that always was and always is. The eternal now is difficult to accept using a perceptual mind that believes in guilt, which is a way of attacking yourself and denying your guiltlessness as the Son of God.

> You are invulnerable because you are guiltless. You can hold on to the past only through guilt. For guilt establishes that you will be punished for what you have done, and thus depends on one-dimensional time, proceeding from past to future. No one who believes this can understand what "always" means, and therefore guilt must deprive you of the appreciation of eternity. You are immortal because you are eternal, and "always" must be now. Guilt, then, is a way of holding past and future in your mind to ensure the ego's continuity. For if what has been will be punished, the ego's continuity is guaranteed. Yet the guarantee of your continuity is God's, not the ego's. And immortality is the opposite of time, for time passes away, while immortality is constant.[675]

The key part of the above quote is "one-dimensional time, proceeding from past to future. No one who believes this can understand what 'always' means...." There is only one now in the reality of Heaven. "Eternity is one time, its only dimension being 'always.' This cannot mean anything to you until you remember God's open Arms, and finally know His open Mind. Like Him, *you* are 'always'; in His Mind and with a mind like His."[676] Eternity is not a limited time that comes and goes. Eternity is unlimited so it has no beginning and no end. Time says you are guilty. Timeless eternity confirms your guiltlessness.

> You are not guiltless in time, but in eternity. You have "sinned" in the past, but there is no past. Always has no direction. Time seems to go in one direction, but when you reach its end it will roll up like a long carpet spread along the past behind you, and will disappear. As long as you believe the Son of God is guilty you will walk along this carpet, believing that it leads to death. And the journey will seem long and cruel and senseless, for so it is. The journey the Son of God has set himself is useless indeed, but the journey on which his Father sets him is one of release and joy.[677]

Eternity is obvious in Heaven because it is directly experienced there. However, since eternity is not experienced by you with your perception based on the ego, it is difficult to understand. The Course tells you that eternity is always now.

> I have repeatedly emphasized that one level of the mind is not understandable to another. So it is with the ego and the Holy Spirit; with time and eternity. Eternity is an idea of God, so the Holy Spirit understands it perfectly. Time is a belief of the ego, so the lower mind, which is the ego's domain, accepts it without question. The only aspect of time that is eternal is *now*.[678]

Since eternity is always now, you may think you understand now and thus understand eternity. But in the section of this book titled "The Holy Instant Elevator," I explained that your typical experience of now is not, in fact, experienced now. You are seeing sunlight 8.3 minutes after it has already left the sun. Similarly, every stimulus travels some small distance and is delayed at least some small period of time before it registers in your brain. You seem to be experiencing a stimulus in the present, when actually you are responding only to what has already happened in the past. This extremely small delay in time may seem negligible, but it is enough to separate you from the eternal now that you do experience in Heaven.

These are the characteristics of time: Things are temporary. There is change. There is movement involved. There are events happening one after another. There are beginnings and endings, such as births and deaths. There is a historical frame of reference based on the past. There is a future that is expected to be caused by the past.

Here are the characteristics of the eternity of Heaven: Nothing is temporary. There is no change. There is no movement. There is no sequence of events. There are no beginnings and no endings. There is no history because there is no past. There is no future. Although God is the First Cause, "It must be understood that the word 'first' as applied to Him is not a time concept."[679] First means the causeless Cause of all that exists from which all of Creation has been extended.

Just as there is no time in the first dimension, there is no space. Your perceptual mind takes for granted that everything is in some place. But reality has nothing to do with space. The first dimension is a dimension that has neither length, width, nor depth. It has no size component. It is everywhere present, encompassing even the other dimensions. Because it has no boundaries that can encompass it, the best way to describe this aspect of reality is "infinity" since it is the idea of being unlimited.

Unlike the idea of space that involves separate places and parts, the infinity of reality is another way of describing the wholeness of Heaven that is not broken up into separate parts. If reality was divided into parts, you could go from one part to another, and there would be space between the parts. However, reality is an undivided whole that is one unlimited awareness, symbolized by an infinitely small dot that is everywhere present. Everything that exists is within this one dot that has no boundaries. Reality is the one unlimited awareness that is present everywhere. Reality is the Mind of God and is the first dimension in which all of creation exists. This first dimension encompasses the second dimension and third dimension. Because reality is infinity without limits and is everywhere, you can never be separate from reality or separate from infinity. Since there is no space or distance, there are no objects, no forms within the "eternal formlessness of God."[680] Your sleeping mind focused on the belief in the third dimension has identified with the illusory form of your body. You can have illusions of being alone and separate from reality and from infinity, but your illusions have no effect on changing your true nature of formlessness in Heaven.

> To be alone is to be separated from infinity, but how can this be if infinity has no end? No one can be beyond the limitless, because what has no limits must be everywhere. There are no beginnings and no endings in God, Whose universe is Himself. Can you exclude yourself from the universe, or from God Who *is* the universe? I and my Father are one with you, for you are part of Us. Do you really believe that part of God can be missing or lost to Him?[681]

Right now you are still in Heaven, only dreaming of exile and separation. Separation is inconceivable in the first dimension because Heaven is above all a state of mind where union is the only condition of life. All of reality is in a state of pure undiluted oneness. All is one because God is One and His Kingdom is One. How can you be alone and separate from the Kingdom of God, when actually "you are the Kingdom of God"?[682] The Course and the Holy Spirit "make no distinction between *having* the Kingdom of God and *being* the Kingdom of God."[683] Reality is God and His Kingdom, and you have His Kingdom and are His Kingdom. God is Light and His Kingdom is Light, so you are this light.

> The ego is legion, but the Holy Spirit is One. No darkness abides anywhere in the Kingdom, but your part is only to allow no darkness to abide in your own mind. This alignment with light is unlimited, because it is in alignment with the light of the world. Each of us is the light of the world, and by joining our minds in this light we proclaim the Kingdom of God together and as one.[684]

When the separation happened, the sleeping parts of the Sonship took some of the Light from Heaven in order to use it as the substance of the dream world they made. Previously I have used the term "light extracted from Heaven" to describe this light. However, this light that was "extracted" from Heaven is not the same as the Light of Heaven. What does "extracted" mean? At the separation, the sleeping Son of God drew "a circle, infinitely small, around a very little segment of Heaven, splintered from the whole, proclaiming that within it is your kingdom, where God can enter not."[685] The light that was extracted from the first dimension is this very little segment of Heaven, and "it is like the smallest sunbeam to the sun, or like the faintest ripple on the surface of the ocean."[686] This extraction of light is described as "this little thought, this infinitesimal illusion, holding itself apart against the universe."[687] From this extraction of light, the whole three-dimensional world has been made with various slower moving variations of light, including the slowest moving "frozen light" called matter. Yet all these variations of faster and slower moving light are illusions that have never left Heaven, as the sleeping Son of God can only dream of separation without ever leaving God as the Source of all Light.

In the previous water analogy, I said that matter is like ice and this "frozen light" is the slowest form of light. I said the blazing light is like the liquid state of water, and it is a faster light. And I said the Light of Heaven is like steam with the fastest moving molecules. But the Light of Heaven is *not* the fastest moving light and is actually motionless. The Light of Heaven is everywhere and infinite, but it is not moving since it and the whole dimensionless first dimension transcend the idea of movement from one place to another. Unlike the extracted light taken from the first dimension and brought into the second dimension, the actual Light of Heaven is not moving. For light to move, it must be in space and time. For example, light typically travels the distance in space of 186,282 miles in the time of one second. It has already been emphasized previously that in Heaven there is no space and no time. Thus Light in Heaven is not moving at all, and yet this Light is everywhere present in the first dimension. Just as God is everywhere, Light is everywhere because God is Light. Similarly, Love is everywhere present, since God is Love. The nature of Light in Heaven is that it is infinite and unlimited. The extracted light must be quite different from the Light of Heaven because it is finite and so has a limited nature. Did the extraction of light make the Light of Heaven lose its infinite nature? No, because it was only an illusion of extraction. The extraction remains part of the wholeness of Light in Heaven. Without the unlimited Light of Heaven, the illusory extraction of light would cease to even be a dream of separation. "Without the sun [Light of Heaven] the sunbeam [extracted light] would be gone; the ripple without the ocean is inconceivable."[688]

The light extracted from the Light of Heaven is the fabric of the second and third dimensions. The blazing light of the real world in the second dimension does not move in one straight line as light moves in the third dimension. The blazing light in the second dimension expands as the two-dimensional area of a circle. When God takes the final step of awakening, He accelerates the blazing light in order to return the extracted light back to its source in the infinite Light of Heaven. When Einstein wrote $E = mc^2$, he was unknowingly describing how mass accelerated to the speed of light squared would result in a leap all the way from the three-dimensional world to Heaven. When the moving light from the third dimension and the second dimension return to Heaven, the *moving* light becomes *motionless* Light everywhere present in the dimensionless first dimension.

Only God can take the final step of awakening each sleeping part of the Sonship who is ready. Eventually at the end of time, everyone will awaken. Then God will bring about the transfer of all the frozen light of matter from the third dimension to the first dimension ($mc^2 = E$). Both the third dimension and the second dimension are illusory dimensions, and both will return to the reality of first dimension. When all of the illusory extraction of finite light finally returns to the infinite Light of Heaven, the other two dimensions will vanish and the sleeping parts of the Son of God will realize that the separation never happened because it did not happen in the reality of God. "The full awareness of the Atonement, then, is the recognition that *the separation never occurred*. The ego cannot prevail against this because it is an explicit statement that the ego never occurred."[689] This section may seem complex, but the Course really has just one simple message that only reality is true, and all your illusions of separation are not real, and therefore never happened.

> This is a very simple course. Perhaps you do not feel you need a course which, in the end, teaches that only reality is true. But do you believe it? When you perceive the real world, you will recognize that you did not believe it. Yet the swiftness with which your new and only real perception will be translated into knowledge will leave you but an instant to realize that this alone is true. And then everything you made will be forgotten; the good and the bad, the false and the true. For as Heaven and earth become one, even the real world will vanish from your sight. The end of the world is not its destruction, but its translation into Heaven. The reinterpretation of the world is the transfer of all perception to knowledge.[690]

The Holy Spirit and Jesus have greatly simplified what is required to wake up to the one reality of God. All you have to do to fulfill your part in the Atonement is to accept the light in your own mind and let go of the darkness. Since Jesus accelerated his body to the speed of light, he broke through the barrier of the third dimension to manifest the face of Christ as your ticket to Heaven. The Holy Spirit gives you Christ's vision to elevate your mind to the real world of forgiveness. "Christ's vision is the bridge between the worlds."[691] Christ's vision enables you to see the divine in everyone and to truly forgive everyone. This process of true forgiveness using Christ's vision leads to seeing the blazing light of the face of Christ at the deepest level of the real world where you will remember your Father. The entire purpose of the Course is to remove all the illusions covering the face of Christ through the application of forgiveness. When all the clouds of illusion are removed, forgiveness has done its job of revealing the face of Christ: "No clouds remain to hide the face of Christ. Now is the goal achieved."[692]

> From the forgiven [real] world the Son of God is lifted easily into his home. And there he knows that he has always rested there in peace. Even salvation will become a dream, and vanish from his mind. For salvation is the end of dreams, and with the closing of the dream will have no meaning. Who, awake in Heaven, could dream that there could ever be need of salvation?[693]

Everyone is seeking Heaven, but perception is so limited that the wholeness of Heaven is difficult to grasp just as God is beyond anyone's full comprehension. However, because the Holy Spirit and Jesus have experienced Heaven, they are qualified to share with your descriptions of Heaven expressed in the words of the Course.

> There is nothing outside you. That is what you must ultimately learn, for it is the realization that the Kingdom of Heaven is restored to you. For God created only this, and He did not depart from it nor leave it separate from Himself. The Kingdom of Heaven is the dwelling place of the Son of God, who left not his Father and dwells not apart from Him. Heaven is not a place nor a condition. It is merely an awareness of perfect Oneness, and the knowledge that there is nothing else; nothing outside this Oneness, and nothing else within.[694]

The reason why Heaven is so unfathomable is that it is the Home of God Who Himself is the absolute highest expression of everything that you value: love, peace, holiness, joy, power, knowledge. You do not actually understand what the absolute expression of any quality of God is because perception allows only partial awareness. Since perception is limited, it excludes the total awareness of knowledge that would be needed to bring complete understanding. For example, think of all the things you value in the three-dimensional world. Now, consider that none of what you value related to form or related to time will continue to be valuable when you wake up in Heaven.

When we are all united in Heaven, you will value nothing that you value here. For nothing that you value here do you value wholly, and so you do not value it at all. Value is where God placed it, and the value of what God esteems cannot be judged, for it has been established. It is wholly of value. It can merely be appreciated or not. To value it partially is not to know its value. In Heaven is everything God values, and nothing else. Heaven is perfectly unambiguous. Everything is clear and bright, and calls forth one response. There is no darkness and there is no contrast. There is no variation. There is no interruption. There is a sense of peace so deep that no dream in this world has ever brought even a dim imagining of what it is.[695]

The most obvious example of what you value in this world is all the illusions you entertain, including the illusion of the world itself and what you imagine the illusions of the world offer you. You do not value the state of mind that excludes all illusions. You cannot even imagine what that state of mind would be like.

Can you imagine what a state of mind without illusions is? How it would feel? Try to remember when there was a time,—perhaps a minute, maybe even less—when nothing came to interrupt your peace; when you were certain you were loved and safe. Then try to picture what it would be like to have that moment be extended to the end of time and to eternity. Then let the sense of quiet that you felt be multiplied a hundred times, and then be multiplied another hundred more.

And now you have a hint, not more than just the faintest intimation of the state your mind will rest in when the truth has come. Without illusions there could be no fear, no doubt and no attack. When truth has come all pain is over, for there is no room for transitory thoughts and dead ideas to linger in your mind. Truth occupies your mind completely, liberating you from all beliefs in the ephemeral. They have no place because the truth has come, and they are nowhere. They can not be found, for truth is everywhere forever, now.[696]

In this world, you value many different kinds of love, depending on your various desires. Instead of accepting that love is eternal, you value love that is temporary, but in doing so you value what is valueless because time cannot take away what is real. You think love can be lost or taken away. You seek love with an eye toward what you can get from it. The Course says that in Heaven there is only one kind of love. Love is only giving and union. It is eternal and can never be lost.

Perhaps you think that different kinds of love are possible. Perhaps you think there is a kind of love for this, a kind for that; a way of loving one, another way of loving still another. Love is one. It has no separate parts and no degrees; no kinds nor levels, no divergencies and no distinctions. It is like itself, unchanged throughout. It never alters with a person or a circumstance. It is the Heart of God, and also of His Son.[697]

There are not different forms of love. But the many kinds of love you believe in are used to describe God's Love in Helen Schucman's book, *The Gifts of God.* Sometimes God is viewed as impersonal, but a closer look will reveal just how personally God loves you.

Rest could be yours because of what God is. He loves you as a mother loves her child; her only one, the only love she has, her all-in-all, extension of herself, as much a part of her as breath herself. He loves you as a brother loves his own; born of one father, still as one in him, and bonded with a seal that cannot break. He loves you as a lover loves his own; his chosen one, his joy, his very life, the one he seeks when she has gone away, and brings him peace again on her return. He loves you as a father loves his son, without whom would his self be incomplete, whose immortality completes his own, for in him is the chain of love complete—a golden circle that will never end, a song that will be sung throughout all time and afterwards, and always will remain the deathless sound of loving and of love. O be at peace, beloved of the Lord! What is your life but gratitude to Him Who loves you with an everlasting Love?[698]

Achieving the goal of awakening in Heaven is inevitable because it is God's Will for you and your own true will. Yet when will you release all the illusions you have made and be able to see the face of Christ and see the blazing light emanating from it? It could happen at any time, but in fact this seldom happens in everyday life for most people. Even if you do experience revelation by seeing the blazing light of the face of Christ and remember God, it will be a temporary experience. You will still have to live your life as before. What you really want is to wake up permanently in Heaven. You will never be satisfied with less than taking your rightful place in the Sonship that is awaiting you.

God is not reluctant to take the last step and transport you to Heaven. Yet it takes a lifetime of preparation to be ready to let go of the ego and the body. I believe the best opportunity most seekers have for seeing the blazing light of the face of Christ is right after the body has ceased to function. Then with the body awareness gone, you will be most open to embracing the blazing light and see in it your own face, your own Self, awakening to the memory of God. If you miss this opportunity to awaken, through reincarnation you will be given another opportunity in another lifetime to awaken. I have focused so much on describing the face of Christ in this book because I am hoping that having this awareness will encourage you to merge with the blazing light and awaken in the Arms of God. As part of your preparation for this moment of truth, you can ask in advance for God's help in your awakening as is recommended below:

God loves His Son. Request Him now to give the means by which this world will disappear, and vision first will come, with knowledge but an instant later. For in grace you see a light that covers all the world in love, and watch fear disappear from every face as hearts rise up and claim the light as theirs. What now remains that Heaven be delayed an instant longer? What is still undone when your forgiveness rests on everything?[699]

You must do your part and give your little willingness to awaken. Put all your faith in God, the Holy Spirit, and Jesus. You will see the vision of the blazing light at a distance in Stage 1 as you cross the bridge. "The new perspective you will gain from crossing over will be the understanding of where Heaven *is*. From this side, it seems to be outside and across the bridge."[700] But then Stage 2 happens as you cross over the bridge, and you merge with the blazing light in oneness and remember God. Then God will take the last step.

Yet as you cross to join it, it will join with you and become one with you. And you will think, in glad astonishment, that for all this you gave up *nothing!* The joy of Heaven, which has no limit, is increased with each [extracted and finite] light that returns to take its rightful place [of being infinite Light] within it. Wait no longer, for the Love of God and *you*. And may the holy instant speed you on the way, as it will surely do if you but let it come to you.[701]

And where is sacrifice, when memory of God has come to take the place of loss? What better way to close the little gap between illusions and reality than to allow the memory of God to flow across it, making it a bridge an instant will suffice to reach beyond? For God has closed it with Himself. His memory has not gone by, and left a stranded Son forever on a shore where he can glimpse another shore that he can never reach. His Father wills that he be lifted up and gently carried over. He has built the bridge, and it is He Who will transport His Son across it. Have no fear that He will fail in what He wills. Nor that you be excluded from the Will that is for you.[702]

PART V

~ • ~

THE PHYSICS OF LIGHT
IN THREE DIMENSIONS

The Course uses the word "light" 498 times. Although the focus of this book you are reading now is on "light dimensions," thus far the aspect of light that has not been addressed is the nature of light from a scientific perspective. This Part V offers a consideration of the science of light as it relates to the three dimensions. Included in Part V are some sections from a future book of mine that will be about "triple dimension physics," which I hope will be the next step in the evolution of physics. Part V employs a new format involving shorter sections with headings that are in the form of questions.

Does light function as a particle or a wave?

The true nature of light, revealed by Einstein and proven in countless experiments over the years, has caused a complete reevaluation of the nature of matter itself. At one time matter was considered to have only a particle nature. Particles were thought to have the definite attributes of position, mass, velocity, and spin. Energy was considered to have a wave nature. Electromagnetic waves were thought to have the definite attributes of no mass, no definite position, and no spin. But waves do possess polarization, energy in proportion to frequency, and a constant velocity of the speed of light. Discoveries in quantum physics have shown that particle nature and wave nature are not in fact separate categories as once thought. Matter and energy have attributes of both a particle and a wave, which is called *wave/particle duality*. Einstein's formula of energy equals mass times the speed of light squared ($E = mc^2$) showed the interchangeability of matter and energy. Matter is mostly emptiness and energy and merely gives the appearance of solidity. In the book, *The Eye of Shiva*, Amaury de Riencourt states:

The world we see and experience in everyday life is simply a convenient mirage attuned to your very limited senses, an illusion conjured by your perceptions and your mind. All that is around us (including your own bodies), which appears so substantial, is ultimately nothing but ephemeral networks of particle-waves, whirling around at lightning speed, colliding, rebounding, disintegrating in almost total emptiness — so-called matter is mostly emptiness, proportionately as void as intergalactic space, void of anything except occasional dots and spots and scattered electric charges... if all the nuclei of all the atoms that make up the whole of mankind were packed tight together, their global aggregate would be the size of a large grain of rice![703]

What is a photon of light?

A unit of light is a photon, described as follows:

As nature's most subtle creation, the photon teeters on a knife-edge. With rest mass equal to zero, if it traveled the slightest bit slower than c, its energy and mass would become zero. It would have ceased to exist. Alternately, if the photon traveled at c but had a rest mass the slightest bit greater than zero, it would have infinite energy and, in effect, could never have been created.... The quantization of light, along with the theory of relativity, forces upon us a new perspective concerning this number we call c. It is no longer just the speed of light but is an inborn characteristic of the universe, of space-time, if you will; it is the speed greater than which nothing can go. Within space-time are created, for reasons we do not know, certain fundamental types of particles. Each is defined by a small set of parameters, one of which is rest mass. (Another is electric charge, a third is intrinsic spin.) The photon is one, perhaps the only one, with zero mass. Hence it may (and it must) travel at c. [704]

What is "unfrozen light" in relation to "frozen light"?

I have previously stated that mass of three-dimensional matter is "frozen light," meaning light traveling slower than its natural state of moving at the speed of light. When mass is accelerated by the speed of light, the frozen light of matter becomes the "unfrozen light" of the second dimension. This "unfrozen light" is simply the photon of light returning to its natural state of traveling at the speed of light. Actually, the term "frozen light" was first theorized by the noted physicist David Bohm. He also talked about an "implicate order" as a higher order, perhaps a divine order, that is implied but not obviously recognized in any observable way. He felt this higher order transcends the lower order of the world of matter. My version of "frozen light" is more specific than

Bohm's theory because it states that *the first dimension is the implicate order.* In addition, my theory identifies the second dimension as what David Bohm would call a lower level "secondary order." Also, I perceive the third dimension as an even lower order transcended by both the first and second dimensions.

Can mass be accelerated to the speed of light to produce a photon?

I have already stated that a small portion of the first dimension Light (Energy) of Heaven has been decelerated by the speed of light (E / c) and the result has been the making of the second dimension. I have also stated that, in spite of modern physics, when mass is accelerated to the speed of light, it switches from the third dimension to the second dimension. Thus the second dimension is expressed as the following reconfiguration of Einstein's formula: E / c = mc. The two-dimensional light of the photon equals E / c and also equals mc.

Why should this be so? I already knew that from the perspective of the world and modern science, mass cannot be accelerated to the speed of light. Therefore, how could my theory be true that mc (mass times the speed of light) equals light or the photon? I had the guidance of my intuition that told me I was right, but I needed to see if I could find something in science to confirm my hypothesis.

I prayed for an answer and let my fingers do the walking through every internet article I could find about the speed of light. Then I found it! What I was looking for was in an internet physics forum titled "Why c^2 ?" The written answer was, "p = mv = mc for a photon."[705] I was delighted at first. Then I was disappointed to find out that the "p" did not stand for photon as I had originally assumed. The "p" stood for *momentum.* Although I was disappointed to discover that the "p" in the formula p = mc represents momentum, I thought more about what momentum really means. In physics, momentum is generally thought to be the amount of motion a three-dimensional object has, meaning mass in motion. The quantity of momentum depends upon how much mass is moving and how fast it is moving. The formula for the momentum of an object is equal to the mass of the object times the velocity of the object written as p = mv. But in the case of photons, which have no mass, the momentum equals *relativistic mass* times the speed of light (p = mc).

What is "rest mass," and what is "relativistic mass"?

There are two different kinds of mass: One is mass at rest, which is usually just called "mass." The other kind of mass is mass in movement, called "relativistic mass." When matter is in motion, it is believed that relativistic mass is increasing. Before the velocity reaches the speed of light, the total energy is a combination of the potential energy ("P") of the rest mass and the kinetic energy ("K") of the mass in motion $(E = P + K)$.

As the velocity of the mass increases coming closer to the speed of light, the potential energy of the rest mass decreases and is balanced out by an equal increase of kinetic energy of the relativistic mass. If the velocity of rest mass increases to the speed of light, all of the potential energy of the rest mass would be gone. At the speed of light with rest mass gone, what remains is the kinetic energy of the relativistic mass.

When mass moves at less than the speed of light, this formula is used: $E^2 = m^2c^4 + p^2c^2$. But when mass reaches the speed of light, rest mass is zero $(m^2c^4 = 0)$. The formula becomes $E^2 = p^2c^2$ and can be reformulated to $E = pc$. The formula $E = pc$ can be combined with the formula $E = mc^2$, so $pc = mc^2$, which is reformulated to $p = mc$. Thus the momentum of a photon equals mass times the speed of light. Conventional wisdom says the photon is a three-dimensional form of energy, such as physical sunlight that has a wavelength. For example, when a photon of light hits a solar sails in space, it transfers its momentum to the spacecraft, serving as a form of propulsion.

According to physics, the momentum of a photon is the energy of the Planck constant (which will be described subsequently) divided by the wavelength. Thus the momentum is inversely proportional to the photon's wavelength. This means the amount of the momentum reduces when the wavelength is longer, and it increases when the wavelength is shorter. In the third dimension, the momentum is the magnitude of the photon's motion in the direction of propagation (as shown on page 199) for the time period of its movement from one end of the wavelength to the other end of the wavelength.

What happens to the momentum if there is no wavelength? If there is no wavelength, there is no forward movement and thus there is no momentum. What if mass times the speed of light produces a two-dimensional photon and not a three-dimensional photon as is assumed by the formula $mc = p$ with "p" meaning momentum? The two-dimensional photon does not have any wavelength and so does not have the movement of momentum in the direction of propagation as is the case with the three-dimensional photon.

For the formula $mc = p$, I have come to the conclusion that mass times the speed of light does not produce a three-dimensional photon with momentum. I believe that when all the rest mass is accelerated to the speed of light and becomes transformed into relativistic mass, it becomes the two-dimensional energy of the two-dimensional photon. In the formula $mc = p$, the "p" intended to represent momentum can ironically stand for the energy of the two-dimensional photon.

How can mass travel at the speed of light?

Scientists say that mass cannot be accelerated to the speed of light. They are correct if the third dimension is the only dimension that is considered. What makes it possible for mass to be accelerated to the speed of light is that mass in the third dimension becomes light in the second dimension. Let's review what has already been said about Einstein's thought experiment of traveling at the speed of light.

As an object comes closer to the speed of light, time slows down, which is called "time dilation." A rocketship that travels close to the speed of light will increase in momentum and in mass. The rocketship will shorten its length in the direction it is moving. This shortening is called "the Lorentz contraction." At the speed of light, the time in the third dimension would stop, the mass would increase to infinity, and the rocketship would shorten infinitely. According to scientists, it would be impossible for the rocketship to go at the speed of light because its functional mass could not expand to become infinitely great. Also, it would take an infinite amount of energy to propel the rocketship to that speed, especially considering that mass is increasing requiring greater and greater amounts of energy to propel the rocketship.

I completely accept that it is impossible to make a rocketship move that fast. Nevertheless, let's imagine it could be possible, what would happen to the rocketship at the speed of light? Its mass would increase toward infinity. What is considered three-dimensional time would end. Of particular interest is the Lorentz contraction because its shortening effect would be for the length to go to zero. Normally this is interpreted to mean that the total size of the rocketship would become zero because the length disappears. But the disappearance of the one dimension of length does not mean that the rocketship must cease to have any size or any form. What about the other two dimensions of width and height that are left after the length is gone?

The hypothetical conclusion I have reached is that the other two dimensions would expand toward infinity, when the rocketship's length has disappeared. Also, all of the energy of the momentum that had been moving forward in the direction of the rocketship would be converted to two-dimensional energy. The law of conservation of energy states that energy cannot be created and cannot be destroyed. Thus energy can only be transformed or transferred from one form to another. Because of the law of conservation, the energy of the momentum can only be transformed into another form, in this case a two-dimensional form since the third direction has been eliminated.

Yes, the rocketship would disappear in size from the world of three dimensions. But with two dimensions remaining, the rocketship would suddenly pop into the two-dimensional world. The rocketship would expand in two dimensions and would take the form of an infinitely expanding circle of light. The mass that had accelerated toward infinity would become transformed entirely into photons of light, thus mc = p, with "p" representing the photon, not momentum. Although it is not possible to build a rocketship that could go at or even close to the speed of light, I believe that at the subatomic level, mass can be accelerated to the speed of light and can make the leap from the third dimension to the second dimension.

How are photons related to holy instants?

Holy instants are in time as the time it takes for a single photon to expand from an infinitely small dot and then contract back to that dot in the first dimension. The second dimension and the photon itself have an infinite third direction. The photon within the second dimension is not moving in this third direction. Thus the two-dimensional photon has no wavelength and no momentum. The photon's expansion and contraction in only two directions is why the holy instant is within time. But the holy instant is also eternal because it is infinite in that third motionless direction of the second dimension. In the following quotation, the word "picture" refers to the holy instant's timelessness, and the word "frame" refers to the holy instant's time-related aspect.

> The holy instant is a miniature of Heaven, sent you *from* Heaven. It is a picture, too, set in a frame. Yet if you accept this gift you will not see the frame at all, because the gift can only be accepted through your willingness to focus all your attention on the picture. The holy instant is a miniature of eternity. It is a picture of timelessness, set in a frame of time. If you focus on the picture, you will realize that it was only the frame that made you think it *was* a picture. Without the frame [time], the picture is seen as what it represents [eternity]. For as the whole thought system of the ego lies in its gifts, so the whole of Heaven lies in this instant, borrowed from eternity and set in time for you.[706]

What is quantum energy?

To understand the holy instant as a hybrid of the first dimension and second dimension, it is helpful to consider the nature of *quantum energy,* which was first discovered by the physicist Planck. He had come up with a formula for the spectral density of radiation. However, he could not find the application of how to use the underlying physics. He settled upon a simple formula theorizing that the quantity of energy equals a constant called "h" times frequency, written as e=hf. The letter "h" is Planck's constant ($6.62607004 \times 10^{-34}$ m^2 kg / s). The letter "f" is the frequency of the radiation. The letter "e" is the energy of a photon.

The energy of a photon is directly proportional to its frequency. Using the equation $e = hf$, the energy ("e") of one photon is equal to the Planck constant ("h") times the frequency ("f") of the photon. If the frequency of the photon is 1, then the energy of the photon is "h," which is Planck's constant itself. Before Planck's discovery, light was believed to be a continuous wave. But after his discovery, science accepted that light is *discontinuous*. This means light acts as a wave, but it also comes in discrete units of energy and therefore light has particle-like qualities. For light, a single packet ("quantum") of energy with wave and particle qualities has the energy of the Planck constant and is a photon.

These packets of energy are very small because Planck's constant is h=0.0000000000000000000000000006626 Joules per second. These bundles of energy in units of $e=hf$ are called "energy quanta." In the experiment that Planck wanted to explain, there were oscillators used. Planck had originally assumed that the oscillators in this experiment would cause the absorption and emission of energy in a continuous range of possible values. Theoretically, the amount of "h" could be reduced to zero, as would be expected from Newtonian physics. But for the formula $e=hf$ to work accurately to reflect the experimental data, Planck had to change his opinion.

To make the math work, Planck theorized that the oscillators must cause the gain and loss of energy *discontinuously* and "h" could not be zero. Instead of the continuous range of possible values of energy, the oscillators showed fixed amounts of energy units. Planck accepted the fluctuations of these discontinuous energy packets but didn't understand them. This was the birth of quantum physics. The word "quantum" refers to the smallest quantity of energy that can be emitted (or absorbed) in the form of electromagnetic radiation. Energy ("e") is equal to the Planck constant ("h") times the frequency of the radiation. Frequency ("f") is the number of discontinuous units (quanta) that occur within a given time period, such as energy units per second.

Since Planck's discovery, physicists have tried to explain quantum fluctuations entirely within the context of the three-dimensional world. In my opinion, all quantum fluctuations are actually interactions influenced by the first dimension and the second dimension connection. I believe a single photon with a frequency of one actually refers to one expansion of a two-dimensional circular photon and one contraction back to the infinitely small dot of the first dimension. Because the frequency is one, the energy of the photon equals the Planck constant ($e = hf$).

Why is two-dimensional time discontinuous?

Scientists have not been able to explain *why* all energy comes in units that must be multiples of the Planck constant. The reason is that the photon must be in a discontinuous unit because it is always forming in the second dimension and collapsing back to the first dimension, making it never continuous. The time aspect of the holy instant lasts only as long as the time it takes for a single photon to form and collapse. The time of the holy instant ends each time the photon returns to the dot in the timelessness of the first dimension, making the holy instant the smallest discontinuous unit of time just as the photon is a discontinuous unit of space and energy. Although discontinuous in its time aspect, the holy instant is continuous in regard to its connection to the timelessness of the first dimension, which is unchanged each time the holy instant is formed and is discontinued. Similarly, although the photon is discontinuous in two directions, the photon is continuous in its third direction that remains infinite even when the photon is expanding or collapsing. The energy of the photon is discontinuous within the context of the second dimension. In spite of the *form* of this energy of the photon being discontinuous, this energy is subject to the law of conversation of energy. Therefore, the energy that is discontinued in the second dimension can be considered to be continuous in the sense that it is not lost, but rather recycled. The discontinued energy is conserved when it returns to the first dimension as the photon collapses. Then that conserved energy in the first dimension is recycled in the second dimension when the photon is formed again.

How much time passes in the second dimension?

In the second dimension, there is just one holy instant of time that is also connected to timelessness. "Merely a tiny instant has elapsed between eternity and timelessness."[707] There is no progression of time beyond one instant. There is no past and there is no future in the second dimension. "Take this very instant, now, and think of it as all there is of time. Nothing can reach you here out of the past, and it is here that you are completely absolved, completely free and wholly without condemnation. From this holy instant wherein holiness was born again you will go forth in time without fear, and with no sense of change with time."[708] You could say that the second dimension has a "clock" with only the one tick of the one holy instant. Within the holy instant, God gave His answer of Correction for all of time, including the separation and all the other illusory mistakes since the separation.

> Time lasted but an instant in your mind, with no effect upon eternity. And so is all time past, and everything exactly as it was before the way to nothingness was made. The tiny tick of time in which the first mistake was made, and all of them within that one mistake, held also the Correction for that one, and all of them that came within the first. And in that tiny instant time was gone, for that was all it ever was. What God gave answer to is answered and is gone.

You may believe each holy instant is a different point in a progression of time, but in the second dimension there is no progression of time from the past to the future. Time lasts only one holy instant and that same holy instant is repeated but never changes and never accumulates into a sequence of time in the second dimension. "You look upon each holy instant as a different point in time. It never changes. All that it ever held or will ever hold is here right now. The past takes nothing from it, and the future will add no more. Here, then, is everything."[709]

In the three-dimensional world, time progresses. A day is twenty-four hours and the days accumulate in the perception of time. Everything changes as time passes in the world. But in the second dimension, time is the holy instant and is *not an accumulation of holy instants*. After the photon collapses, the next holy instant is the same single holy instant being repeated and relived changelessly. The holy instant in the second dimension can be experienced in the third dimension with Christ's vision. This holy instant is the same one that occurred in the separation when you gave up timelessness and replaced it with the illusion of time.

> You who believe that God is fear made but one substitution. It has taken many forms, because it was the substitution of illusion for truth; of fragmentation for wholeness. It has become so splintered and subdivided and divided again, over and over, that it is now almost impossible to perceive it once was one, and still is what it was. That one error, which brought truth to illusion, infinity to time, and life to death, was all you ever made.[710]

When time was first introduced as an illusion of separation from the reality of timelessness, the Son of God could have laughed at such a meaningless idea and could have instantly awakened from his dream of separation. But instead, the sleeping Son of God took the belief in time seriously and is still taking this illusion seriously believing it is real.

> Into eternity, where all is one, there crept a tiny, mad idea, at which the Son of God remembered not to laugh. In his forgetting did the thought become a serious idea, and possible of both accomplishment and real effects. Together, we can laugh them both away, and understand that time cannot intrude upon eternity. It is a joke to think that time can come to circumvent eternity, which *means* there is no time.[711]

You are right now reliving that first holy instant of the separation, which is called "the time of terror" in the following quotation: "Each day, and every minute in each day, and every instant that each minute holds, you but relive the single instant when the time of terror took the place of love. And so you die each day to live again, until you cross the gap between the past and present, which is not a gap at all."[712]

How does your frame of reference affect time and space?

The reality of Heaven is the absolute Truth of God, which is the same truth for everyone. Reality offers no possible alternate frame of reference because truth has no opposite. Reality is known in Heaven because everyone has the total awareness of knowledge. Illusions are unreal because they offer an alternative to truth that depends on the partial awareness of perception. Perception requires you to have a space between a perceiver and an object of perception. A separation in space always involves a time element that consists of time equaling distance divided by speed. When you fully awaken in Heaven, you will have total knowledge in which the ideas of space and time are meaningless. However, with your current limited awareness of perception, what you perceive depends entirely on your frame of reference based on where you believe you are located in space and time.

Let's consider what you would experience in your perception if you have the frame of reference of being on a rocketship traveling at 87% of the speed of light. At this specific speed, your time would be 50% slower that time observed on earth. In this case, your clock on the rocketship will record one minute of time, while the same clock on earth will record two minutes.[713] When you return to the frame of reference of earth after traveling one year in your rocketship, you will be told that two years had elapsed on earth when you had only aged one year.

Now let's imagine as your frame of reference, you are a photon of light in the second dimension. As a photon, you are "born" as an expanding circle. Then you are a contracting circle. Finally, your circle becomes a dot, so the circle "dies." But next you are "reincarnated" and have no memory of the past. From this frame of reference of a circular photon, your "lifespan" is always the same holy instant of time." The holy instant is the only time there is in this frame of reference. Thus from your frame of reference, your holy instant contains all the worldly time of human history. If you are a photon in the second dimension, you also have a third direction where you are infinite, motionless, and timeless. When you apparently "die," all your two-dimensional energy becomes just like that third direction being infinite, motionless, and timeless. When you are in the second dimension as a circular photon, you have one frame of reference that is a perfect reflection of the Light of Heaven. When you return to being a dot in the first dimension, you have the divine frame of reference of reality itself. From the frame of reference of the second dimension, you as a photon can only conceive of two limited dimensions and a third unlimited dimension. But you could not possibly conceive of a different frame of reference with three limited dimensions. On the other hand, if you perceive yourself as part of a three-dimensional world, you would find yourself seeing the second dimension as though it was three-dimensional. You would see the third direction of two-dimensional photons as though they were limited by wavelengths, even though that direction is infinite.

How are holy instants and photons perceived within the frame of reference of the third dimension?

Within the frame of reference of the second dimension, time is just the formation and collapse of every photon, which lasts for one holy instant. Then that same holy instant is repeated with no real change having occurred. The photon that collapses and disappears is identical to the next photon that is formed, just as each holy instant is also identical to the next one. Therefore, there is no past different than the present and no future different than the present. If you experience the real world of the second dimension, you will be as close to the eternal *now* as you can be outside of the first dimension of Heaven.

But from the frame of reference of the third dimension, time will seem to be progressing. Why? Perception of the third dimension is seen through physical eyes and is not capable of perceiving the unlimited third direction of the photon and the holy instant. From the viewpoint of the third dimension, the infinite third direction of the photon is perceived as being just as limited as its length and width. Thus the photon, while remaining two-dimensional, is perceived as being a three-dimensional discontinuous energy unit (quantum). The photon's unlimited third direction is perceived as having a limited length, which is its wavelength. Likewise, the eternal aspect of the holy instant in the second dimension is perceived as the progression of time from the frame of reference of the third dimension.

Within the second dimension, the holy instant remains partially connected to timelessness and the photon remains partially connected to the infinite. The two-dimensional holy instant and the two-dimensional photon always remain connected to the first dimension, in spite of being misperceived within the third dimension. This two-dimensional light of the real world connected to the first dimension is what the Course calls "true light," which has been explained on pages 86 to 88. You cannot see true light with your physical eyes since this light is not three-dimensional. But you can use Christ's vision to see true light.

All the teachings of the Course are designed to encourage you to make a shift in your frame of reference. The most typical frame of reference is the obvious one of using the physical body and its senses, which are limited and can only perceive the limitations within the third dimension. The other frame of reference relies on Christ's vision and not on using your physical eyes. "Let me not look to my own eyes to see today. Let me be willing to exchange my pitiful illusion of seeing for the vision that is given by God. Christ's vision is His gift, and He has given it to me. Let me call upon this gift today, so that this day may help me to understand eternity."[714] The shift from vision of physical light of the third dimension to true light of the second dimension is also a shift in emotion from fear found in the world to only loving thoughts in the real world, as a preparation for the infinite love found in the first dimension. "You have but two emotions, and one [fear] you made and one [love] was given you. Each is a way of seeing, and different worlds arise from their different sights. See through the vision that is given you, for through Christ's vision He beholds Himself."[715]

The physical world and the real world are illusions that are within your mind as dream worlds you have projected. The physical world in the third dimension is an illusion of apparent opposites, such as love and fear, truth and falsehood, and light and darkness. The real world is an illusion since it has only the partial awareness of limited perceptions. But within the illusion of the real world, those perceptions are unified to express only love, light, and truth that are reflections of Heaven.

You can ask for the gift of true light in order to see the real world. "True light that makes true [Christ's] vision possible is not the light the body's eyes behold. It is a state of mind that has become so unified that darkness cannot be perceived at all."[716] Every form in the third dimension has a two-dimensional counterpart in the real world. "The real world holds a counterpart for each unhappy thought reflected in your world..."[717] Each two-dimensional counterpart has a third infinite direction, and each counterpart can be seen shining in true light with Christ's vision. "The smallest leaf becomes a thing of wonder, and a blade of grass a sign of God's perfection."[718] Physical eyes can only see a three-dimensional version of light, which has a limited wavelength as its third direction. Christ's vision enables you to see true light, which is two-dimensional light that has an infinite third direction, connected to the first dimension as a reflection of Heaven. The forms you see with Christ's vision are still illusions, but their loving content is eternal and will go with you when you awaken in Heaven. "Every loving thought that the Son of God ever had is eternal. The loving thoughts his mind perceives in this world are the world's only reality."[719]

Is the two-dimensional photon still two-dimensional when it is seen in the third dimension?

For photons of light to be seen with the physical eyes within the third dimension, those photons would have to be perceived as being three-dimensional. Certainly, photons are subjectively perceived as being within the three-dimensional world. These perceived photons do produce noticeable three-dimensional effects, such as heat and light. Nevertheless, these effects produced by photons are the result of the fact that the second dimension itself overlaps and influences the third dimension, which it transcends because of its unrecognized infinite third direction. Although photons are perceived with the physical eyes as being three-dimensional, photons remain two-dimensional while being connected to the infinite first dimension. The second dimension is the real world, which the Course calls "the world of light." This is where the two-dimensional photon remains while it is seen as being three-dimensional within the frame of reference of the third dimension. "This world of light, this circle of brightness is the real world..."[720]

The two dimensions of length and width of each photon are limited as the photon expands and contracts. This means that photons are discontinuous two-dimensional units of energy, which could be called "two-dimensional quanta." The third direction of the photon is infinite and motionless because it reaches to the first dimension. But from the perspective of the third dimension, this infinite third direction is seen as being finite and moving at the speed of light rather than being the motionless light of the first dimension. Instead of photons being recognized as two-dimensional discontinuous quanta, the photons' third direction is divided into discontinuous pieces so its wavelengths are perceived as "three-dimensional quanta."

All light perceived in the third dimension never really leaves the second dimension, except after each holy instant when all light leaves the second dimension as it returns to the first dimension from which it originated. The second dimension is an illusory reflection of reality that relies on its connection to the first dimension. The third dimension is an illusion within the illusion of the second dimension. Although the third dimension relies on the two-dimensional illusion, it distorts the infinite third direction of the second dimension by limiting it.

If a rocketship travels for 93 million miles from the sun to the earth at the speed of light, a hypothetical rocketship captain would experience time slowing down so much due to time dilation that time would stop. Zero time would pass for the rocketship captain from his frame of reference, while 8.3 minutes would pass from the world's frame of reference. In addition, due to the Lorentz contraction, the rocketship captain himself and his rocketship would shrink to zero length in the direction it is traveling. From the frame of reference of the captain, the rocketship would have traveled zero distance to go from the sun to the earth, while the rocketship would have traveled 93 million miles from the worldly frame of reference.

Of course, a rocketship cannot travel at the speed of light, but a photon can and does. A photon of sunlight travels 93 million miles to go from the sun to the earth and the trip takes 8.3 minutes of time from the worldly frame of reference. Now imagine you are this photon traveling from the sun to the earth. Just as the hypothetical rocketship captain would experience no three-dimensional passage of time and no distance between the sun and earth, you in your role of being the photon would have an entirely two-dimensional experience. You would be aware of only one holy instant of time in two directions. From your frame of reference, your third direction would be just as timeless and infinite as usual since it is your connection to the first dimension. You, as the photon of sunlight, would experience zero time in your third direction and you would experience zero traveling distance.

This analogy has been provided to illustrate that from the frame of reference of the photon, every photon remains entirely two-dimensional, even while it is perceived as traveling in time and space from the frame of reference of the third dimension. The photon remains likewise entirely infinite in its third direction, even while its third direction is perceived as being limited to a very wide range of wavelengths from the frame of reference of the third dimension. This means that if a photon travels the entire length of the physical universe, that photon is always traveling zero distance for one holy instant from the frame of reference of the second dimension. In regard to the photon, the frame of reference of the second dimension can be said to be more valid than the worldly frame of reference since the second dimension is a true reflection of Heaven, as is revealed by Christ's vision. However, there is only one absolute arbitrator of what frame of reference is truly valid, which is God's frame of reference recognizing all illusions, including time, do not exist.

How are dimensions related to wave/particle duality?

Although the photon appears to be both a wave and particle from the perspective of the third dimension, this is just a misperception of what the photon really is. The photon is perceived in the third dimension, but it never actually leaves the second dimension. The true nature of the photon is that it is just a dot from the first dimension expanding into a two-dimensional disc and contracting back to the infinitely small dot. The third direction of the photon is infinite, but from the three-dimensional perspective, the expanding and contacting flat disc will appear to be moving forward perpendicular to the other two dimensions. The distance the photon seems to be moving forward is the distance the speed of light can travel as one two-dimensional photon is formed by expansion and is dissolved by contraction. This distance is the wavelength.

Appearing to move forward for one holy instant at the speed of light, the circular two-dimensional photon will appear to take the shape of a horizontal "S" shaped wave. If the photon is only a two-dimensional expansion and contraction of a circular energy field, it would appear in the third dimension as two horizontal cones as shown in the illustration on the following page. As the photon expands, it would be seen within the third dimension as the horizontal cone on the left. As the photon contracts, it would appear as the horizontal cone on the right.

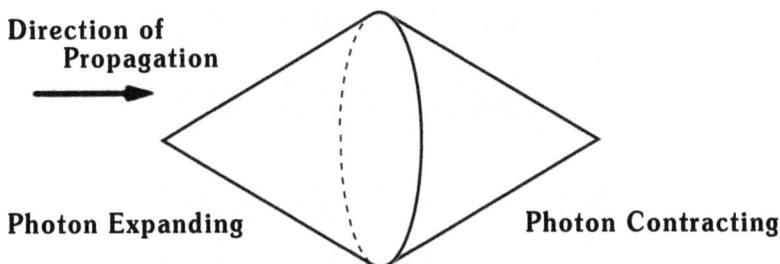

Electromagnetic waves are not perceived as shown in the imaginary illustration above. The illustration below is of the photon perceived as a horizontal "S" shaped electromagnetic wave. There is a reason why the two horizontal cone shapes are not perceived and why the horizontal "S" shaped wave is perceived in the third dimension.

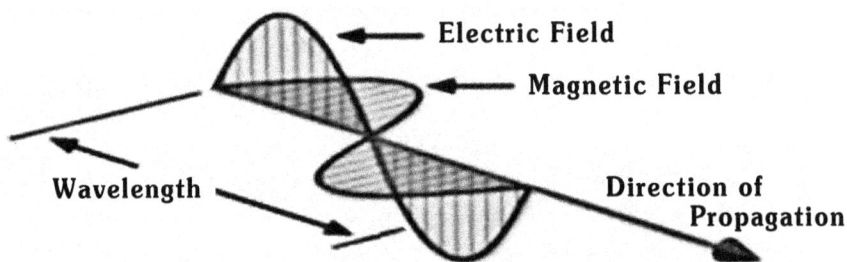

The reason why the two-dimensional photon is perceived in the third dimension as an "S" shaped wave is that the photon is more than just an expanding and contracting circle of energy. The two-dimensional photon consists of a flat electric field and a flat magnetic field existing within its circular shape as it expands and contracts. In addition to the photon expanding and contracting, its electric and magnetic fields are *rotating*. Thus the photon is constantly changing in both *size* and *rotation*, which is the reason why the two-dimensional photon is perceived in the third dimension as an "S" shaped wave. There are actually two waves: One is an "S" shaped wave for the electric field, and the other one is an "S" shaped wave for the magnetic field. As the two-dimensional photon expands in size from a dot to a circle, its electric and magnetic fields rotate 180 degrees. As the photon contracts in size from a circle to a dot, its fields rotate another 180 degrees, returning the photon to the first dimension. This takes one holy instant of time. The next photon that forms and collapses in the second dimension is identical in its form and in its location to the previous photon.

Because the two-dimensional photon rotates, it appears in the third dimension as the horizontal "S" shaped wave. When the *expanding* and rotating photon is perceived as moving forward, it gives the impression of the first half of the horizontal "S" wave. When the *contracting* and rotating photon is perceived as moving forward, it brings about the impression of the second half of the horizontal "S" shaped wave. The length from the beginning of the horizontal "S" shape to the end is its wavelength. The wavelength is defined as the distance over which the wave's "S" shape repeats. The wavelength indicates one expansion and one contraction of the circular two-dimensional photon. The photon in the second dimension always has the energy of the Planck constant. However, in the third dimension, the actual length of the wavelength determines the forward-moving energy of the photon as its momentum. The momentum is the energy of the Planck constant divided by the length of the wavelength in meters.

Unlike the two-dimensional photon that returns to its same location and time, this three-dimensional photon moves to a new location. Since space/time is one thing, any change in spatial location will produce a change in time. Thus just as the photon is perceived as moving forward in location, it is also perceived as having moved forward in time. From the frame of reference of the third dimension, when the next photon expands and contracts, it cannot return to the same space and time as it does in the second dimension. This is why there is a progression of movement in space and also a forward progression in time in the third dimension that does not occur in the second dimension.

This explains the paradox of how a photon possesses wave/particle duality. The photon is perceived as being a wave while it is rotating and expanding and contracting. It is perceived as being a particle when it barely starts to expand from the dot leaving the first dimension and also when it has contracted and is about to disappear into the dot in the first dimension. The fact that each photon must expand, contract, and disappear back to the first dimension explains why the wave cannot be a continuous wave and must consist of discontinuous quantum energy packets that are multiples of the Plank constant.

How much time is the holy instant?

Although the holy instant is connected to the timelessness of the first dimension, the holy instant in the second dimension is the smallest unit of time. What is the exact amount of time of the holy instant? I have my own theory about this, which will be explained in my future book about "triple dimension physics." However, for now, let's assume that the holy instant is the same as *Planck time*, which is the smallest unit of time that has any meaning. It is written as $5.391\ 16 \times 10^{-44}$ seconds. If the holy instant equals Planck time, it would be the following part of a second —.00000000000000000000000000000000000000000539056. Time is calculated by dividing distance by speed. Modern science defines Planck time as the time it would take a photon moving at the speed of light to travel a distance equal to the *Planck length*. Just as the photon itself is discontinuous because it forms and disappears, Planck time and Planck length represent discontinuous units of time and of distance respectively. Although Planck time and Planck length have been computed theoretically, they are too small to be confirmed due to the current limitations of experimental measuring.

It was originally believed that energy was continuous, yet it was later proved energy comes in discontinuous quantum packets. Time also gives the appearance of being continuous, but the holy instant is the single discontinuous unit of time that makes time the smallest deviation from eternity, which itself is continuous timelessness. Whatever the exact measurement of the holy instant happens to be, the most important thing to remember is that the holy instant is the fundamental discontinuous smallest unit of time just as the Planck constant is the single smallest discontinuous energy unit. Just as all energy comes in single or multiple quantum units of the Planck constant, all time comes in quantum units of the holy instant or misperceived multiples of the holy instant.

What does the holy instant have to do with the illusion of a holographic universe?

In the second dimension, there is only one holy instant blinking on and off, but without seeming to accumulate time. In the third dimension, that holy instant is seen as being accumulated in an endless progression of time. Therefore, the eternal now of the first dimension is divided into countless pictures of time, like individual frames in a movie film. Science currently believes Planck time is the time required for light to travel, in a vacuum, a distance of one Planck length. If the eternal now were divided like frames in a movie film, Planck time would be the individual pictures of time that would be projected for us to see. If you were seeing a movie projected onto a flat screen, you would never see any one individual frame. You would only see the movie in motion, which is an illusion of movement. You would even interpret the two-dimensional movie screen as if it were a three-dimensional space. The holy instant as Planck time is like these individual frames of the movie that are blurred together so you never see their quantum units of individual frames. It appears to you that time is passing continuously. Because of your context of space, you cannot see the discontinuous nature of each individual duration of time, meaning each discontinuous quantum of time, which is the aspect of the holy instant that is within time.

You would not know if photons of light are flickering at the subatomic level, especially when you consider how much slower fluctuations of light are not consciously experienced. In order to understand time and light fluctuation, consider what you appear to see when you watch television (or a computer monitor) in contrast to what is actually occurring without your awareness. What you appear to see when you watch television is a continuous picture. What you are actually being presented with is a screen of pixels or units of light. Instead of a steady stream of continuous light, you experience a flickering of light on and off. This is the "flicker rate" or "refresh rate," which is the rate of time it takes for the screen to reset itself. This flickering is happening so fast you cannot see it. This is called "the flicker fusion threshold" or "flicker fusion rate" that is defined as the frequency at which *intermittent* light stimulus appears to be a *continuous* light stimulus to the vision of an average person. The refresh rate of how often an older model television changes an image on screen is called a "frame," and it is 60 times per second (60 Hertz). Often modern television sets will have a refresh rate of 120 Hertz (120 frames per second), but some have a refresh rate of 240 Hertz.

When you are looking at a television screen, you are looking at the phosphorescent glow of over hundreds of thousands of tiny pixels or dots so you are not looking at a picture. You might assume that when the lights come on, you are seeing a picture and when the lights go off, the picture disappears. Yet even when the lights are on, there is not really a picture there to see in any objective sense. Your subjective mind needs to interpret those lights as a picture built up over time. In the case of a television, all the lights don't go off all at once together even though the frame is refreshed. Which dots are left on and which dots are turned off determines the frame of the screen that you see. A scanning system is used to refresh the screen. This scanning is not recognized visually just as the flickering is not consciously seen. The television scanning system is described below as a series of lighted dots that you interpret subjectively as a picture, when really there is objectively no single picture there.

> Proceeding along a line from the upper-right-hand portion of your screen across the top to the left, the scan lights some dots and skips others, depending upon the image to be conveyed. Then the scan goes down another line, starts at the right again and goes across to the left and so on. What you perceive as a picture is actually an image that never exists in any given moment but rather is constructed over time. Your perception of it as an image depends upon your brain's ability to gather in all the lit dots, collect the image they make on your retina in sequence, and form a picture. The picture itself, however, never existed. Unlike ordinary life, in which whatever you see actually exists outside you before you let it in through your eyes, a television image gains its existence *only* once you've put it together inside your head.[721]

As you watch what appears to be pictures, the flickering dots and scanning of the screen that affect these dots can't be observed directly. Everything you perceive is seen at a rate of speed that exceeds the full processing abilities of the physical apparatus of nerves between your brain and retina. You can only see what's in the slower range of speed. If this whole world is a hologram with a refresh rate of Planck time as the holy instant, it would be impossible for you to notice the flickering of this worldly three-dimensional hologram. Each photon in the second dimension forms and collapses in unison making for one holy instant. Thus all parts of the whole second dimension are flicking on and off at the same rate. Since the refresh rate of the second dimension is one holy instant, when you enter the real world, you are just one holy instant away from experiencing the eternal *now* in Heaven. But time in the third dimension is much more complicated. Light of different wavelengths flickers on and off at different refresh rates. Yet time in both dimensions is illusory and only seems real. "Time is a trick, a sleight of hand, a vast illusion in which figures come and go as if by magic. Yet there is a plan behind appearances that does not change. The script is written. When experience will come to end your doubting has been set."[722]

What is light that appears in the third dimension?

The second dimension is not independent of the first dimension. The third dimension is not independent of either the second dimension or the first dimension. The oneness of the divine Light from the first dimension is fragmented into two-dimensional circular photons that expand, contract, and rotate before returning to the first dimension. This two-dimensional light is projected into three-dimensional forms that appear as light or as the frozen light of mass. This projected light forms a holographic universe according to some physicists. There are five fundamental ideas about this three-dimensional hologram that are important to consider:

1. The first dimension is the only reality and the only true source of Light. The two other dimensions borrow dimensionless infinite Light of the first dimension and alter that unlimited light so it is perceived as being limited. The second dimension is a lesser light than the Light of the first dimension, but it is a reflection of the first dimension, similar to the way the moon receives reflected light from the sun.

2. The second dimension is itself a two-dimensional hologram of light projected from the first dimension. As all holograms, the whole is present everywhere within each of its smaller parts. In the second dimension hologram, microcosmically each photon is a small circle of light with an infinitely small dot as its center point. Macrocosmically, the second dimension as a whole is one giant circle of light with an infinitely small dot in the center, identical to each photon making up its parts.

3. The reflected light originally from the Light of the first dimension is projected to and then through the second dimension to produce the three-dimensional world in which light is fragmented to make up the holographic physical universe. Yet the whole is everywhere present in each fragmented part of the light of the holographic universe.

4. All two-dimensional photons are formed in the same holy instant and return simultaneously to the first dimension. Thus all of the second dimension as a whole is flickering on and off at the same exact start and end of one holy instant. The flicker range is from the holy instant to zero time of the eternal now. The three-dimensional photon has a flicker rate dependent on its frequency, which is the number of wavelengths that are repeated for a given period of time. The longer the wavelength is, the lower the frequency will be. The shorter the wavelength is, the higher the frequency will be. Since the frequency varies, the refresh rate will vary in the third dimension but will always be a faster rate than the holy instant that is the unchanging refresh rate of the entire second dimension.

5. When light in the second dimension is perceived in a holographic third dimension, *the two-dimensional photons are fragmented in their three-dimensional appearance but not changed in their two-dimensional and one-dimensional substance.* Perception of light from a worldly frame of reference is a distortion of the true nature of two-dimensional photons that remain connected to the first dimension. Christ's vision removes this distortion so you can perceive the true light of the second dimension that includes its connection to the infinite third direction.

What is a hologram, and what is a holographic image?

Making a hologram requires two beams of focused light. A hologram is a recording of the difference between two beams of coherent light. The hologram diffracts light into the form of a picture of light that is called a "holographic image." The term "hologram" can include both the encoded material and the resulting image.

What is important to remember about a hologram is *that the whole is present in every part of the entire hologram.* A hologram on a glass plate is made as follows: Two beams of laser light are shined onto a glass plate coated with a light sensitive emulsion. One beam is the original laser light. Another beam is bounced off an object and onto the glass plate. The two overlapping waves of light result in an interference pattern. The two beams interfering with each other make a holographic image. Unlike a normal photograph, light from every point on the object is absorbed at every single point on the holographic plate. Thus the entire image of the object is recorded as a whole, but more importantly is recorded at every point on the holographic plate.

After a holographic plate is developed, the image first appears to be just a swirl of light. But when a third laser is shined onto the developed plate, it produces a three-dimensional effect. When a normal photograph is cut into pieces, the wholeness of the photographic image is lost. What if you cut a holographic image into small pieces? Every fragment of the holographic plate will reveal an image of the whole object because every part of a hologram contains the information of the whole.

Is the universe a holographic image?

The fact that science has revealed that interference patterns of light can produce holographic images raises the question of whether or not this holographic principle could be a fundamental part of the universe. If the holographic principle applies to the universe, it means that the entire wholeness of the macrocosmic universe is contained within every individual microcosmic point in the universe. An increasing number of physicists are exploring the possibility that the universe is a holographic image. This theoretical research related to a holographic universe may lead to a greater awareness of the nature of reality. Jacob Bekenstein, professor of Theoretical Physics, wrote the following:

> Remarkably, recent developments in theoretical physics answer some of these questions, and the answers might be important clues to the ultimate theory of reality. By studying the mysterious properties of black holes, physicists have deduced absolute limits on how much information a region of space or a quantity of matter and energy can hold. Related results suggest that our universe, which we perceive to have three spatial dimensions, might instead be written on a two-dimensional surface, like a hologram. Our everyday perceptions of the world as three-dimensional would then be either a profound illusion or merely one of two alternative ways of viewing reality. A grain of sand may not encompass our world, but a flat screen might. [723]

What does the holographic nature of light have to do with the face of Christ?

The subtitle of this book is "See the Face of Christ and Awaken" to emphasize this idea: "*The face of Christ* has to be seen before the memory of God can return."[724] Since you cannot awaken unless you see the face of Christ, it is helpful to understand as much as possible about what this means, especially in relation to the holographic illusions of the second and third dimensions. The term "the face of Christ" is not just a poetic term. The face of Christ must have form. "All thinking produces form at some level."[725] The entirely loving thoughts of the real world have taken the form of the face of Christ expressed as "the bright Rays of His Father's Love that light His [Christ's] face with glory."[726] If the face of Christ did not have a form, it might be an elusive intellectual concept of divine love. How could you "see" the face of Christ as you must do to awaken if His face has no form? Since all perception must manifest form at some level, what form does the face of Christ take so it can be seen? The form the face of Christ takes is the image of an expanding circle of light. Another name for the face of Christ is the "vision of the Son of God" that is described in the following way:

Beyond the body, beyond the sun and stars, past everything you see and yet somehow familiar, is an arc of golden light that stretches as you look into a great and shining circle. And all the circle fills with light before your eyes. The edges of the circle disappear, and what is in it is no longer contained at all. The light expands and covers everything, extending to infinity forever shining and with no break or limit anywhere. Within it everything is joined in perfect continuity. Nor is it possible to imagine that anything could be outside, for there is nowhere that this light is not.[727]

The quotation above describing the vision of the Son of God refers to light in the form of "an arc of golden light that stretches as you look into a great and shining circle." This expanding circle of blazing light is the form of the face of Christ. The next two lines describe how this two-dimensional circle is connected to the infinity of the first dimension: "The edges of the circle disappear, and what is in it is no longer contained at all. The light expands and covers everything, extending to infinity forever shining and with no break or limit anywhere." This whole first paragraph describes the form of the real world of only light and loving thoughts where the face of Christ is seen. The macrocosm of the real world is one giant expanding circle of light seen in the second dimension as the face of Christ, and this circle of light is the form that must be seen to remember God and awaken to His Love.

In the microcosm of the real world, which is the second dimension, the individual photon is a circle of light seen in the holy instant. Every hologram has the same image in each part that is also the image of the whole. The real world is a holographic illusion that shows you the face of Christ as a circle of light in the wholeness of the second dimension and the same face of Christ as a circle of light in each microcosmic photon. Why is it important for you to see the same face of Christ both macrocosmically and microcosmically in order to awaken? The answer is that this two-dimensional holographic image reminds you of your own wholeness and your part-ness in Christ. You will see your wholeness in Christ in the wholeness of the two-dimensional face of Christ. You will see your part-ness in Christ in each individual two-dimensional photon. In this dual reflection, you are seeing how your Father thinks of you as a part of Christ and the whole Christ. "The recognition of the part as whole, and of the whole in every part is perfectly natural, for it is the way God thinks, and what is natural to Him is natural to you.[728] The face of Christ needs to be seen to awaken because this two-dimensional hologram in form reminds you that *you are a formless one-dimensional hologram*. God gave you a part/whole Identity so you are the *living holographic Christ*. The face of Christ, seen as the vision of the Son of God, awakens the memory of your *divine holographic Identity*.

This is the vision of the Son of God, whom you know well. Here is the sight of him who knows his Father. Here is the memory of what you are; a part of this, with all of it within, and joined to all as surely as all is joined in you. Accept the vision that can show you this, and not the body. You know the ancient song, and know it well. Nothing will ever be as dear to you as is this ancient hymn of love the Son of God sings to his Father still.[729]

Though only an unreal holographic image, the vision of the Son of God is the face of Christ that shows you your own *holographic reality* of part-ness and wholeness as Christ. This holographic vision is where you will remember "what you are" and awaken. "Here is the memory of what you are; a part of this, with all of it within, and joined to all as surely as all is joined in you." Notice the words "a part of this, with all of it within" are a holographic reminder that you are a part of Christ with all of the whole Christ within your part. This vision can only be seen with Christ's vision, not the body's eyes. "Accept the vision that can show you this, and not the body." Hidden within your mind is the memory of an "ancient hymn of love the Son of God sings to his Father still." This "ancient hymn of love" will inevitably come to your mind when you finally see the face of Christ in the vision of an expanding circle of light. "And they will look upon the vision of the Son of God, remembering who he is they sing of. What is a miracle but this remembering? And who is there in whom this memory lies not?"[730]

This memory of the song of love you sing to your Father is only blocked by the separation you feel between your brother and you. To remove the block to the awareness of your love for your brother and for your Father, you need to welcome Christ's vision and forgiveness. "Forgiveness lets the veil be lifted up that hides the face of Christ from those who look with unforgiving eyes upon the world. It lets you recognize the Son of God, and clears your memory of all dead thoughts so that remembrance of your Father can arise across the threshold of your mind. What would you want forgiveness cannot give?"[731]

How is the face of Christ like the picture of the Son of God?

Just as the vision of the Son of God is another way of describing the face of Christ, the Course's description of the "picture of the Son of God" is another way of describing the face of Christ. This picture is first described as the "broken picture of the Son of God," which is the picture of Christ seen in the three-dimensional world. Then the Course refers to this as the "holy picture" that the Holy Spirit heals in the real world so it is no longer broken. "The Holy Spirit's function is to take the broken picture of the Son of God and put the pieces into place again. This holy picture, healed entirely, does He hold out to every separate piece that thinks it is a picture in itself."[732] Each sleeping Son of God has exaggerated his part-ness in Christ so each separate piece of the broken picture "thinks it is a picture in itself" and disregards the wholeness of Christ that the whole picture stands for. But the Holy Spirit's function is to point to the holy picture of wholeness and to remind each sleeping Son of God of his true Identity as the whole Christ instead of being just a broken and separated little piece. "To each He [the Holy Spirit] offers his Identity [Christ], which the whole picture represents, instead of just a little, broken bit that he insisted was himself. And when he sees this [whole] picture [of his Identity] he will recognize himself."[733] Seeing the healed and holy picture of the Son of God restores his memory of his true nature as the whole Christ, just as seeing the face of Christ will restore your memory of your Father and memory of your true Self as His Son. This remembering awakens you and opens the door to your Father Who will take the final step of welcoming you back to complete awareness of your home in Heaven. "And here the Father will receive His Son, because His Son was gracious to himself."[734]

In the next paragraph, Jesus expresses his gratitude that the "broken pieces" of the Christ are brought together in wholeness. Each individual part of the one Christ is recognized as equal to every other part and "the whole is in each one." The quote below clearly emphasizes the holographic principle that the whole is within each part.

> I thank You, Father, knowing You will come to close each little gap that lies between the broken pieces of Your holy Son. Your Holiness, complete and perfect, lies in every one of them. And they are joined because what is in one is in them all. How holy is the smallest grain of sand, when it is recognized as being part of the completed picture of God's Son! The forms the broken pieces seem to take mean nothing. For the whole is in each one. And every aspect of the Son of God is just the same as every other part.[735]

How can you prepare for finally seeing the face of Christ?

You can have an awakening experience in any holy instant. But the passing of the body will be your best opportunity to see the face of Christ, *fully* awaken in Heaven, and not be reincarnated again. Yet if you react with fear when seeing the face of Christ, the appropriate response of awe might be mistaken for fear. If that happens, you will not awaken. Instead, you will be reincarnated. The best way to prepare for your final seeing of the face of Christ will be using the seven instruments of the Holy Spirit. These seven instruments have previously been identified as forgiveness, Christ's vision, the holy relationship, the holy instant, miracles, meditation, and the Atonement. Although these learning tools have separate names, they are the same because they share a common purpose. "What shares a common purpose is the same. This is the law of purpose, which unites all those who share in it within itself."[736] These instruments are like a hologram because each one is a different name for the same oneness represented by the wholeness of all seven.

Their individual and collective purpose is to reveal to you that every aspect of Christ is a part of Christ and the whole Christ. Perception will tell you a part cannot be the whole, but these tools prepare you for awakening and accepting the total awareness of knowledge. Just as every part of Christ is whole, every aspect of knowledge is whole. "Every aspect is whole, and therefore no aspect is separate. You are an aspect of knowledge, being in the Mind of God, Who knows you. All knowledge must be yours, for in you is all knowledge."[737]

Since the seven tools of the Holy Spirit have the same purpose of removing the separation between your brother and you, they are used together. Meditation is an inner form of forgiveness in which you look for the divine and overlook distracting thoughts. Forgiveness is an outer form of meditation in which you look for the divine and overlook any distracting thoughts. Christ's vision enables you to see the face of Christ in your brother, which forgives him by removing your judgments and reestablishing your eternal holy relationship with him. By accepting the Atonement for yourself, you let the miracle of love be extended not *by* you but *through* you, healing your brother and you. With Christ's vision, you will see an aspect of Christ, but you will also see the whole Christ because *every* aspect is the whole. When you see the same face of Christ in every brother, that generalized learning is your ideal way of preparing for the final vision of seeing the face of Christ and awakening. "This is the miracle of creation; *that it is one forever.* Every miracle you offer to the Son of God is but the true perception of one aspect of the whole [Christ]. Though *every* aspect [of Christ] *is* the whole [Christ], you cannot know this until you see that *every* aspect [Son of God] is the same, perceived in the same light and therefore one."[738]

Instead of misperceiving your brother as a body, Christ's vision lets you literally see light in him, and "if you see light in him, your sins have been forgiven by yourself."[739] Your brother carries God's presence that can be recognized by perceiving true light. "And as you see him shining in the space of light where God abides within the darkness, you will see that God Himself is where his body is. Before this light the body disappears, as heavy shadows must give way to light. The darkness cannot choose that it remain. The coming of the light means it is gone. In glory will you see your brother then, and understand what really fills the gap so long perceived as keeping you apart."[740]

You are the means for God; not separate, nor with a life apart from His. His life is manifest in you who are His Son. Each aspect of Himself is framed in holiness and perfect purity, in love celestial and so complete it wishes only that it may release all that it looks upon unto itself. Its radiance shines through each body that it looks upon, and brushes all its darkness into light merely by looking past it *to* the light. The veil is lifted through its gentleness, and nothing hides the face of Christ from its beholders. You and your brother stand before Him now, to let Him draw aside the veil that seems to keep you separate and apart.[741]

Is seeing Christ's face and your awakening for you alone?

Your remembering of God and your awakening is not for you alone because awakening is the full recognition that you are never alone as part of God's Family. "The light in one awakens it in all."[742] Your final awakening will bless every Son of God, yet your preparation requires that you learn to bless your brother now. "The holy instant is this instant and every instant. The one you want it to be it is. The one you would not have it be is lost to you. You must decide when it is. Delay it not."[743] Healing happens in the holy instant. "The holy instant's radiance will light your eyes, and give them sight to see beyond all suffering and see Christ's face instead. Healing replaces suffering."[744]

In the holy instant, you can see "glimpses" of Christ's face in your brother. "If you see glimpses of the face of Christ...you will behold your brother's face and recognize it."[745] You must welcome Christ's vision to perceive your brother in the holy instant without his body and without guilt. "And each one finds his savior when he is ready to look upon the face of Christ, and see Him sinless."[746] How you see your brother is how you see yourself. "If he be lost in sin, so must you be; if you see light in him, your sins have been forgiven by yourself."[747] By seeing the face of Christ in your brother, you will see your own face. "And you will see Christ's face...in reflection of your own."[748] After all, "you *are* light"[749] and so is your brother. Seeing the face of Christ is not limited to seeing just one brother and seeing yourself reflected there. "The light in one awakens it in all. And when you see it [light] in your brother, you *are* remembering for everyone."[750] You will want to bear witness to the light of the face of Christ you have seen in the holy instant so you can help all parts of the sleeping Son of God to awaken.

> The interval [holy instant] suffices. It is here that miracles are laid; to be returned by you from holy instants you receive, through grace in your experience, to all who see the light that lingers in your face. What is the face of Christ but his who went a moment into timelessness, and brought a clear reflection of the unity he felt an instant back to bless the world? How could you finally attain to it forever, while a part of you [your brother] remains outside, unknowing, unawakened, and in need of you as witness to the truth?[751]

FINAL THOUGHTS

~ o ~

A helpful way to prepare yourself for awakening is to remind yourself many times during the day that you are loved by God. To express gratitude for God's Love, every morning I start my day by repeating the prayer below that has grown over time to be a long one. At first, my prayer of gratitude was just the first two sentences, which summarize the idea that God's Love must be acknowledged within and then extended to everyone. I am not recommending that you repeat my prayer, but I do suggest that you formulate your own short prayer in your own words. The words you choose are not as important as your sense of gratitude and willingness to open your heart and mind to the divine within and without.

Father, thank You for loving me. Let Your love flow through me to bless all my brothers and sisters everywhere. They are the holy Son of God Who deserve to wake up in Heaven. They are Christ. They are the light. They are love. I am the holy Son of God Who deserves to wake up in Heaven. I am Christ. I am light. I am love. I am just as holy now as when You created me without guilt in my eternal Home in Heaven. With Jesus beside me on my journey of awakening, Holy Spirit, guide my mind, decide for God for me, and be in charge of my meditation experience of the holy instant. Holy Spirit and Jesus, with your help, I forgive all my brothers and sisters and I forgive myself because we deserve only love and not the illusions of guilt we have fabricated to unfairly punish ourselves. I am free of all my mistakes and their effects because I gratefully accept the perfect love and healing of the Atonement that corrects all errors. I am not a body. I am free for I am still as You created me. I am still a spirit created in Your Thought and in likeness to Your character. Help me to appreciate and manifest the things of spirit: peace, kindness, love, patience, faith, hope, charity and humility. Help me to let go of the things of the ego and attachments to the body, such as fear, anger, pain, guilt, shame, pride, specialness, and judgment. Father, help me to do Your Will and understand that Your will is my true will, which is all the loving expressions I would create if I were fully aware of all the love You are giving me right now. Help me to love everyone. Father, let Your Light and Love flow through me to bless (names of those in need of prayer).

[1] *A Course in Miracles* quotations in this book come from the second edition that is currently in public domain. Helen Schucman referred to herself as the "scribe" of the Course. She considered Jesus Christ to be the true author of the Course because he dictated the Course to her. The second edition of the Course was first copyrighted and published by the Foundation of Inner Peace, P. O. Box 598, Mill Valley, CA 94942-0598.

[2] T-22.III.2:1

[3] T-12.V.8:3

[4] T-6.IV.1:1-2

[5] T-6.IV.6:1-2

[6] T-12.IV.5:5

[7] T-6.IV.6:3-8

[8] T-8.III.1:3

[9] C-4.7:4

[10] T-26.IV.3:3

[11] T-26.VIII.9:1

[12] T-5.II.10:5,7

[13] T-26.VIII.9:9-10

[14] W.ep.3:3

[15] W-pII.8.2:1-3

[16] T-18.II.9:4

[17] T-13.VII.9:1-2

[18] W-pII.in.2:2-5

[19] T-17.VI.2:2

[20] T-13.VIII.3:1-2, 7-9

[21] W-71.6:4

[22] T-20.IV.8:3-9

[23] T-27.II.10:1-6

[24] T-9.III.6:1-4

[25] T-19.IV.D.3:3

[26] T-19.IV.D.3:4

[27] T-26.V.8:4

[28] T-26.V.13:1

[29] T-26.V.13:2

[30] T-26.V.13:3

[31] T-26.V.13:4

[32] T-26.V.9:1

[33] T-26.V.8:1-2

[34] T-26.V.6:1

[35] T-26.V.6:2-3

[36] T-26.V.6:4-5

[37] T-26.V.6:6

[38] T-26.V.9:3-5

[39] T-26.V.9:6-8

[40] W-138.2:1

[41] W-138.3:1-2

[42] T-26.V.1:9-12

[43] W-138.4:1-2

[44] W-138.4:5-8

[45] T-26.V.2:1

[46] T-26.V.2:3

[47] T-26.V.2:4-5

[48] T-19.IV.A.4:7-10

[49] W-252.1:1-3

[50] T-12.VI.5:4

[51] T-13.III.10:2
[52] T-19.IV.D.3:4
[53] T-13.VIII.5:3
[54] T-8.VIII.1:10-15
[55] T-13.VIII.2:1-4
[56] T-14.X.1:1
[57] T-16.II.3:2-3
[58] T-8.III.4:1-8
[59] T-8.VII.5:7
[60] T-11.IV.1:1-2
[61] T-11.IV.1:3
[62] T-11.IV.1:4-5
[63] T-11.IV.1:6-7
[64] T-11.IV.3:1-3
[65] T-11.IV.3:4-7
[66] T-11.IV.4:1-2
[67] T-11.IV.4:4-6
[68] T-11.IV.5:1-3
[69] T-11.IV.5:4-6
[70] T-11.IV.8:2-3
[71] M-22.1:1
[72] T-12.VIII.8:6
[73] T-5.I.6:5-6
[74] T-12.VI.5:9, 6:1-4
[75] T-7.VI.4:6
[76] T-12.VIII.7:10-11
[77] T-2.II.5:1-2
[78] T-2.II.6:8-10
[79] T-2.II.6:10
[80] T-2.VI.7:8
[81] T-2.V.5:1-3
[82] T-12.VIII.8:8-9
[83] T-9.IV.2:1
[84] T-9.IV.2:5-7
[85] T-9.IV.1:1
[86] T-9.IV.3:1-3
[87] T-14.IV.3:8-10
[88] T-14.IV.4:1-2
[89] T-14.IV.4:3-5
[90] T-14.IV.4:6-9
[91] T-14.IV.4:10-11
[92] T-14.IV.4:12
[93] T-14.IV.5:1
[94] T-14.IV.5:2-3
[95] T-14.IV.5:4
[96] T-14.IV.5:5
[97] T-14.IV.5:6
[98] T-14.IV.6:1-3
[99] T-14.IV.6:4
[100] T-14.IV.6:6-8
[101] T-14.IV.8:4-5
[102] T-14.IV.8:6
[103] T-14.IV.9:1
[104] T-14.IV.9:2
[105] T-14.IV.9:3

[106] T-14.IV.9:4-5
[107] T-14.IV.9:6-8
[108] T-14.IV.10:1-2
[109] T-14.IV.10:3-4
[110] T-14.IV.10:5-7
[111] M-22.3:1
[112] T-16.II.3:3
[113] T-3.V.9:1
[114] W-pII.1.1:1-6
[115] T-9.IV.5:3-6
[116] T-in.2:2-3
[117] T-9.IV.4:1, 4-6
[118] W-46.1:1
[119] T-24.V.3:1-6
[120] Kenneth Wapnick, *Absence From Felicity*, Copyright 1991 by the Foundation for *A Course In Miracles*, R.R. Box 71, Roscoe, N.Y. 12776-9506, p. 287
[121] T-4.VI.8:2-3
[122] M-16.4:7, 5:1-5
[123] T-1.I.1:3
[124] T-18.VII.4:7-11
[125] T-18.VII.7:7-9, 8:1-5
[126] T-8.III.6:1
[127] T-8.III.5:7-8, 12
[128] T-8.III.7:1-4
[129] T-21.IV.3:4-5
[130] T-22.in.4:2-3
[131] T-22.in.4:6
[132] T-19.IV.1:5
[133] T-1.I.41:1
[134] T-1.I.3:1-3
[135] T-2.IV.1:2-5
[136] T-1.I.36:1, 37:1-3
[137] T-1.I.9:1-3
[138] T-14.X.2:1-3
[139] T-14.X.2:4
[140] T-14.X.2:5-7
[141] T-14.X.3:1-3
[142] T-11.VI.10:5-9
[143] T-14.X.3:4-5
[144] T-14.X.12:1
[145] T-14.X.12:2
[146] T-14.X.12:3
[147] T-16.II.4:1
[148] T-16.II.4:2
[149] T-16.II.4:3
[150] T-16.II.4:4
[151] T-14.X.12:4-6
[152] T-14.X.12:7
[153] T-13.VIII.5:1-3
[154] T-14.X.12:8
[155] T-14.X.12:9
[156] T-13.VIII.6:1-5
[157] T-15.V.10:8-10
[158] T-13.IV.5:1-2
[159] W-158.4:1

[160] T-15.II.2:1-2
[161] T-15.II.3:5-6
[162] T-15.IV.4:4
[163] T-15.IV.6:3-5
[164] T-15.IX.2:3-5
[165] T-15.IX.2:6
[166] T-15.V.3:1-2
[167] T-15.V.1:1-3
[168] T-15.VI.5:3-5
[169] T-15.VI.5:6-7
[170] T-15.VI.5:12
[171] T-18.VI.11:1-6
[172] T-18.VI.11:7-11
[173] T-18.VI.13:1-6
[174] T-15.VI.6:1-3
[175] T-15.VI.6:4-5
[176] T-15.VI.6:6-8
[177] T-15.VI.6:9
[178] T-27.V.3:1
[179] T-17.IV.11:1
[180] T-17.IV.11:4-5
[181] T-15.II.2:1-2
[182] T-18.V.2:1-2
[183] T-13.V.10:1-6
[184] T-12.VI.4:4-6, 8
[185] W-159.8:1
[186] W-159.4:1-6
[187] W-161.9:1-4
[188] T-7.XI.5:2
[189] T-25.I.3:4
[190] W-158.7:1-5, 8:1
[191] T-9.V.6:5
[192] T-25.I.4:5-6
[193] C-3.4:1
[194] T-5.I.6:1-4, 7:1
[195] T-18.V.1:2
[196] T-14.III.12:4
[197] T-14.III.12:5-7
[198] T-14.III.13:1-2
[199] T-4.V.3:2
[200] T-14.III.13:3-5
[201] T-2.VI.7:8
[202] T-3.V.9:1
[203] T-1.I.44:1
[204] T-25.VI.3:1
[205] T-1.IV.3:6
[206] T-6.II.10:1-8
[207] T-5.IV.2:11-13, 12:1-3
[208] M-22.6:1-2
[209] W-pII.8.5:1-4
[210] C-4.3:5-9
[211] T-10.I.2:1-6
[212] T-13.VII.6:3
[213] T-13.VII.6:3
[214] T-13.VII.6:5

[215] T-13.VII.6:6-7
[216] T-13.VII.7:1-3
[217] T-13.VII.7:4-5
[218] T-13.VII.7:4-7
[219] T-13.VII.8:1-2
[220] T-13.VII.8:3-4
[221] T-13.VII.8:5-7
[222] T-11.VII.3:9
[223] T-13.VII.9:1-2
[224] T-13.VII.9:3-5
[225] T-13.VII.9:6-8
[226] T-14.V.7:6-7
[227] T-14.V.8:1-2
[228] T-14.V.8:3
[229] T-14.V.8:5-6
[230] T-14.V.10:8
[231] T-14.V.10:9
[232] T-14.V.10:10
[233] T-14.V.10:11
[234] T-14.V.11:1
[235] T-14.V.11:2-3
[236] T-14.V.11:4
[237] T-14.V.11:5
[238] T-14.V.11:6
[239] T-14.V.11:8-9
[240] T-11.VII.2:1-7
[241] Edgar Cayce, Reading 1152-4, paragraph 12
[242] T-2.VI.9:13-14
[243] T-30.V.7:1-8
[244] M-4.X.2:7-13
[245] C-3.4:1-12
[246] W-15.2:2
[247] T-8.III.1:3
[248] T-7.VI.4:6
[249] W-167.12:1-7
[250] W-167.12:5
[251] C-4.6:9-10, 7:1-7, 8:1-3
[252] T-18.I.5:1-6
[253] T-27.VIII.6:2-5
[254] T-25.III.4:1-3, 5:1-3
[255] T-2.VI.9:14
[256] C-4.3:1-9
[257] C-3.4:1
[258] T-19.IV.D.2:3
[259] T-21.I.9:1
[260] W-15.2:2-4, 3:1-7
[261] https://groups.google.com/d/forum/talk.religion.course-miracle
[262] T-21.I.8:1-3
[263] T-21.I.8:4-6
[264] T-21.I.9:1-2
[265] T-21.I.9:4-6
[266] T-21.I.10:3-5
[267] T-21.I.10:6-7
[268] T-27.VII.13:3-5
[269] T-12.VI.7:1-7

[270] Thomas Matus, *Yoga and the Jesus Prayer Tradition* (Mahwah, New Jersey: Paulist Press, 1984), p. 106-107 (currently published by Asian Trading, Bangalore, India; distributed by Hermitage Books, New Camaldoli, 62475 Coast Highway One, Big Sur, CA 93920)
[271] Ibid., p. 141
[272] C-6.1:4-5
[273] C-6.3:1-9
[274] T-4.II.10:1
[275] T-5.I.6:4-5
[276] T-15.V.11:5
[277] T-16.VI.7:1
[278] T-26.III.2:1
[279] T-26.III.2:3
[280] T-12.III.6:6-7
[281] T-12.III.7:1-3
[282] T-12.III.7:4-5
[283] T-12.III.8:2-3
[284] T-12.III.8:4
[285] T-12.III.9:8-10
[286] T-in.2:2-3
[287] T-5.III.7:4-7
[288] T-8.III.1:3
[289] C-6.3:5
[290] T-13.V.11:1-2
[291] T-7.III.5:1
[292] T-13.VIII.5:4-6
[293] T-13.V.8:1
[294] T-25.VI.3:1
[295] W-108.2:1-3, 3:1-3, 4:1-2
[296] W-15.2:2-4
[297] W-15.2:3:1-6
[298] T-5.III.7:5
[299] T-13.VI.7:1-3
[300] T-7.V.11:3-5
[301] T-13.VI.7:4
[302] T-13.VI.7:5-6
[303] T-2.V.5:1
[304] T-2.VI.7:8
[305] T-15.VI.2:1
[306] T-3.I.6:5-6
[307] T-2.III.1:1
[308] W-67.4:3
[309] W-342.1:8
[310] T-13.VI.8:1-3
[311] T-13.VI.8:4
[312] T-13.VI.8:5
[313] T-13.VI.8:7-8
[314] T-13.VI.9:1-2
[315] T-13.VI.9:3-6
[316] T-13.VI.10:1-3
[317] T-13.VI.10:4-6
[318] T-14.III.5:8
[319] T-13.VI.10:7-9
[320] T-13.VI.11:1-4
[321] T-13.VI.11:5-7

322 T-13.VI.11:8-10
323 T-13.VI.12:1-2
324 T-13.VI.13:1-3
325 T-13.VI.13:4-6
326 T-14.VIII.2:10-11
327 T-14.VIII.2:12-13
328 T-14.VIII.2:14-16
329 T-14.VIII.3:1-3
330 T-14.VIII.3:4
331 T-14.VIII.3:5-8
332 T-14.VIII.4:1-3
333 T-14.VIII.4:4-7
334 T-14.VIII.4:8-10
335 T-14.VIII.5:1-2
336 T-11.II.5:1
337 T-11.II.5:4
338 T-14.VIII.5:3-5
339 T-14.VIII.5:6
340 T-2.III.4:1-5
341 T-12.III.10:3-6
342 T-12.III.10:7-9
343 T-26.III.2:1-5
344 C-1.6:3:1
345 T-4.II.11:1-3
346 T-4.I.9:10-11
347 W-167.12:1-7
348 W-67.4:3
349 T-8.III.1:3
350 C-3.7:6-8, 8:1-6
351 C-3.4:1
352 T-10.IV.8:1-3
353 T-10.IV.8:4
354 T-11.in.3:1-7
355 T-15.IX.1:1-2
356 T-15.IX.1:5
357 T-12.VI.7:2
358 T-10.IV.8:5-7
359 T-10.IV.8:5-7
360 T-11.II.5:4
361 T-3.III.4:1-6
362 T-21.in.1:1
363 T-3.III.5:10
364 T-1.II.1:5-7
365 T-3.IV.2:1
366 T-31.VI.4:7-8
367 T-30.V.4:1
368 T-11.III.3:3-7
369 T-1.II.1:7
370 T-1.II.3:1-3
371 T-1.VII.5:8
372 W-194.1:3
373 T-25.III.6:1-8
374 W-138.9:1-2
375 W-138.10:3-4
376 T-30.V.9:5-10

377 T-26.VIII.9:1
378 T-26.VIII.3:1
379 W-121.13:6
380 W-116.3:4
381 W-100.7:3-6
382 T-26.VIII.9:9-10
383 T-1.II.1:5
384 T-1.II.2:1-2
385 T-1.II.2:7
386 M-26.3:4
387 T-16.III.8:1-3
388 T-16.III.8:4-5
389 T-16.III.9:1
390 T-16.III.9:2-3
391 T-1.VII.5:1-11
392 T-3.IV.7:4
393 T-5.III.5:5-6
394 T-1.II.2:5
395 T-3.IV.3:3-4
396 T-14.VII.7:1-6
397 C-in.1:1-3
398 T-14.VII.7:7
399 T-5.I.6:3-4
400 W-79.3:3-5
401 W-79.2:1-2
402 W-79.1:4-5
403 W-79.1:1-3
404 T-15.X.4:2-4
405 W-80.2:1
406 T-14.IV.9:2-8
407 T-2.VI.7:8
408 T-5.I.6:3
409 T-5.I.5:1-7
410 T-19.IV.B.8:2-5
411 T-17.VII.4:1-6
412 T-19.IV.B.6:1-6
413 T-8.IV.6:2-9
414 T-2.II.4:2-3
415 T-2.II.5:1
416 T-2.II.4:3-5
417 T-3.I.1:2-9
418 T-11.VI.4:1-3
419 T-6.I.7:1-4
420 T-3.V.1:3
421 C-5.3:1-5
422 T-1.III.4:1
423 T-12.VII.6:1
424 C-6.1:1-5
425 T-2.II.5:1
426 W-138.2:5
427 T-30.V.7:5-7
428 W-15.1:1-7
429 W-159.4:1-6
430 W-108.2:1
431 W-94.2:1-6

[432] T-25.VI.3:1
[433] W-159.6:1
[434] T-12.VI.4:1-10
[435] T-15.X.1:8
[436] T-15.X.2:3
[437] T-15.X.2:4
[438] M-23.5:1-11
[439] T-6.I.6:6-7
[440] T-15.X.2:5
[441] T-4.II.6:3-6
[442] T-15.X.2:6
[443] T-15.X.3:1-2
[444] T-4.IV.8:2-3
[445] T-8.I.2:2-3
[446] T-27.VIII.10:1
[447] T-21.II.2:5
[448] T-16.VI.12:2-7
[449] T-4.IV.11:1-5
[450] T-4.IV.8:5-10
[451] T-15.X.3:3
[452] T-15.X.3:4-5
[453] T-15.X.3:6-7
[454] W-159.5:1-4
[455] T-16.VI
[456] C-3.5:3
[457] T-16.IV.13:4-6
[458] T-16.VI.7:1
[459] T-18.IX.9:1-7
[460] T-18.II.6:1-3
[461] T-5.III.1:1-5
[462] T-26.VII.13:1
[463] W-19.1:4
[464] T-2.II.4:2-5
[465] C-6.1:1-5
[466] W-331.1:9-11
[467] M-28.1:1-5
[468] M-28.1:6
[469] M-28.1:7-8
[470] M-28.1:9-10
[471] T-1.III.4:1
[472] M-23.4:1-2
[473] M-23.2:8
[474] T-14.V.2:1
[475] T-14.V.9:3-5
[476] T-14.V.11:1-5
[477] T-16.IV.10:1-4
[478] T-16.IV.13:1-11
[479] T-9.I.1:3-5
[480] T-9.I.2:1-2
[481] T-9.I.3:6-8
[482] T-9.I.4:2-4
[483] T-9.I.5:2-4
[484] T-9.I.6:6-7
[485] T-9.I.9:1-2
[486] T-9.I.9:7-9

487 T-9.I.10:1-4
488 T-9.I.9:3-6
489 T-9.I.11:5-6
490 T-9.I.11:7-8
491 T-9.I.12:1-2
492 T-9.I.13:1-3
493 T-9.I.14:1-4
494 T-9.I.14:7
495 T-13.III.1:4-6
496 T-13.III.1:7-8
497 T-13.III.1:9-10
498 T-13.III.2:1-2
499 T-13.III.2:3-4
500 T-13.III.2:5-7
501 T-13.III.2:8-9
502 T-13.III.3:1-2
503 T-13.III.3:3-4, 4:1-2
504 T-13.III.4:3-5
505 T-13.III.5:1-5
506 T-13.II.8:1-6
507 T-13.II.9:2-3
508 T-10.III.1:1-4
509 T-13.II.9:4-5
510 T-13.II.9:6-7
511 T-15.VI.2:1
512 T-13.III.6:1-3
513 T-13.III.6:4
514 T-13.III.6:5-6
515 T-13.III.7:2-4
516 T-13.III.7:5-6
517 T-13.III.8:1-3
518 T-13.III.8:4-5
519 T-13.III.8:6-7
520 T-13.III.9:1
521 T-13.III.9:2
522 T-13.III.9:3-4
523 T-5.I.3:2-6
524 T-4.I.4:7
525 T-4.I.5:1
526 T-4.I.13:4
527 T-4.I.13:10
528 T-1.II.3:7-9
529 T-1.II.3:10-13
530 T-1.II.4:3-6
531 T-1.III.4:1-2
532 T-1.III.1:1-5
533 T-13.VII.16:1-3
534 T-13.VII.16:4-7
535 T-13.VII.17:1-3
536 T-13.VII.17:4-5
537 T-13.VII.17:6-9
538 T-8.IV.7:3-4
539 T-7.V.10:9-10
540 T-8.V.1:6-8
541 T-8.V.2:7-12

542 T-8.V.2:3
543 T-8.VI.8:3
544 T-8.V.3:1-2
545 T-8.V.3:3-6
546 T-8.V.3:7
547 T-7.V.10:6
548 T-7.III.4:10, 5:1
549 T-4.IV.9:3-6
550 T-8.V.4:1-2
551 T-8.V.4:3-6
552 T-8.V.5:8-9
553 T-8.V.6:4-6
554 T-8.V.6:8-10
555 T-9.II.7:1-4
556 T-6.I.5:1
557 T-8.IV.2:3
558 T-8.IV.2:6
559 T-8.III.1:3
560 T-8.IV.2:10-12
561 T-8.IV.2:13
562 T-8.IV.3:1-2
563 W-161.4:1-2
564 T-8.IV.3:4-5
565 T-8.IV.3:6
566 T-8.IV.3:7-9
567 T-8.IV.6:8-9
568 T-8.IV.5:12-14
569 T-4.VI.6:5-7
570 T-8.IV.7:5-7
571 T-8.IV.7:8-11
572 T-8.IV.8:1-2
573 T-8.IV.8:4-5
574 T-8.IV.8:6-8
575 T-8.IV.8:9-11
576 T-8.IV.8:12-13
577 T-8.IV.3:10-11
578 T-8.IV.4:8
579 T-8.IV.5:1
580 T-8.IV.5:3-5
581 T-8.IV.5:6-8
582 T-14.V.9:1-10
583 T-16.III.6:1-3
584 T-16.III.6:4-5
585 T-16.III.6:6-7
586 T-16.III.6:8
587 T-16.III.7:1-3
588 T-16.III.7:4
589 T-16.III.7:5
590 T-16.III.7:6-7
591 T-16.III.7:8
592 T-16.III.9:2-3
593 M-1.1:1-2
594 M-9.2:1-4
595 M-10.2:5-7
596 M-10.3:1-7

[597] M-16.4:7
[598] M-16.5:6-8
[599] M-18.4:1-9
[600] M-22.6:1-2
[601] M-22.2:1-5
[602] M-22.3:1
[603] M-22.4:5-8
[604] T-11.VII.2:6-8
[605] T-11.VII.3:1-4
[606] W-152.2:6-7
[607] T-11.VII.3:5-6
[608] T-11.VII.3:7-8
[609] T-11.VII.3:9
[610] T-11.VII.4:1
[611] T-11.VII.4:3
[612] T-11.VII.4:4-6
[613] T-11.VII.4:7-8
[614] T-11.VII.4:9
[615] Donald James Giacobbe, *Memory Walk in the Light: A Christian Yoga Life as "A Course in Miracles,"* p. 481
[616] T-26.III.1:1-4
[617] T-26.V.6:1-2
[618] T-26.V.11:4-5
[619] T-26.V.11:6-7
[620] T-26.V.11:8-11
[621] T-16.VI.6:2-3
[622] T-16.VI.4:6-7
[623] T-16.VI.6:4-5
[624] T-16.VI.7:4-7
[625] T-16.VI.8:1-8
[626] T-26.V.12:3
[627] T-26.III.3:1-8
[628] T-26.III.1:10
[629] T-3.III.2:2
[630] T-26.III.4:1-10
[631] T-26.III.5:4
[632] T-In.2:1-3
[633] W-138.4:1-8, 5:1-4
[634] T-3.V.7:7
[635] W-152.3:1-9
[636] T-23.II.2:1
[637] W-152.4:1
[638] W-152.4:3
[639] T-14.II.1:1-3
[640] T-16.V.6:5
[641] T-14.II.1:4
[642] T-14.II.1:5-7
[643] T-14.II.1:8-9
[644] T-14.II.1:10-11
[645] T-14.II.2:1-2
[646] T-14.II.2:3-7
[647] T-14.II.3:2-9
[648] T-14.II.4:1-3
[649] T-14.II.4:4-5
[650] T-14.II.4:6-7

[651] T-14.II.4:8-9
[652] W-126.7:4-5
[653] T-14.II.5:1-3
[654] T-14.II.5:4-5
[655] T-14.II.5:6-8
[656] T-14.II.6:1
[657] T-14.II.6:2-5
[658] T-14.II.7:1-2
[659] T-14.II.7:3-4
[660] T-14.II.7:5-6
[661] T-5.III.7:5
[662] T-14.II.7:7-9
[663] T-14.II.8:1-2
[664] T-14.II.8:3-5
[665] T-14.II.8:6
[666] T-14.II.8:7-8
[667] T-16.V.16:1
[668] T-6.V.C.1:1-5
[669] T-16.V.17:1- 3
[670] T-2.VIII.5:6-11
[671] T-17.II.4:1-5
[672] T-4.VII.5:1-5
[673] W-161.2:1-6
[674] W-161.4:1-7
[675] T-13.I.8:1-9
[676] T-9.VI.7:1-3
[677] T-13.I.3:2-7, 4:1
[678] T-5.III.6:1-5
[679] T-7.I.7:4
[680] C-6.5:8
[681] T-11.I.2:1-6
[682] T-4.VI.7:7
[683] T-4.III.9:7
[684] T-6.II.13:2-5
[685] T-18.VIII.2:6
[686] T-18.VIII.3:3
[687] T-18.VIII.3:5
[688] T-18.VIII.4:6
[689] T-6.II.10:7-8
[690] T-11.VIII.1:1-9
[691] W-159.5:1
[692] M-4.X.2:7-8
[693] T-17.II.7:1-5
[694] T-18.VI.1:1-6
[695] T-13.XI.3:1-3
[696] W-107.2:1-5, 3:1-6
[697] W-127.1:1-7
[698] Helen Schucman, *The Gifts of God*, p. 129
[699] W-168.4:1-5
[700] T-16.VI.11:1-2
[701] T-16.VI.11:3-7
[702] T-28.I.15:2-9
[703] Amaury de Reincourt, *The Eye of Shiva*, (New York, NY: William Morrow, 1981) pp. 28-29.
[704] Michael I. Sobel, *Light*, (Chicago, IL: University of Chicago Press, 1987) p. 207.

[705] da_willem, "Why c² (speed of light squared)?" Text - Physics Forums Library, http://www.physicsforums.com/archive/index.php/t-41354.html.
[706] T-17.IV.11:1-8
[707] W-234.1:2
[708] T-15.I.9:5-7
[709] T-20.V.6:1-5
[710] T-18.I.4:1-4
[711] T-27.VIII.6:2-5
[712] T-26.V.13:1-2
[713] Jacey Menzies Ong, August 2, 2015, https://www.quora.com/Does-a-photon-experience-time-Relativity-shows-that-as-objects-approach-the-speed-of-light-they-experience-increased-relative-mass-and-time-dilation-Since-a-photon-is-massless-and-travels-at-the-speed-of-light-does-time-pass-for-a-photon
[714] W-59.2:3-6 (42)
[715] T-13.V.10:1-3
[716] W-108.2:1-2
[717] W-pII.8.2:1
[718] T-17.II.6:3
[719] T-11.VII.2:1-2
[720] T-18.IX.9:1
[721] Jerry Mander, *Four Arguments for the Elimination of Television: The Effects of Watching TV*, 1979, http://www.motherearthnews.com/nature-and-environment/effects-of-watching-tv-zmaz79mazraw.aspx
[722] W-158.4:1-4
[723] Jacob D. Bekenstein, "Information on the Holographic Universe," April 1, 2007, http://www.scientificamerican.com/article/information-in-the-holographic-univ/
[724] C-3.4:1
[725] T-2.VI.9:14
[726] T-19.IV.D.2:3
[727] T-21.I.8:1-6
[728] T-16.II.3:3
[729] T-21.I.8:1-6, 9:1-6
[730] T-21.I.10:3-5
[731] W-122.3:1-3
[732] T-28.IV.8:1-2
[733] T-28.IV.8:3-4
[734] T-28.IV.8:6
[735] T-28.IV.9:1-7
[736] T-27.VI.1:5-6
[737] T-13.VIII.2:3-4
[738] T-13.VIII.5:1-3
[739] W-158.10:4
[740] T-29.III.3:6-10
[741] T-25.I.4:1-6
[742] T-21.I.10:6
[743] T-15.IV.1:3-7
[744] T-27.V.6:5-6
[745] T-20.I.4:2
[746] T-20.IV.5:6
[747] W-158.10:4
[748] W-124.9:5
[749] T-8.III.1:2
[750] T-21.I.10:7
[751] W-169.13:1-4